£1.50

# ALL THE HOURS GOD SENDS?

PRACTICAL AND BIBLICAL HELP
IN MEETING THE DEMANDS OF WORK

## PETER CURRAN

Inter-Varsity Press

INTER-VARSITY PRESS
*38 De Montfort Street, Leicester LE1 7GP, England*

*First published 2000*

**British Library Cataloguing in Publication Data**
A catalogue record for this book is available from the British Library.

ISBN 0–85111–656–6

Set in Garamond
Typeset in Great Britain
Printed and bound in Great Britain by
Creative Print and Design (Wales)

*Inter-Varsity Press is the book-publishing division of the Universities and Colleges Christian Fellowship (formerly the Inter-Varsity Fellowship), a student movement linking Christian Unions in universities and colleges throughout Great Britain, and a member movement of the International Fellowship of Evangelical Students. For more information about local and national activities write to UCCF, 38 De Montfort Street, Leicester LE1 7GP.*

# ALL THE HOURS GOD SENDS?

# Dedication

*To Clare, David and Alison*

## Acknowledgments

My wife Clare, and our children David and Alison for their patience and support.

Mum and Dad for their example of a lifetime's hard and honest work.

Dave Leal for starting me writing and Richard Higginson for encouraging me.

Lyn Richards for giving me my first job in personnel, and Dot Griffiths from whom I have learnt so much about management.

The people of St John's Church, Stoke-next-Guildford for their fellowship and support.

The many people with whom I have had the pleasure to work, and whose experiences have helped shape this book.

The team at IVP for editing and producing this book

And for the waitress in a hotel in Cape Town who, seeing me editing a chapter (when I thought I would never finish), said 'I've never met a real writer before.'

# Contents

1. All the hours God sends  9
   *Working to live and living to work*

2. Work in its place  16
   *Stemming the tide of workaholism*

3. Keeping all the plates spinning  30
   *Handling the pressures of work*

4. With all your heart  49
   *Making a difference in work*

5. What gets you out of bed in the morning?  73
   *Staying motivated*

6. Riding the rollercoaster  91
   *Coping with change at work*

7. It takes two to tango  111
   *Working at relationships*

8. Is the world my oyster?  136
   *Finding the right job*

9. On the scrapheap?  153
   *Responding to redundancy,
   unemployment and retirement*

10. Leading the way  172
    *Directing, inspiring, motivating,
    enabling, caring … serving*

11. Reaching for the skies?  192
    *Handling ambition and wealth, status and power*

    Conclusion  215
    *A Christian path through the world of work*

    Bibliography  217

# CHAPTER 1

# All the hours God sends

*Working to live and living to work*

## Between pressed men and workaholics

Liz was at her wits' end. Her husband was seldom in before eight o'clock despite being on the early train to London every day. 'I'm left to do everything at home and I have to sort out all the children's activities. I can't remember the last time he was in early enough to put them to bed. I'm surprised they still recognize him!' She commented that his job meant that he sometimes had to work late, but surely that didn't mean he had to do a twelve-hour day every day? 'I've had about as much as I can take,' was her closing remark, and she made it clear that it was not just his relationship with the children that was suffering.

Does this sound familiar? Perhaps it induces a pang of guilt? If so, the fact that you have found time to pick up this book is a good sign. The cruel dichotomy that seems to have entered the world of work is that either you do not have any work (due to redundancy, unemployment, early retirement) or you have too much. For those in work, it seems to be encroaching on all other areas of life, squeezing them out, pushing them to the end of the day when you are just too tired. The trend of reducing formal working hours that has been negotiated and fought for since industrialization now seems to be in reverse in many sectors. The issue is about not only increased working hours, however, but increased workload (more work done by fewer people) and often greater stress.

If you are in work, you are likely to be working harder and for more hours than ever before. This may be because you feel under pressure to do so (to keep a job, to pay the bills, because of peer pressure), or because you want to (to advance your career, because you enjoy your job). While it is helpful to be able to work a little more if money is tight, or to spend more time at the office when a project is stimulating or approaching a deadline, more and more people are finding themselves nearer the extremes of this spectrum; feeling like pressed men trapped into working long hours, or slipping into a lifestyle of workaholism. In either case, they are working all the hours God sends.

For you, long hours may be necessary to earn a decent living. You may need to work long and hard, and perhaps even to undertake several jobs, to make ends meet. Perhaps your workload has increased. The global market has opened up trade, letting developing countries get a bigger stake in the world economy, and giving us greater choice as consumers. But it has also created greater competitive pressure for the products and services we provide through work. Hence, organizations are constantly looking for ways to cut costs and find efficiencies. They want their people to be more productive, to do more with less.

Therefore, although long hours should be 'voluntary', you may feel obliged to work them for fear of being caught in the next redundancy round; there is the perceived need to show willing. Or it may be to increase your chances of promotion, to avoid letting others down, or because you find it difficult to say 'no' to the boss.

You may work long hours because you want to; perhaps you are ambitious and work hard to progress, or you love your job and there is nothing you would rather be doing, or you feel that what you do is so worthwhile you want to go the extra mile. These can be perfectly good reasons to work hard and long, but you need to be aware of the danger of workaholism – a life that revolves around work to the exclusion of everything and everyone else.

I cleared my desk, switched off the computer and packed up my things. Why did I have to be sitting in an open-plan area next to the head of the unit? It was five o'clock and I wanted to catch the 5.20. I slipped on my coat and hurried towards the lifts, hoping not to meet too many people on the way. They were all still working, as if they hadn't moved since I had arrived that morning. From the corner of my eye, I noticed one or two heads lifting; no comments, but I knew what they were thinking. Couldn't they see I had my laptop and would probably work at home tonight anyway? But I still felt guilty, as if I was slinking off like a skiving schoolboy.

Having run the gauntlet of stares and nods, I reached the lifts. The doors opened and a colleague stepped out. 'See you tomorrow,' I said as

I entered and pressed the 'ground floor' button.

'Half day today, then?' he jested.

Peer pressure can be positive and reinforce the 'culture' of an organization for good, but it can also impose upon us working practices and attitudes with which we may disagree. It is not easy to leave the office when you know everyone else will be there for another two hours, especially if they all started earlier than you did. You feel you are letting the side down, and although your boss supports 'family friendly' working practices (in theory, anyway), you can't help feeling that you are jeopardizing your career prospects. And in many work settings it is regarded as committed, even macho, to be seen at the coffee machine at 7pm, or to send e-mails dated late at night or over the weekend.

Many of us feel trapped in a pattern of work that seems difficult or impossible to change. It is not easy to counter a culture of working all the hours God sends. We need a basis for change, some principles to guide the changes we wish to make, some practical tips, and a little help. This chapter and the next two attempt to point the way.

# Working to live or living to work?

*Polarized perspectives*

We were in the middle of our finals. During a break between exams, we chatted about the future. Rick seemed to have everything worked out. He was tall and good-looking, played rugby for the college 1st XV, was on course for a good degree, and had a job lined up in the offshore oil industry. 'That's where the big money is,' he said confidently. He outlined his ambition to get a large house, a fast car and lots of money so that he could give up work altogether.

Paul was responsible for the production of airline meals, and for their loading on to the aircraft. His organization had contracts with several major airlines, and if they were to keep their jobs, they couldn't afford for a Jumbo jet to leave without its food! His job did not use his engineering education, or match his talents. But it was a living and the means to pursue his interests outside work, which included helping with the youth work in the church. However, the lack of stimulation in what he was doing, together with the hassle of the job, resulted in frustration. He eventually retrained for a career in a subject in which he was truly interested.

A former boss said his work really gave him a buzz. And there was no doubting he was good at it; he had risen to a senior position, and gained a lot of respect on the way. 'I work seven till seven because I want to,' he told me, 'but I don't expect other people to work the hours I do.' I believed him, and his attitude to my work patterns confirmed his sincerity. But this did not stop people looking to him as a role model. They linked his success not only to his skill, but also to his single-minded dedication to work. But at what cost?

Different people have widely different ideas about work, the place it should have in their lives and the hours they should devote to it. They are influenced by the traditions they have inherited, their need to survive, changes happening in work, and peer pressure. These factors may change at different times in their lives.

If we are to avoid working all the hours God sends we need to be clear about the place work is to have in our lives. God does have a place for work in creation, and a purpose that will benefit us and the world in which God has placed us.

### Work: curse or idol?

Most people need to work. Work provides life's necessities (food, clothing, shelter), and, whether paid or unpaid, enables life to continue and ideally makes it more pleasant. This is the only purpose that many see for work; a means of support and a means to supply some of life's luxuries. They look to life outside work for meaning and fulfilment. Work is to be endured as a necessary evil; if they won the lottery they could dispense with it altogether. They *work to live*.

At the other extreme, some view work as the reason for living. They feel satisfaction and fulfilment as they use their skills, complete tasks, achieve and succeed. They immerse themselves in work, and it becomes the dominant component of their lives, in fact an idol. They *live to work*.

Most of us *work to live* to a degree, but how much importance should we give to this material motivation ? Work can be a great source of fulfilment, but is it meant to be the driving factor of our lives so that we *live to work*? What does the Bible say?

Work is shown to be important by God's own example in creating and sustaining the world. And we, made in God's image, are to continue God's work. We are placed in the world to work it and to take care of it with delegated authority from the Creator (Genesis 1:28; 2:15). Through work, we participate in God's creative activity. That Jesus spent much of his earthly adult life as a carpenter (Mark 6:3) endorses the significance of human work. Although work is made harder by human wrongdoing and frustrated by a world tainted by sin (Genesis 3:17–19), from the beginning God ordained work as something both necessary and good for humankind, and it remains an integral and natural part of life (Ecclesiastes 5:18; Psalm 104:23). Because of the fall, our experience of work will include both good and bad. However, God's redemptive activity extends to the world of work, and we can bring his rule into the work we do and win it back for him.

The biblical view of work is that it is neither curse, necessary evil nor panacea for all ills. Rather, it is a part of our humanity that is essential and potentially good. It is the principal means of *sustenance*, so that we can secure food, clothing and shelter from the world God has given (Genesis 1:29–30; 3:19), and on top of these a decent way of life for ourselves and our dependants (1 Timothy 5:8; Proverbs 28:19). The apostle Paul upholds the principle that, where possible, people are to supply their needs through their work (2 Thessalonians 3:10, 12), so that they are not dependent on anybody (1 Thessalonians 4:11–12). He points to himself as an example (Acts 18:3; 20:34). Correspondingly, Proverbs exhorts us to work and not be idle (e.g. 6:9–11). Work is how we provide for our needs, support our dependants and improve our lot; in the words of the theologian Karl Barth, people work 'to earn their daily bread and a little more' (1961: 525).

Through work, we should be able to use and develop our gifts and thereby find *satisfaction* in the achievement of our tasks. Such satisfaction is hinted at when God rested after the work of creating: 'God saw all that he had made, and it was very good' (Genesis 1:31). The writer of Ecclesiastes outlines the frustration and meaninglessness of much toilsome work, yet recognizes that satisfaction can be found within it: 'That everyone may eat and drink, and find satisfaction in all his toil – this is the gift of God' (Ecclesiastes 3:13). E. F. Schumacher comments that an important purpose of work is 'to enable every one of us to use and thereby perfect our gifts like good stewards' (1979: 3). For many (though sadly not for all), work draws on their talents and skills, enabling them to gain fulfilment through work. There is probably greater potential to do this in modern society than in agrarian societies, although there are still many who are consigned to mindless, soul-destroying jobs. When satisfying, work helps to build our character and contributes to our self-esteem.

Work also enables us to support the enterprises of our community, society and the world at large, and thereby offer *service* to and with others. As Christians, we live under the command 'Love your neighbour as yourself' (Matthew 22:39), and are called to demonstrate this love through service (Philippians 2:3–7; Matthew 20:26–28), defining our neighbour as anyone who needs our help (Luke 10:25–37). Jesus' exhortation to be the 'salt of the earth' and the 'light of the world' (Matthew 5:13–16), together with Paul's words on being good citizens (Romans 13:1–7), underline our responsibility to society as a whole. The Old Testament echoes this in its concern for the poor, widows and orphans (e.g. Deuteronomy 15:1–7).

One of the key ways we serve others is through work. The thief is told to cease stealing and start working, not only to do something useful for himself but also 'that he may have something to share with those in need' (Ephesians 4:28). As John Stott points out, 'Certainly the Bible regards work as a community project, undertaken by the community for the community' (1999: 191). Biblical examples are the making of articles for the tabernacle (Exodus 36) and the rebuilding of Jerusalem's walls (Nehemiah 3 – 6). Here we see people using their gifts in complementary ways. Paul's model of the church as a body with many parts (1 Corinthians 12) carries a similar message that people need to work with each other if they are to achieve what is necessary. It also makes work more enjoyable. The apostle Peter's words are a good summary: 'Each one should use whatever gift he has received to serve others, faithfully administering God's grace in its various forms' (1 Peter 4:10).

Ultimately, work is *service to God*, done for his glory and offered as worship to him. We should strive in whatever we do to 'do it all for the glory of God' (1 Corinthians 10:31). In fact, this is the overarching purpose of work: as Paul instructed Christian slaves ('workers'), 'Whatever you do, work at it with all your heart, as working for the Lord, not for men' (Colossians 3:23).

As we align our thinking with a Christian view of work, we start to see how it takes its place within the whole of human existence as God has established it, and contributes, as Bishop Graham Dow writes, to 'what God is making human beings to be' (1994: 6). It is a necessary part of the whole with important purposes which include sustenance, satisfaction and service, but it needs to be held in balance alongside life's other obligations and activities. If work has a place in our lives that should be neither curse nor idol, how can we put some sensible boundaries around it? How can we achieve a biblical balance? The next chapter tackles these questions in practical terms.

## The action column

Does work dominate your life so that you *live to work*? Or do you view work merely as a means to get money, so that you *work to live*? Think about what God would have you do with your life and how your work can contribute to his purposes.

# CHAPTER 2

# Work in its place

## Stemming the tide of workaholism

God calls us not only to work but also to rest. He sets us not only in workplaces but also in families. And he wants us to spend time with him and with our Christian brothers and sisters in the community of his people. Let's look at these aspects of our lives in turn.

## Getting some rest

### Take a break

'Come with me by yourselves to a quiet place and get some rest,' Jesus said to his disciples after a busy day (Mark 6:31). Here lies the key to achieving a balance between work and life's other essential ingredients. Jesus was reiterating the Old Testament principle of stepping aside from work to get some rest. The Bible expresses the balance needed by contrasting the obligation to work with the command to rest. Just as God is said to have rested, we are to rest from our labours, as the sixth commandment makes clear (Exodus 20:8–11; Genesis 2:2–3).

Whatever view you hold on Sunday as the day of rest, the underlying principle is clear; we are to work and we are to rest. Just as human work finds its basis in the being and activity of God, so does rest. In its broadest sense, rest is *cessation from work* – stepping aside from necessary tasks to make space and time for refreshment, recreation, relationships and worship. It is this principle which helps us create an appropriate balance between work and the other activities of life.

Lyn was conscientious and professional at work, taking seriously her role as Head of Personnel for a site of 2,000 employees. The pressure on her would sometimes show as she worked tirelessly to maintain a good service, and to ensure that managers and staff were treated with fairness and respect and that points of principle were defended. Despite a week of activity that at times looked as if it might overwhelm her, Lyn always managed to return fresh the next Monday. The secrets of her survival in such a demanding role seemed to include some oases of calm: a regular Friday meal out with her husband, a sport she enjoyed, and weekends away that gave her a complete break. She came back each Monday rested, eager to plunge energetically into another week.

Rest provides a *limit* to work, allowing us time for physical rest and refreshment of body and mind. Having such a limit is the key to successful work *and* enjoyable rest. Rest is needed so that the quality of our work is not compromised through tiredness or exhaustion. After any sustained activity we need to replenish our reserves, and give our bodies and minds time to recuperate. We can do this by taking a lunch break, relaxing with a cup of tea between chores, or having an evening's entertainment or a good night's sleep – whatever is needed to provide the required refreshment.

Rest provides a necessary protection from, in Karl Barth's words, being 'possessed, controlled and impelled' by work (1961: 552). Rest helps to keep work in perspective, giving it a time and a place, thus enabling us to avoid being enslaved by it. The story of Mary and Martha (Luke 10:38–42) portrays Martha as consumed by her work, and Mary, by contrast, as having chosen what was more appropriate at that time: a break from her work obligations. Rest retains our autonomy and freedom in relation to work, preventing us from becoming too identified with our work and from taking it (and ourselves) too seriously. Hence rest from work meets not only physiological but psychological needs. One of the ways it achieves this is by relieving us of work's demands for a while, together with its associated tensions and stresses.

### Finding space

Elbows tucked in, attempting to eat a meal on a crowded flight, we talked about our lives outside work. Don said that if it wasn't for activities he pursued with his family, and playing in a rock group (who would have guessed?), work would easily soak up all his free time. I understood his struggle only too well. He added that getting involved in the Parent–Teacher Association and the sailing-club committee were welcome distractions that helped him to leave the office at a reasonable time. For myself, it is my family, church and sport that help me to draw some boundaries.

Rest, then, also provides a *diversion* from work. Some rest is inactive (to replenish bodily reserves), but some is active: our leisure and recreation. They help us to forget about work for a while and add interest and colour to our lives.

Rest gives us space to build, nourish and enjoy the most significant *relationships* in our lives, with our loved ones and those who depend on us. Rest also provides time for *leisure*, allowing us to enjoy the results of our work, often with our family and friends. This can be through all manner of activities (interests, hobbies, sports) which we don't have to do but choose to do, for their own sake rather than for another purpose. They provide relaxation, enjoyment, fun and a 'good time'. The Bible emphasizes the importance of celebration and festivity. Although most of the festivals in the Bible are, in Ryken's view, 'leisure of a specifically religious kind', they are 'leisure nonetheless' (1989: 195). The people of Israel celebrated God's deliverance (Exodus 12:14–17), God's provision (Exodus 23:16), and other significant events for which they were thankful (e.g. 1 Samuel 11:14–15; 1 Chronicles 15:29). True celebration and festivity have their basis in worship.

Most significantly, then, rest has a spiritual purpose: to provide time for *contemplation and worship*, recognizing our need of God. The link between rest and worship is implicit in the biblical idea of the Sabbath rest. Observing a specific day of rest demonstrates that God's people do not trust in their own work or achievements but in God, and can, in freedom, abstain from work to rest. As Jesus made clear, the Sabbath is for our good (Mark 2:27). For the Christian, a day of rest does not represent the finishing-line as one works towards the end of the week, but rather a launch-pad for the week ahead: the way of ensuring that we start as we mean to go on, with God's rest entering every day because of Sunday. And in this way, we can partake of God's future rest through developing a relationship with him now (Hebrews 4:9–11).

## Family matters

### *Working parents*

Working at the same time as raising a family is nothing new (otherwise the world would not have lasted so long). But the roles parents are asked to play, together with the changes occurring in the world of work, pose threats and challenges as well as opportunities. In our modern world we have drawn a line between work at home (caring for children, housework), and work in the workplace (usually synonymous with paid employment). We have assumed that women will do all or most of the former, while men undertake what are often perceived as the more important roles of outside worker and breadwinner. But changes in attitudes by and towards women, the opportunities open to them, and new patterns of work, are causing us to rethink these stereotypes. The boundaries between work in the workplace and work at home become less clear when people have their office at home, are self-employed, undertake part-time work, provide consultancy, and so on. Back in history and in agrarian cultures, the division was similarly less marked as whole families lived off the land and contributed to their own sustenance.

There is a biblical mandate to provide for dependants, but the Bible does not assign this role solely to men or husbands. Nor does the Bible assign the role of parenthood to one sex. Fathers and mothers are charged with the upbringing of children, teaching them and setting an example, caring for them and nurturing their growth towards adulthood (Ephesians 6:1–4; Proverbs 3:12; 22:6).

Starting a family will have an impact on the work of *both* partners. Pregnancy (as it advances) places some obvious restrictions on the mother-to-be, and there is legislation to help provide support, time off work, and employment protection during this time. This extends into the early months after the birth, when it is the mother who has the most direct role. However, the father also has responsibilities during this time – to offer support in the run-up to the birth, to share the load of caring for a baby, to make time to form a relationship with a growing child. Adjustments need to be made by *both* partners, and it's good to start as you mean to go on.

### Work and home

Returning to work after the birth of a child has become increasingly common. For you it may be necessary to make ends meet. Or you may feel it is right to continue the career for which God has gifted you, or at least to keep it ticking over during the early years of parenthood. So if you are working, and have a family, how do you balance work and home?

A number of large employers have developed more flexible policies to attract back their own former employees or as an aid to recruitment.

These vary from career breaks following maternity leave to various forms of part-time working. More parents wish to return to work, and companies are increasingly making flexible working available – so what's the problem?

Louise was hard-working and conscientious. Although her company operated a flexible working policy, her busy operational role ruled out part-time work. She had negotiated a return to full-time work with two out of five days working from home. 'I've given people my home number, but they don't ring. I feel guilty when I'm at home spending time with the baby, but I do my hours. If anything, I work harder.' She felt left out of things in the team when she was at the office.

Clare went back to work as a pharmacist two evenings a week. 'It does me good to dress smartly and play a professional role,' she said. 'I know parenting is important, but when you are at home people treat you as if all you're interested in is nappies and teething. Going to work, even though it's only six hours a week, is a real boost to my self-esteem. My career has been on hold for ten years, but being able to "keep my hand in" has helped.'

Those of us who continue in our profession, almost untouched by having children, do not realize the sacrifices made by those who play the primary carer role at home.

Linda was a single parent raising two lively boys. With a keen desire (and need) to develop professionally, she found herself balancing a full-time job, external study and the roles of parent and breadwinner. 'Although people say it doesn't matter, I feel awkward not being able to arrive at work until after I have taken the boys to school. Mum picks them up after school but I have to leave promptly in the evening to relieve her.'

So all is not well. Those who return to work part-time can feel under pressure or not fully part of the team because they are not physically present for as many hours as their full-time counterparts. Being left out of key events, forgotten in staff communications or not included in training programmes reinforces the 'outsider' feeling as well as making it harder to do the job.

Those who return to work full-time probably have the restraints of child-care arrangements, and can feel at a disadvantage because they are tied to regular hours and are less able to work late, to travel, or to be away overnight. (Of course, this can also be a blessing, helping them to draw boundaries around work.)

Those who simply keep their career ticking over during parenting can find it difficult to watch colleagues continue to progress while they themselves are left out of development programmes, or overlooked for promotion. They may end up working for someone many years their junior who has far less experience of both work and life. They feel (and are sometimes regarded as) second class.

While many organizations have introduced more flexible working policies, these are not always available in practice – either because the role actually requires someone to be there full-time, or because the manager is uncomfortable with someone working differently (from home, or for fewer hours).

Childcare may be a constant headache – it's not available, or the hours don't fit, or it's so expensive that it is hardly worth working, or it involves an awkward journey. Because of work, young parents may have moved many miles away from their own parents' home, so they lack the help of the extended family.

Those who have had a long break from work may feel that their confidence has slid to an all-time low. 'Can I still do this? Are my knowledge and skills still relevant?'

As the children grow and progress through school, people start to ask, 'Are you working again yet?' As friends with children of the same age start to go back to work, it can get lonely at home.

Meanwhile, employers often expect partners who are not primary carers to continue as normal despite the new challenges and pressures at home, though some countries have introduced a right to unpaid parental leave, and the UK is likely to follow this lead.

Parenting is an important role and, as all parents know, hard work. Full-time parenting is a valid form of work; many would say it is more challenging and involves more skills than many so-called 'full-time' jobs. Full-time parents are nurse and counsellor, teacher and chauffeur, manager and, of course, slave. Their shifts are twenty-four hours long and they rarely get a day off. At the most frantic times, just when they thought toilet training was cracked, there is a puddle. Staying at home is not the easy option.

However, for a range of valid reasons linked to work's purposes (sustenance, satisfaction, service) returning to (paid) work while raising a family may be the right thing and perhaps the necessary thing for some. How can it be handled in a way that results in a good balance between work and home? How can those who combine these roles do them successfully and make some time for rest?

### Starting as you mean to continue

David's sports day had been in my diary for months. But I had just taken on a new responsibility at work, and a meeting had been called at head office at which I was to represent my organization for the first time in this role. I apologized to my son, but I couldn't seem to make him understand why I would not be present at the most important event in his school year. The meeting came and went; it didn't change the world and there have been many similar meetings since. But that sports day was unique. My son will never be in a Year 1 sports day again. He was upset that I wasn't there and still remembers it as the event I did not attend. I had let him down; after all, I could have got someone else to stand in for me at the meeting, but not at the school. I have not missed a sports day since.

Here are some guidelines which recognize that the family matters. They apply to *both* partners.

- Recognize that while roles at home may differ, both of you as parents are responsible for the upbringing of your children, and that this is an important task in its own right.
- Your day is now bounded and interrupted by events that you cannot control, yet which are often more important and urgent than anything else: your child waking, getting hurt, needing to be fed and, occasionally, going to sleep. Chapter 3 offers some tips.
- Know your limitations. The desire to do some paid work during this time can drive some to take on too much, so that they get over-tired and neglect quality time with their children.
- Reach a deal with your employer (or, if you are self-employed, with your clients), which is fair and workable.
- If you are the manager of people trying to balance work and family commitments, treat them fairly and equitably. Do not expect them to do a five-day week if they are contracted to do three. Be aware of constraints upon them: do you really need to hold meetings early, or after work hours, that you know they will find difficult to attend? Do not exclude them from the necessary aspects of work such as team meetings, training opportunities or development processes.

## Achieving a balance

### *A question of priorities*

We met for breakfast. Sandra and I were in busy roles supporting staff in remote sites across the world. Nearly everyone around us was working long hours, made worse by lots of time away from home. But we had taken similar stances on not allowing work to swamp our lives completely. I was encouraged that Sandra could manage to do this, and do her job to a standard that others found hard to match. In good humour, but seriously, we made a pact that we would encourage each other to maintain the balance we thought to be important. We agreed that working long hours was not always a sign of higher output or greater commitment; it could be the result of inefficiency or the lack of organizational skills, poor time management or an unwillingness to delegate. Although we now work for different organizations, we still make contact from time to time, and continue to encourage each other not to conform.

We may insist that our spouses are more important to us than our work, but continually to work late suggests the opposite to them and will make them feel devalued. We may love our children deeply, but never to make time for them because we are always working will make them feel that our job is more important than they are. One day, their jobs will be more important than coming to see us, and we will question their priorities. True, there are times when the pressure is on and extra effort or more time away from home than we would like is required; spouses and children can usually understand this. But this should not be allowed to become the norm. Those closest to us are just too important, and our relationship with them goes beyond any job or work task. Our children need the continuity of our presence if they are to flourish. And as they are young for such a short time, we should count every opportunity with them as precious, and try to make each of them count. How do we decide on some priorities?

Many of the successful people in my organization seem to be those who are prepared to give up everything for work. They work long hours, are regularly away from home and appear totally committed to the progress of the company. How surprised I was to find a senior role model who was bucking the trend. I organized a one-day meeting for Andrew, to which people travelled from far and wide. At the start of the day I enquired when he would like us to finish. He answered that when he was working near home, he liked to be there to see his children to bed, so we would finish by 5.30pm. On another occasion, after he had been made a director of the company, I met him in the gym. Despite the demands upon his time he maintained his frequent exercise sessions, and by so doing made it acceptable for everyone else there to take a break at lunchtime.

The apostle Paul wrote: 'Do not conform any longer to the pattern of this world, but be transformed by the renewing of your mind. Then you will be able to test and approve what God's will is – his good, pleasing and perfect will' (Romans 12:2). There is huge pressure to conform. Rather, let us do God's will allowing our thinking to be transformed and aligned with his principles so that we get the balance right.

## A balancing act

'Hard work never hurt anyone' is only really true when there is a balance to our lives. This balance will vary from person to person. Being prescriptive about how much time or attention people should give to their work is therefore unhelpful. Our capacity for work varies, as do the gifts and abilities we possess. We carry different responsibilities, and the nature of our work and the interest we have in it vary. The balance between work and other aspects of life will vary with time and circumstances: for example, a college leaver in a first job may wish to devote proportionally more time to working than someone in mid-career with family responsibilities. However, more demands will be placed on a chief executive than on a junior member of staff.

What is the best balance for one person may be stressful or constraining for another. We each need to seek a good balance for ourselves at each particular stage of life and in relation to our circumstances. This will enable us to function best in all of life's activities. Straying too far from this can lead to the dangers of boredom or stress, demotivation or workaholism. How are we to decide on the appropriate balance for our lives? We need to examine our work balance against a Christian set of priorities, ensuring that we make time for God, others, church and ourselves.

1. *Time for God.* Time spent working is just as much God's time as that spent in 'spiritual' activities, but we need to make space for special time with God in order to develop our relationship with him through prayer (Matthew 6:6; Colossians 4:2) and worship (Hebrews 10:24–25; Acts 2:46–47). Our relationship with God underpins all we do in work: it is fundamental to finding peace in times of pressure (chapter 3), and

to honouring God in the way we do our work (chapter 4). It is necessary for godly motivation (chapter 5), for handling change (chapter 6), for finding guidance (chapter 8), for leading (chapter 10), and for handling ambition, status, power and wealth in a Christian way (chapter 11).

A group of us had arrived in Angola early that morning and were due to start the workshop at 10am. The venue had been changed. This presented several logistical challenges, the first of which was finding it. We had not worked together as a team before, or met many of our clients. It was a high-profile project to be delivered in two languages. We were tired and nervous. As the team's leader, I was beginning to think we had bitten off more than we could chew. I showered and, before joining the others, found space to pray. God heard my prayer, and gave me the assurance I needed. Despite the difficulties, we pushed ahead and came away a week later satisfied that we had done a good job.

2. *Time for others.* Christian love places other people and their well-being high on the priority list (Matthew 22:39). The following 'hierarchy of loyalties' (based on Higginson 1988: 214) may help: after God, with whom we have a relationship for eternity, come family, dependants and closest friends – those with whom we have lifelong ties. Then come others with whom we have significant but shorter-term contact, such as work colleagues, friends and neighbours. Those in need also deserve our attention, and when this is acute, may come high on this list. Circumstances will sometimes make balancing such loyalties more complex than this hierarchy suggests, but it is nevertheless a good overall guide.

3. *Time for church.* Being available for the work of God's church in the world is part of a Christian's responsibility. The New Testament makes it clear that the church is a priesthood of all believers (Ephesians 4:11–16; 1 Peter 2:9), not a few professionals and a lot of spectators, but a team where everyone is a playing member. While our service in the church may vary according to circumstances and other demands on our time (remember, work itself is serving God), it remains an obligation through our membership of Christ's body.

4. *Time for self.* As the saying goes: 'All work and no play …' It is important to build in time for rest and relaxation, for interests, hobbies and leisure (Exodus 34:21; Mark 6:31). These can be pursued with family or friends, and also through church activities, and so can be coupled with the items above.

# Work in proper perspective

## What is work?

So far I have described the purposes of work: a means of sustenance for ourselves and our families, to provide satisfaction as we use and develop our God-given abilities and aptitudes, to serve others and, underlying all of these, to serve God. Work is a God-ordained part of our lives, part of creation's pattern and a key way in which we subdue the earth and work out God's purposes for ourselves and the world. People, as those who undertake work, give work meaning as they continue, in God's image, the ongoing work of creation and sustenance of the world. Work also has meaning because of the purposes it achieves. And, as we have seen, for work to be good for us, it needs to be different from, and balanced by, rest.

Taking these aspects into account, my practical definition of work is *purposeful human activity to achieve necessary tasks* or, in short, *purposeful activity*. Work is not everything there is to life; to regard it as such is to make it into an idol and to become its slave; it is a hard taskmaster because there is always more work to do. Nor is it merely a necessary evil in order to survive; this is to deny the value and satisfaction of creative work. It can be the purposeful activity of running a business, assembling a car, or writing a computer programme; of raising children, organizing a household, or studying for exams; of leading a church, being a professional cricketer or undertaking voluntary work. Because work depends on both the person undertaking it and on its object, what is work for one may be leisure to another. One person does gardening for a living, while for another it is a hobby. Or someone may undertake an activity which is work in one context (as a stamp dealer), but a form of leisure in another (as an avid stamp collector).

Work can be paid employment, voluntary work, housework, raising children, studying at college, learning at school or even, for the unemployed, the process of applying for jobs. These are all purposeful activities undertaken for specific and necessary reasons related to our survival and well-being – to enable, sustain and fulfil life.

## By the sweat of your brow

This is all very well, but some find work boring and soul-destroying, or dirty and dangerous. Work is ordained by God, but as Genesis 3 depicts and as our experience confirms, it is often characterized by toil and sweat rather than by significance and dignity (Genesis 3:19). To eke out a meagre living to survive is a long way removed from grandiose notions of subduing the earth. Genesis 3:17 paints an even harsher picture: 'Cursed is the ground because of you; through painful toil you will eat of it all the days of your life.' Given the struggle often associated with work, the words of the Preacher in Ecclesiastes ring true: 'What does a man get for all the toil and anxious striving with which he labours under the sun? All his days his work is pain and grief; even at night his mind does not rest. This too is meaningless' (Ecclesiastes 2:22–23).

The creation pattern establishes human dignity and responsibility in subduing the earth, but the fall renders work a struggle to survive. This is depicted in the Garden of Eden account by a curse on the ground. 'So the two essential principles offer us opposite extremes and the whole range of human work lies somewhere in the range between them, interpreted in the light of both' (Dow 1994: 6).

When work becomes toil it is often unwelcome and frustrating, and sometimes dehumanizing. However, there are some aspects of toil which may be interpreted in a more positive way. First, the toil of work is one way in which we share in the suffering of Christ as we daily follow him (Luke 9:23). This is a common theme in the writings of Paul, where suffering is seen as part of the cost of living a godly life and spreading the gospel, but also as a way of building Christian character and later of sharing in Christ's glory (e.g. 2 Timothy 3:10–12; Romans 5:3; 8:17; Philippians 3:10–11).

Secondly, experience shows that job satisfaction often stems from overcoming difficulty in a task, or working hard at something until it is solved, or creating something good through effort and perseverance. While hard work and effort are not synonymous with toil (the former can be very enjoyable whereas the latter implies a degree of drudgery or futility), a certain amount of toil is often associated with them. In many instances the job satisfaction would have been lessened had the task not involved some difficulty to overcome. So, even when work is mostly toil, God can use it for our good.

Whereas we all have some 'toilsome' aspects to our jobs, some work is intrinsically bad: for example, when we ourselves are treated as a mere 'means' (exploited, oppressed, discriminated against, de-skilled, under-employed), when work is relentlessly toilsome, when its products or processes are evil or when it destroys the world with which we are entrusted.

E. F. Schumacher focuses on the damaging effects of some types of bad work, stating that people 'should be encouraged to *reject* meaningless, boring, stultifying, or nerve-racking work in which a man (or woman) is made the servant of a machine or a system. They should be taught that work is the joy of life and is *needed* for our development, but that meaningless work is an abomination.' He makes the point that it destroys initiative, discourages people from using their brains and degrades 'the moral and intellectual qualities of man', thus damaging 'his soul and his spirit' (1979: 36, 119). God is opposed to the oppression caused by bad work, as exemplified by his rescue of the Israelites from slave labour in Egypt (Exodus 1:11–14), and so should we be. If our work is like this, we should seek to change it or find ways of making it more challenging and meaningful (as described in chapter 5); or, if this is not possible, to seek to move on (chapter 8) and find where God would have us use our skills.

### *All is not lost*

Creation, despite its fallen nature, is still God's (Psalm 24:1–2): created, sustained, loved and redeemable by him. Revelation 21:1 pictures a new heaven and a new earth, representing redemption in its consummate completeness. The incursion on earth of God's kingdom rule through Jesus (Mark 1:14–15), and subsequently through his church, shows that Christians have a part to play in this redemptive activity (Colossians 1:9–14). Every time we act in conformity with God's purposes, espousing his reign in our lives, we contribute to establishing his kingdom on earth and his redemptive activity of drawing the world back to himself. Work, as one of life's major activities, is a means by which we can take part in this redemption and help usher in God's kingdom. This happens every time we make a good product, solve a problem, provide excellent service, complete a task well, defend a principle, help to develop others, promote good relationships, expose wrongdoing or do a good job.

## The action column

1. Do you make time for 'rest' – time and space away from work, ensuring you have opportunity to replenish reserves, enjoy relaxation and spend time with family and friends and with God? If not, decide how you will change things.
2. How do you manage your responsibilities at work together with those to your family?

3.  Is the way you handle your work balance consistent with a Christian set of priorities? Do you have time for God, for others, for church and for yourself?

4.  Do you have work in proper perspective – understanding its good purposes, working to redeem it when it goes bad?

CHAPTER 3

# Keeping all the plates spinning

*Handling the pressures of work*

## Under pressure

*Calm amid the storm*

We have looked at the challenge of establishing a balance in line with a Christian view of life and work. Some of us have experienced the tension already when we have held to our principles to get home at a reasonable time. The problem is that as we become more disciplined about the balance in our life, we may feel under increased pressure at work, or feel bad about putting more pressure on others in the team. As if there was not enough pressure already! Having reasserted our priorities, we may wonder, 'How can I do all I need to get done in the working day? How can I keep all the plates spinning?'

There are some ways of tackling this problem that, coupled with our resolve to maintain a healthy balance for our life and work, can enable us to establish ways of working that will help when we are under pressure. The solutions are not always easy to implement and we will not always succeed. But underlying them all, God promises to help us when we are hard pressed, as the psalmist expressed: 'God is our refuge and strength, an ever-present help in trouble. Therefore we will not fear, though the earth give way and the mountains fall into the heart of the sea' (Psalm 46:1–2). In fact, as Paul found, when we are under pressure in our work and feel weak, Christ's power rests on us all the more and makes us strong (2 Corinthians 11:23–30; 12:7–10). Where we are anxious, we turn to him and find that his peace is available to guard our hearts and minds (Philippians 4:6–7). When the disciples were caught in a storm, they woke Jesus and he brought calm. But then he asked them, 'Where is your faith?' (Luke 8:25), implying that if they had trusted, they could have known calm in the midst of the storm.

God helps us to find a firm place to stand in the midst of trouble and pressure by his strength within us. Gordon MacDonald make this point powerfully in his book *Ordering your Private World*, arguing that it is as we make time and space for God and develop our 'inner life' (based on our relationship with the indwelling Christ) that we are strengthened to face better the pressures that come upon us. He speaks of the biblical writers, whose work has endured: 'For what they wrote they received from the Creator *who made us to work most effectively from the inner world toward the outer*' (1985: 31). As we think through some practical ways of handling pressure, it is within the context of a caring God working alongside us and within us.

### All stressed up and nowhere to go

It was the world's largest industrial merger and the pressure was on. For ninety-nine days it was unrelenting. My colleague was at full stretch and, like the rest of us, was just coping. We were bringing together complex organizations, helping to select people for jobs, dealing with the politics, making people redundant and, on top of it all, dealing with our own uncertainty. But there was a particularly unreasonable request that pushed my colleague too far and he found himself experiencing symptoms of intense stress. The doctor decided to sign him off sick.

'But I can't be off, there's too much to do,' my colleague protested.

'Are you the only employee your company's got, then?' asked the doctor.

'No, but … '

'How many other employees are there?'

'Well, about a hundred thousand, but …'

'And they can't do without one of them?'

'But I'm part of the merger work …'

'So you're indispensable, then?'

'No, but it's all hands to the pump.'

'What, even dead ones?'

My colleague took some time off; the company survived and so did he.

A certain amount of pressure prompts action and increases performance as our minds and bodies respond to the stimulus. But if it is intense and/or prolonged, those responses keep us in a pattern of alertness, and cause physical, emotional and behavioural symptoms that signal that we are under stress and may be doing ourselves harm.

It is one thing to recognize the symptoms of stress and take action to alleviate them. It is another to identify the *sources* of stress and to tackle them, so as not to run the risk of continually returning to the same over-stressed state. This requires some discipline and some creativity on our part, and some help from others, to manage better the pressures upon us and the stress they create. The diagram is based on a model used by The Return Consultancy to help people balance work and home. It shows some ways to handle both the symptoms and the sources of stress and to achieve a right balance in our lives.

**On top under pressure**

Creates some space → **Managing stress**

Stops you going under

**Managing time**

**Keeping close to God**
*Calm amid the storm*

**Sharing the load**

Clarifies boundaries, builds confidence → **Saying 'no'**

Provides additional help

(Modified from The Return Consultancy)

Each of these is an activity in its own right, but they are linked together. If we can manage stress better, we avoid going under and are in a stronger position to take control of our situation and get the necessary help. Sharing the load gets tasks adequately resourced, makes us realize we are not indispensable and gives us the confidence to say 'no'. Being more assertive helps to establish with others the way we intend to work, builds our confidence and helps us to manage our time better. Managing time helps to create some space to be proactive and to relax.

# Managing stress

There are ways to manage stress and there are lots of books that can help (for example, *Pressure Points* by Peter Meadows). Here is a brief summary.

## *Ask God for his help and strength*

As underlined at the outset of this chapter, turning to God is the Christian's first port of call, not the last resort. God promises us protection when we are assailed, his strength when we feel weak, and his peace amid the storm. As we feel stress encroaching, we should turn to God first. As the psalmist declared: 'When I said, "My foot is slipping," your love, O LORD, supported me. When anxiety was great within me, your consolation brought joy to my soul' (Psalm 94:18–19).

## *Recognize the symptoms*

There are well-documented symptoms of stress and these affect people in different ways:

- *Physical:* headaches, sleep disorders, chest pains, breathing problems, etc.
- *Behavioural:* inability to concentrate, inability to relax, rushing everything, anger and aggression, crying, complaining, escape activities (drinking, smoking, eating disorders), etc.
- *Emotional:* loss of self-esteem, loneliness, pessimism, depression, etc.

## *Look after yourself*

If you recognize you are under stress, you need to take steps to look after yourself. This will help to alleviate the symptoms, and may also help to address some of the sources. There are some well-tried ways:

- *Rest and relaxation.* If you are to survive under pressure, establish a balance, and get a right perspective on your work. These are a biblical imperative.
- *Exercise.* Whether exercise takes the form of a sport or just a regular walk, it benefits body and mind, and also helps you to use up the excess energy associated with stress. Recognize that your body is a temple of the Holy Spirit (1 Corinthians 6:19), to be treated with care and respect.
- *Diet* can be neglected or abused because of stress. Maintaining a good diet helps the body cope with the pressure it is under.

- *Sharing your feelings with others:* the act of expressing how you feel can be therapeutic in itself, but also draws out the support of others.

### Identify and tackle the sources

Addressing the symptoms helps, but we must also identify the sources of stress. Sometimes this is easy, and the real problem is not having the will to do something about them. If we have grown used to being a 'martyr to the cause' and are quite proud of coping with an impossible workload, we may see shedding some of that work as a sign of weakness. Sometimes identifying the sources is more difficult; perhaps the problem is not any single task but the fact that there are lots of them, so that even a small demand feels like the straw that breaks the camel's back. Perhaps we are distracted from the true cause by another factor: we see our boss as the cause of stress when really it is our own perfectionism, or some tension in another area of our lives.

The following sections suggest how we can tackle the sources of stress through sharing the load, saying 'no' and managing time.

## Sharing the load

### You cannot handle it alone ...

No-one wants to do himself or herself out of a job, but many of us are under more pressure than we need to be because we do not *delegate* effectively. Moses received wise counsel from his father-in-law Jethro: 'The work is too heavy for you; you cannot handle it alone' (Exodus 18:18). Jethro advised him to delegate much of it to others who were able to help. If he had not heeded the advice, important things would not have got done and he would have suffered through doing too much. There are just not enough hours in the day for one person to do everything that needs doing.

Delegation is doubly beneficial, since, in addition to relieving the person under pressure, it encourages others to use and develop their skills. Jesus delegated some of his mission work to his disciples (Luke 9 and 10). His trust affirmed them in their mission roles and fostered their growth in the work. But delegation is not the 'dumping' of unwanted or low-level tasks on junior colleagues. To be undertaken well and with commitment, delegated tasks need to be manageable with some shared benefit, or they will not get done properly and the person who delegated them will be held accountable. Moses delegated some of his tasks so that he would 'be able to stand the strain' (Exodus 18:23) and so that the tasks would get done to everyone's satisfaction.

A few years ago my boss Martin asked me to represent him in some discussions at an overseas office. He told me that he was more than happy for me to stand in for him on such occasions. His willingness to delegate increased my confidence and at that stage gave me some valuable experience. It saved him from another journey away from home in an already busy schedule.

Why do we often find it difficult to delegate? Sometimes it is because we feel the need to keep control of all we are responsible for. We may think only *we* can complete the task and that it has to be done *our* way. It may be something we really enjoy, our 'baby'. We may feel insecure about our position and threatened by the competence of others. These are common, and usually unjustifiable, fears. If we try to cling on to everything in an attempt to keep all the plates spinning, some will inevitably drop – or we will. We may also gain a reputation for being unwilling to accept help, or selfish, protective, or overly pedantic. To delegate, we must be willing to rely on others and to give up some of our work. This involves trust (will they be able to handle the task?) and self-sacrifice (am I willing to relinquish control?). But if we succeed, the load will be reduced, those entrusted will benefit and everyone's time will be better used.

*Giving away power*

Another method of sharing the load is to give a task fully over to another person, together with the resources to undertake it and responsibility for the result. The delegated task of mission work that the disciples undertook when Jesus was with them later became fully theirs (Matthew 28:16–20; Acts 1:8) for which they were given the resources (the power of the Holy Spirit) and the freedom of action to accomplish it. *Empowerment* is another of those jargon words that is now slipping into normal language through its popularity with management gurus and its adoption by organizations. It means freeing people from instructions and controls, allowing and encouraging them to take decisions themselves and to use their own initiative. Why the emphasis on this in recent years? In an environment of rapid and continual change (chapter 6 outlines the background to this), it can help to make an organization more responsive (people can make decisions without getting approval), reduce costs through taking out management layers (delayering), and improve collaboration between people who are free to communicate 'horizontally' across the organization rather than just 'vertically' up and down a hierarchy.

Empowerment can be abused by pushing unwanted responsibilities upon people: not all want more autonomy, challenge and responsibility at work; they may have enough in other areas of their lives. Also, empowerment has to be appropriate to the type of job, the tasks in hand, the company culture and the ability of the individual concerned. However, if used conscientiously it can help to take pressure from over-busy people while enabling others to exercise more initiative in the work they do and to use their talents better. It is very close to the principle of subsidiarity, which states that it is right and just for responsibility to be handed down to the lowest possible level.

Empowerment is not a matter of getting someone to help you with *your* task; rather, you give the task to them and it becomes *theirs*, or you encourage them to take control of the tasks already theirs. It is a way of treating people with respect and trust: 'The philosophy of empowerment recognizes that nobody knows a job better than the person doing it, and that most people want to be involved and take a pride in the work that they do' (Smith 1996: 7). The appointing of the 'seven' in Acts 6:1–6 is an example of empowerment, since the apostles turned the responsibility in question wholly over to them. In relation to the church, Paul states that people have different gifts and should be able to use them ('If it is serving, let him serve; if it is teaching, let him teach …' Romans 12:7). Empowerment, when used well, encourages people to do what they are good at, and hence upholds this principle. Empowerment is also a hallmark of God's dealings with humankind since creation: 'God uses power to empower' (Goldingay & Innes 1994: 10). Just as God empowers us, we should empower those around us and encourage them to empower themselves, so that their skills are used to best effect and so that we can survive under pressure. Whereas empowerment in the business world is often driven by an organization's need to become more efficient (which can lead to more pressure upon people and sometimes to abuse), a Christian view of empowerment puts people before profit and uses empowerment responsibly for people, not against them.

A high-profile two-week event needed organizing. It was my idea and my project. But I didn't have the time to do it. Diane was a gifted organizer and loved a challenging task to tackle and complete. She was already responsible for the project's administration. Somewhat reluctantly, I handed over to her the organizing. If I am honest, it was not so much 'Can she handle it?' as 'Am I able to let it go?' Diane did a superb job, and grew in confidence and ability as a result. She said it was one of the most satisfying tasks she had ever undertaken. When the idea was taken up by another site, it was Diane they asked for, not me; and what had started as delegation became empowerment.

It can be difficult to empower because we feel we are losing control. Yes, we do lose hands-on control of the activity, but, by setting the direction and the boundaries, we can retain the control necessary to ensure the task is done; that is, we control the context in which empowered decisions are made. This represents a cultural shift, and in part reflects a move from managing to leading (as described in chapter 10), so that the role of supervisor is one of 'team leader and coach, not driver and controller' (Burdett 1991: 27). The culture necessary is one of mutual support and learning; it may require changes in attitude (so that we all take more responsibility for our work), relationships (sharing power, responsibility, communication, expectations and rewards), and organizational structure (policies and practices to encourage empower-ment) (Scott & Jaffe, 1992: 10, 40). Delegation and empowerment are both key aspects of leading and motivating others; done well, they convey dignity and respect, and lighten our own load.

### Getting some help

I was worried about committing the team, already overstretched, to further work. But the issue of resource planning had been raised by employees, and we knew that senior management wanted it addressed. I wondered how the conversation with my boss would go, especially since I had already expanded the team and was struggling to manage the budget. But he recognized the need for the new work and, before I could protest, added, 'If you need additional people to do it, that will not be a problem.'

You can use your time better, delegate and empower others and still find that you cannot cope with the workload in a reasonable time frame. If this is continual rather than sporadic, and if you are to establish a decent balance to protect yourself and your family from harm, further action is needed. You may need to make a case for further help, or for reducing the workload, or both. These are sensitive areas; no-one wants to tell their boss they cannot cope, and most organizations like to feel they are getting leaner through efficiency, not increasing staff numbers. The way you handle such issues will depend on your place in the organization, or, if self-employed, what increases in people or cuts in work can be made without harming your business.

In a supervisory role, you may have a direct influence over staffing levels or the amount and type of work undertaken. As a team member, you will need a conversation with your boss. There is a positive way to frame the discussion, since taking on more people or reducing the number of tasks can add value in addition to lessening the load on those under pressure (which also adds value in the long term). Reducing work is a tried and tested management technique for enhancing efficiency. The skill lies in deciding which tasks can be dropped or be better done elsewhere without putting people's safety or the business at risk. If you are self-employed or in unpaid activity you will need to make a disciplined and realistic appraisal of your work commitments. Temporary or short-term contract help can be brought in during busy times; such labour-market flexibility should not be used only for the benefit of organizations.

One of my first projects in a personnel role was to run the annual employee share scheme. On top of my normal workload, which was heavy in the new job, I was responsible for distributing and processing the share-scheme forms for 2,000 people – a relatively straightforward yet seemingly endless task that ate up my evenings for two weeks, made me grumpy and delayed other important work. Because I did such a good job (if only my boss had known what I had said to my wife at the time!), I was given the honour of doing the same the following year. This time I hired some temporary help, an ex-employee who welcomed the work. Some additional costs were incurred, but these were effectively cancelled out because I was free to complete other pressing tasks. It went well and became the pattern for the years that followed.

There is also a moral argument for hiring or contracting more help when the pressure gets too great. And this is true not just for the workplace, but for work in the home also; if the pressure is such that we need help with the cleaning or the gardening, let's not be 'inverse snobs' and reject the notion as in some way demeaning for those who would do it – they may be glad of the work. It is absurd and unjust that those in work are increasingly overstretched and overstressed while thousands who would dearly love to work remain unemployed. This amounts to an abuse of those in work through relentless pressure and a waste of the talents of those out of work. It serves to divide society further into the 'haves' and the 'have nots'. If we return to the biblical purposes of work (to provide sustenance, satisfaction and a way of serving God and others), then all people have the right to work. We have a responsibility to uphold this right for each other, and when our own work is so great as to bury us, we should be looking for ways to share it so that others can work too.

## Saying 'no'

### Firmness under fire

We were talking about the pros and cons of family-friendly policies when a female manager said of a male colleague, 'He would always call the management meetings early in the morning, even though he knew I had to sort the children out. I asked him if he could schedule them later; he said yes, but then called the next one at 7.30am. It got to the point where I didn't like to keep asking, so I just got to most of the meetings late, feeling disadvantaged and guilty.'

How can you handle the demands of others upon you, which is crucial if you are to establish a better balance in life? Even if you are successful at handling the pressure of work, you will find that others will want to fill the time you have created. Or you may find yourself tempted to fill this new space with more of your own work. If you are to gain ground and then retain it, you must be able to say what you feel about a situation, and be able to say 'no'.

Saying 'no' means stating your view clearly, in line with the balance you wish to achieve. In popular jargon it means being *assertive*, although such terminology is sometimes disliked by Christians because it can suggest a selfish attitude: getting one's own way at another's expense. Indeed, many assertiveness courses do stress the need to exert your own rights and to get what *you* want. But there is a proper place for assertiveness which is not selfish, but upholds what is fair and is in line with the principle of achieving a balance. Many of us find it difficult to say 'no' because we have interpreted the Christian characteristics of humility and meekness as softness and weakness. Jesus showed how humility and courage, meekness and forthrightness, could be held together and in fact complement each other. He was forthright in standing up for what was right when evicting the money-changers from the temple (John 2:12–17), bold in his dealings with the teachers of the law (Matthew 9:1–8) and frank in his condemnation of the hypocrisy of the Pharisees (Matthew 23). Yet he did this without boasting, without the selfishness of wanting his own way and without the desire to put others down.

During a course on assertiveness, a participant said, 'It's OK for you.

My job's already been outsourced. If I say "no" to doing something I'll lose my job altogether. It's better to do as you're told than to be made redundant.' Good point. We may need to tread carefully, particularly when our skills are easily replaced. But we do still have rights. As another participant observed: 'If we all keep saying "yes" to the impossible, then it will only get worse and we will get the organization and working patterns we deserve.'

Saying 'no' does not have to be an expression of selfishness or one-upmanship, but can be a way of aligning how we wish to live with the principles we hold. It is being honest and straightforward about what we think. How many times have we said 'yes', when what we meant or wanted to say was 'no'? As Jesus said in the context of making oaths: 'Simply let your "Yes" be "Yes", and your "No", "No" ' (Matthew 5:37). The principle is that we should be as good as our word, and confident enough to state our view without having to justify it in great detail. To do this requires us to be courageous and bold, something God promises to help us with (Psalm 138:3). But the *way* we state our view is important if we are not to appear rude or arrogant. As when sharing the gospel, it is to be with 'gentleness and respect' (1 Peter 3:15–16), acknowledging the views and feelings of others.

I find it hard to say 'no'. In an effort to please rather than offend, I find myself saying 'yes' to things that I know will put me under pressure. An example occurred when writing this chapter. Could I attend a two-day meeting followed by a three-day course? I was already committed to time away from home that month. More absences would create further stress for my wife and more upheaval for the children. But I did not want to let the team down, particularly as I was its leader. Anyway, it was only for five days. I said 'yes'. My daughter wept in my arms the week before I left: 'Daddy, why do you have to go away again? Why can't they come to our country? I hate it when you are away.' I changed my schedule so that I was away for two days instead of five. I had managed a 'half-no'.

How can saying 'no' work in practice? A good friend of mine, Dot, who runs courses on assertiveness, uses an example like the following. Suppose you have been asked to work late, but tonight you have promised to be in at a reasonable time to attend a parents' evening at the school. The response that tries not to give offence, and is not true to the way you feel, is: 'It's difficult, but if you can't find someone else, I suppose I can stay late.' A response at the other extreme would be: 'You always ask me; can't you get someone else this time?' This denies the boss even the right to ask. A straightforward way of saying 'no' would be: 'No, I'm sorry. I know you have a problem in getting someone, but I'm unable to help tonight.' You may wish to help the boss to find an alternative solution, but you must not feel guilty that you cannot solve the problem personally, and you must resist the need to explain to the last detail why it is difficult for you. Most people are reasonable when a member of their staff says 'no', and will accept that there must be a good reason. This approach takes an 'assertive' rather than a 'passive' or 'aggressive' position. Terry Gillen gives other examples of this approach in his book *Assertiveness* (1997).

What is the key to saying 'no' effectively? Some guidelines may help:

- Be open and honest with yourself and others (Matthew 5:37).
- Listen to others and acknowledge their concerns. 'Look not only to your own interests, but also to the interests of others' (Philippians 2:4).
- Express your own view clearly and succinctly. Avoid apologizing or justifying. Ask God for help – he makes us 'bold and stout-hearted', 'as bold as a lion' (Psalm 138:3; Proverbs 28:1), and can give us the right words in a difficult spot (Luke 21:15).
- Treat others with respect and gentleness (1 Peter 3:15–16): 'Let your conversation be always full of grace' (Colossians 4:6).
- Stay calm, and repeat the point if it seems not to have been heard or understood. Put on God's armour (truth, righteousness, faith, etc.) so that 'you may be able to stand your ground' (Ephesians 6:13).

Saying 'no' takes some practice, so we must not worry if we fail some of the time. It may also involve some loss, since there is always someone willing to work longer or for less, and the boss may choose that person for the next project or promotion. But we trust God with such matters, attaching greater value to keeping the right balance. Unless we learn how to say 'no' simply and honestly, the balance we are striving to achieve may be hijacked by those who see us as an easy option to offload some of their own poorly handled pressure.

## Managing time

*A time for everything ...*

I started coming into work earlier in an attempt to get a report written that I had kept putting off. Its deadline was now fast approaching. But each day there were pressing tasks that demanded my attention and gobbled up the 'extra' time I had sought to create. By the time I had checked the in-tray and the e-mail, the post and the voice-mail, the phone had begun to ring. Soon, everyone else had arrived and the round of meetings had started. I stayed late to keep on top of the day's happenings. Into the briefcase went the report, to be done that evening, but there was not much of the evening left. It was postponed to the weekend, but we had visitors. I completed it late on Sunday night.

Just as money needs managing, so does time if we are to have any of it left at the end of the day. The business training course that has affected my own work habits more than any other was a one-day programme on time management. As is obvious from the incident described above, I was in dire need of it. 'Consultant' jargon, you might think; but when some simple guidelines (mostly common sense) can have such a positive effect, it is wise to heed them. In fact, the Genesis picture of creation gives us a model of perfect time management; the work of creation is described as a planned and ordered set of activities, with time at the end for rest. Whereas business time management is often about being more productive, the biblical principles underlying our use of time are more fundamental.

Time is the medium in which we live our lives, and as such it has some distinct characteristics. First, as Michel Quoist states in his poem 'Lord, I have time' (1963: 77), it is a *gift* from God, and as such it is our responsibility to be good stewards of it. Like all gifts from God, we get the best from them as we offer them back to him, without selfishness or reservation. Jesus articulated such a principle with the words 'whoever loses his life for me will find it' (Matthew 16:25). If we can say as the psalmist said, 'My times are in your hands' (Psalm 31:15), we will have begun to recognize that our time really is God's, and that we can trust him to help us use it well.

Secondly, it is limited, in terms both of our overall life-span ('The length of our days is seventy years – or eighty, if we have the strength'; Psalm 90:10) and of the time we have each day. 'There are only twenty-four hours in the day,' one boss used to tell me when I tried to take on too much. And, as the builder of bigger barns in Jesus' parable found, we may have less time than we think (Luke 12:13–21), and this focuses even more attention on how we use it. The Bible also places a cosmic limit on the time available, because of the promised return of Christ. Jesus' message was that his return will come unexpectedly, and therefore we need to be prepared (Matthew 24:42). Paul encouraged people to live in the light of Christ's return (1 Thessalonians 5); that it could happen any day is not an excuse for idleness but gives us the motivation to work hard and use well the time we have (2 Thessalonians 3:6–13).

Thirdly, as the writer of Ecclesiastes noted, 'There is a time for everything, and a season for every activity under heaven' (3:1), the implication being that there is a right time for life's different activities or events to occur, and a right way to use the time we have each day. As Steve Chalke points out in his book *Managing Your Time*, 'The biblical idea of stewardship applies just as much to time as it does to money and other resources' (1998: 12). So our prayer becomes, 'Lord, how can I best use the time I have to serve you today?' In the Gospels, we see Jesus busy and pressured, but he made choices about the use of his time, sometimes stepping aside from what people would have him do to minister to an individual (Mark 10:46–52; Luke 8:40–48; 19:1–10), making time to underline an important lesson for the disciples (Luke 9:18ff.), to encourage others in their use of time (Luke 10:38–42), or to find quiet (Mark 6:46).

## Taking control of your time

Managing time amounts to organizing and prioritizing your work so that it is done in an optimum way, distinguishing what is really necessary from what is discretionary. Some fear that being organized and having a structure can stifle creativity and initiative. Certainly, our different personalities and preferences mean that a well-laid plan that will reduce stress for one person will feel like a strait-jacket to another. To a certain extent it is 'horses for courses'; we each need to find methods that will help us, whatever our preferred style of working, to use our time to best effect.

While there are many events that we have little or no control over, within work most people have some control over how and when things are done; we need to manage our time at work to minimize the pressure we feel and to contribute to the balance we are aiming to achieve. If we don't manage our own time, others will manage it according to their priorities. Marian Haynes (1996: 16–17) describes three tests which can help:

- *The test of necessity.* Is this task necessary? The *what*.
- *The test of appropriateness.* Am I the most appropriate person to be doing this task? The *who*.
- *The test of efficiency.* What is the best way of doing the task? The *how*.

Here are some guidelines for managing your time.

### Make a list

During a training event in Nigeria, I met Falaki, who had helped to arrange our visit. She was a PA in a busy role supporting several senior managers. They made constant demands on her time, most of which were, of course, urgent. The addition of a further manager to support caused the plates she was spinning to wobble and start crashing down. She was struggling to balance multiple tasks, beginning to miss things out, and not satisfying anyone, least of all herself. But she made it to the session on time management. The next day, she had made a determined attempt to prioritize her work and get it under control. She enjoyed showing me the most urgent items of her 'to do' list written in ink on her wrist.

Making a list captures and clarifies the tasks we have to do and, for those who enjoy the feeling of task completion, gives the opportunity to tick them off as they are done. Result: as well as feeling more in control of our time, we will not forget things as easily, and will experience job satisfaction as some items are cleared off the list. Some people use 'to do' lists; others have time-management diaries or electronic planners to help them to list tasks and projects. Whatever method is used, having a list helps, and finding a way to carry over unfinished tasks means that we will not drop important ones. Updating the list at the end of the day is a good way of being ready to start the next day.

The same principle applies to longer-term activities and projects. These need capturing as soon as we know about them so that we can plan how and when to do them. A lot of work pressure is caused because we have not looked ahead and anticipated what will be required in a week or a month's time, and so should be started now.

### Prioritize tasks

Given the choice between doing an interesting, easily completed task and a difficult but important one, many of us will choose the former. Expressing our view on a straightforward topic, supplying some information we have at our fingertips, or tackling e-mails that we can quickly delete is easier than meeting a member of staff who thinks he is underpaid, analysing complex and conflicting results or writing that contentious report.

We need to *prioritize tasks*, otherwise the more interesting, less difficult or most urgent tasks will get done before the most important ones. Here are guidelines to prioritizing:

- First do tasks which are both urgent *and* important.
- Then do urgent tasks.
- Then do important tasks (having planned when to do them).
- Finally, do routine tasks, but ask yourself: 'If it is not urgent or important, should I be doing this?'

When we have our priorities established, the less important work and the interruptions get directed into the available gaps, rather than the other way round.

### Break tasks into manageable pieces

I had spent a year with the company, and it was my first big project to undertake unassisted. A month had gone by with little to show for it, and I was panicking. There was so much to do, but I couldn't seem to get started. I felt swamped by information and flitted from topic to topic, seemingly unable to make an impact. It felt as though I was trying to put my arms around an elephant. The panic made things worse and the hurdle got higher. Cramming my problem into a moment's thought made the elephant appear even bigger, and I felt depressed. Some advice from my boss Mike broke the log jam; he helped me to see that, divided into its constituent parts, the project was achievable, and he suggested which pieces to tackle first.

We need to break tasks into manageable pieces, otherwise the psychological barrier to even starting them can be insurmountable. Writing this book, for example, seemed a daunting undertaking, but broken into its smaller parts (a plan, chapter headings, research into specific topics, a first chapter, etc.) made it less of a mountain to climb.

### Plan quality time for important tasks

Peter was as busy as the rest of us but he could always find the time to design a workshop or write some notes for a training programme. I wondered how he managed it. When I asked for a meeting with him concerning some work we were doing together, I got an insight into his diary. For important tasks that needed pre-work, he would count back from the due date and block out some preparation time in his schedule. He would then book a quiet room away from his desk to do this work, and treat the appointment with himself as being as important as any other; he would not give up that time lightly. Not surprisingly, he met his commitments.

Some tasks need concentrated attention, an uninterrupted period of time when we are at our best. This sort of time needs to be carved out of our schedule and then kept sacrosanct if we are to get the task done. During such time, we need to choose or create an environment that helps us to work, and interruptions need to be controlled (divert the telephone, leave e-mail or the in-tray alone, find somewhere quiet if necessary) so that we can give the task our undivided attention. Ideally, we need to plan this time when we work best. We each have our own preferred work cycle, and it is worth understanding your own.

### Beware procrastination

When I occasionally complete a DIY task (there are lots of stories without endings in this area of my life) and before I get complacent, my wife Clare reminds me of the mirror that waited eighteen months to be hung, and of the many other jobs put off because of bad weather or lack of materials or the right tools. Here, above all, I am prone to procrastination; to put it bluntly, there are other things I would rather be doing!

So it often is with our work; it is tempting to find other things to do rather than tackle that difficult and important task that lies waiting. Some procrastination can be helpful if it drives you to get lots of small tasks done while you muster up the will to tackle the important one, and a looming deadline can help to focus the mind. But this is often simply time-wasting. And beware: the longer you put things off, the harder they can become and the more pressure you will put yourself under as the deadline draws closer.

Some people relish the feeling of working 'on the edge', and enjoy being under the pressure of time; their energy builds as the deadline approaches and they give their best in the final flurry of activity. This works for some, but carries the danger of not completing the task on time, or of turning pressure into stress.

### Do things once

Picking up that memorandum and reading it for the third time, then putting it back in the pile because it is too difficult to deal with, wastes time. Starting a job that you know you cannot complete can be frustrating. It is best to deal with each piece of paper, e-mail or request *once*, or else to put it in the pending tray to be dealt with when you have the necessary information. When deciding to embark on a task, you need to ensure that you can move it along or complete some phase of it. Otherwise it's best to leave it for now and plan when you will be able to tackle it.

## Build in some contingency time

When I asked a group what were the stumbling-blocks in their management of their time, one of the strongest responses was, 'Other people.' There may have been some passing of blame here, but they gave enough examples to show that the complaint was real: the manager who asked for the report just before an employee was about to leave the office, the person who promised to supply information which didn't arrive, the client who turned up late so that a rep missed his next appointment. We could all add to the list from our own experiences, and, if we are honest, admit the times we have sabotaged someone else's well-planned day.

There will always be unexpected demands from others, and emergencies that mean we have to put our best-laid plans aside. We cannot prevent every unscheduled happening (life would be rather boring if we could), but we can increase our ability to handle them by building in some *contingency time*. A little slack in your schedule means that there is some room to cope with the unexpected, and also recognizes that most things take longer than we allow. But beware: too much unplanned time can become a dumping-ground for the tasks of disorganized colleagues.

## Lead by example

There was a point during the merger when, after lots of travelling and constant demands, I became tired, irritable and inefficient. People started to tell me how terrible I looked, and I knew I was overdoing it. But it was difficult to get off the treadmill. In the end my boss told me he was worried about me and he intervened to reduce my workload and provided additional support. I was setting a poor example to those who worked with me; it needed someone to say, 'Enough's enough.'

In a leadership role, we must recognize that we have a responsibility to protect our team members from harming themselves by working too many hours; there are times when it is appropriate to lighten their load or to tell them to go home.

In any role, you can set an example by not being late for appointments and by sticking to deadlines so that you do not waste other people's time. You can say 'no' to unreasonable demands that jeopardize your balance. Such demands often arise because those making them have not maintained their own balance.

Self-discipline and creativity are two characteristics mentioned in the Bible. They are necessary to manage time well. Self-discipline (the ability to control ourselves responsibly and order our lives in line with God's standards) helps us to make lists, prioritize, plan quality time, and so on. Creativity (that part of us which, in the image of God, enables us to innovate and take initiative) helps us do more with the time we have by finding the best ways to do our tasks.

## The action column

1.  Are there tasks you can delegate? Perhaps there are some projects you can hand over completely to another member of the team, to his or her benefit?
2.  Do you need additional resources, or are there some tasks that can be dropped altogether? Find someone with whom to discuss the options.
3.  Plan to say 'no' in a situation that keeps putting you under un-necessary or unfair pressure. Ask God to give you the courage and the right words.
4.  Think how your time at work is organized. Update your 'to do' list, assign priorities, and put quality time aside for important tasks. Commit all your time to God and ask him to help you to use it wisely.

# CHAPTER 4

# With all your heart

*Making a difference in work*

## In search of excellence?

### Does my work count?

'I'm only a shop assistant,' Angela said. Behind her comment was the implication that because of her junior position in the organization she didn't have much influence and couldn't do much good. More than this, she felt she wasn't very important, in fact that she was insignificant in the order of things.

'Do you think you should be doing something else?' a friend asked me. 'Does God want you working for a multinational for ever?' Perhaps he does, perhaps he doesn't, I thought. What concerned me more was the assumption that working for a large company was somehow not wholesome or worthwhile. Further conversation revealed my friend's premises that 'full-time Christian work' was the ideal and everything else was really second best.

You may feel that your role or position, or the end product of your work, is not very significant. Perhaps it does not seem to serve God or others directly. It is easy to slip into thinking that your work doesn't count, that you will never be able to do anything worthwhile or that what you do will never really make a difference. Feelings of dissatisfaction like these can then lead to boredom, poor performance and seeking roles for which you are not particularly suited as a way out.

We need to seek what God has for us to do, and for the best ways to serve him. That may be in the job we have now. Even if it isn't, we can still serve him in that role until we find the next. Here are some biblical principles which underline the fact that whatever our work is, provided it is honest work, it can be undertaken in the service of God, and

49

therefore can make a difference.

## Working for the Lord

As Christians, we are exhorted to do our work 'as working for the Lord, not for men' (Colossians 3:23). This was Paul's instruction to the slaves (workers) in his letter to the Colossians, and is the underlying motivation to do a good job, to do things well. We know the effect of being asked to do a task by someone very senior, who has made a point of personally requesting that we undertake the job. It becomes a privilege and an honour, and we want to do it well. In a very real sense, it is God who is asking us to do our work, so ultimately he is the one for whom we are working. Instead of a chore or a duty, when our labour is done out of love for God and a corresponding desire to serve him in everything, it 'becomes joyous and free service and the source of deep satisfaction' (Richardson 1963: 47).

Paul states that we should strive in whatever we do to 'do it all for the glory of God' (1 Corinthians 10:31). To elaborate, God is served and glorified when people, made in his image, fulfil their role as trustees of his creation, subduing it, developing and using it as God intended, hence more clearly reflecting God's being. God has arranged creation so that it needs the participation and co-operation of people, through delegated authority and empowerment, to fulfil his purposes for it (Psalm 8:3–8). When we play our role correctly, God is served as his purposes are achieved, and his being is revealed and magnified through his creation.

## All manner of things

As I cleaned out the toilets I couldn't help thinking that perhaps they hadn't recognized all the other gifts I had. After all, I had recently graduated with an honours degree. I was starting a voluntary year, working at an outdoor centre in North Wales, and hoped to be 'used by God' in work with the visiting groups of young people. But the cleaning continued. After a particularly hard session – the group had been out in the rain and trodden mud everywhere – John, the centre manager, took me aside and complimented me on the job I had done, and said it was just as important to do the cleaning well as to work with the groups. It made me feel good about the sparkling showers and loos. The next day I was asked to help with the canoeing!

If we view the work we do as work for God, it follows that all good and legitimate work can be done for his service. It has been argued that 'all truth is God's truth' (Holmes 1979: 8); in a similar way it has been said that '*all* work is God's work, whether it is full-time church service or not' (Catherwood 1987: 16). More correctly, all *good* work is God's work. This means that to be glorifying to God, the work task does not need to be overtly Christian or in the form of direct service. Providing for oneself and one's dependants through an honest day's work brings glory to God. If this also brings personal fulfilment and serves others, the wider community and humankind, then all the better.

And it doesn't have to be 'important' in the eyes of this world to be service to God. The parable of the talents (Matthew 25:14–30) makes the point that being trustworthy in small things is just as worthy as managing large things, and may be preparation for the latter. The servants were given money to use according to their ability (verse 15). To the person given five talents and to the person given two, the master's response for their work was the same: 'Well done, good and faithful servant! You have been faithful with a few things; I will put you in charge of many things' (verses 21, 23). Furthermore, we must take hold of the responsibilities we are given, no matter how small. The servant who had been given one talent did not do anything with it, fearing he would lose even that, and was condemned by the master for being wicked and lazy. Some people do not realize that they can serve God in their work even though the position they hold is a lowly one; they regard work as simply a 'necessary evil', and concentrate on other areas. Work becomes a means of support and nothing more.

There may be times when our paid work subsidizes our 'work' in other areas of our life because the latter is our principal calling, but does not earn us enough to live on. Paul's principal work was his calling to be an apostle (1 Corinthians 9:1–2), and while he maintained that those who serve the church should be rewarded (1 Corinthians 9:14), he also held that, where possible, people should be able to support themselves (2 Thessalonians 3:7–10). He himself did this when necessary (e.g. tent-making; Acts 18:3). Ideally, the two areas are one, so that we can concentrate on what God wants us to do and earn our living at it; but this is not always possible, at least early on.

### In any and every situation

You may find yourself in a role which is not what you want to do for ever, or which you feel obliged to take because there are no other opportunities at present and it is your only way of earning a living. Paul's instruction to stay in whatever situation (calling) one finds oneself (1 Corinthians 7:20) was interpreted by Luther as remaining in and accepting one's particular 'station' in life. It is probably not the correct explanation of the verse (see chapter 8) and, in today's world, vocational mobility is increasingly necessary as work changes. It is important to seek the right role, but that does not negate your responsibility to do your best in the current role.

We may find ourselves in less than ideal circumstances. We are not judged on our circumstances (over which we may have no control), but on what we do in them. Paul speaks of making the best of circumstances: 'I have learned the secret of being content in any and every situation, whether well fed or hungry, whether living in plenty or in want.' What is Paul's secret? He continues: 'I can do everything through him who gives me strength' (Philippians 4:12–13). Applying this to work, we can find contentment and make the best of any job with God's help, and can therefore serve God in our work. This does not mean we accept unsafe conditions, soul-destroying work, or a role for which we are unsuited. But if we find ourselves in such circumstances, we can serve God as we work to change what is bad, or as we seek God's next step for us.

### Serving others is serving Christ

Jesus' parable of the sheep and the goats makes the point that when we help and serve other people, we serve God: 'I tell you the truth, whatever you did for one of the least of these brothers of mine, you did for me' (Matthew 25:40). The majority of jobs serve other people through provision of services or products. We may question some types of work because of their harmful products or the pollution they cause, or because of the way an organization undertakes its activities. But for most of us, if we undertake a job in good conscience and fulfil our work honestly, then, whatever our work, it can be used by God.

John V. Taylor makes a similar point by describing the breadth and range of the Holy Spirit's 'mission' activity through a wide range of occupations and work activities: 'The missionaries of the Holy Spirit include the probation officer and the literacy worker, the research chemist and the worn-out schoolteacher in a remote village, the psychiatrist and the designer, the famine-relief worker and the computer operator, the pastor and the astronaut' (1972: 38). If the majority of jobs can be honouring to God, there is little justification for viewing some jobs as more important than others. Their importance lies in how people serve God in them. As Derek Tasker states: 'He does not grade the work of the parson as more important than the work of the policeman, nor the work of the teacher as more important than the work of the taxi-driver. All are necessary to a right ordering of His world – to the redemption of what He has made' (1960: 39–40). This challenges the importance society places on the status and value of jobs, discussed in chapter 11.

As 2 Timothy 3:16–17 stresses, our grounding in the faith through Scripture is to equip us for 'every good work'. So, whatever the work, it can be done as service for God, which is a prime motivation to do it well.

### Doing things well

*In Search of Excellence* was a 1980s management book by Tom Peters and Robert Waterman Jr which extolled the drive for excellence as a way to corporate success. In their view, excellence in an organization 'comes from treating people decently and asking them to shine, and from producing things that work' (1982: xxv). As Christians, should we be in search of excellence in our work?

The Bible teaches that we are to do our work well, to work at it with all our heart, because ultimately it is for God (Colossians 3:23; Ephesians 6:7). Derek Tasker comments that a Christian 'ought to bring a distinctive attitude of mind to his work. He should be conscious of the fact that in rendering goods or service to others he is serving God' (1960: 55). Viewing work in this way helps us to see even mundane tasks in a new light.

The Bible underlines this by extolling the work of skilled people: 'Do you see a man skilled in his work? He will serve before kings; he will not serve before obscure men' (Proverbs 22:29). The skilled craftsman Bezalel was chosen with others by God to build the ark, the tent of meeting and its furnishings (Exodus 31:2). Kenaniah the head Levite was in charge of the singing 'because he was skilful at it' (1 Chronicles 15:22). Elsewhere in the Bible there are examples of other people chosen to undertake all manner of tasks well (Moses, Joseph, Nehemiah, David, Daniel, Paul, etc.). Although we view these figures as spiritual heroes (and they were), it is important to remember they were undertaking their work as a leader, an advisor in government, a soldier, a shepherd, a king, a missionary. And one of the reasons they did their jobs well was that they had God's help through the Spirit (e.g. Genesis 41:39–41; Exodus 31:3; Daniel 1:17).

So, as Tasker comments, work 'should be done as conscientiously, as thoroughly and as skilfully as it possibly can be done, for we should offer to God nothing that is not as perfect as we can make it' (1960: 58). However, the 'perfection' must be appropriate to the task in hand; we should not aim at a 'gold-plated' level of product or service when the requirement is for something different. It must relate to the overall requirement and context of the task, which will include good management of the available resources, including our time. I can remember when Tony and I, as young geology students, had three square miles of the Rhinog Mountains in Wales to map in just three weeks. Tony was good with the detail, but left to his own devices may have still been working in the field outside our chalet at the end of the allotted time. On the contrary, I missed most of the detail, and would have finished in the first week and failed the course. Together, we did the task to about the right level of detail and produced a good map in the time allowed, and we both passed.

Doing things well does not mean that we have to be the best at everything we do. Clearly, we are differently endowed, and do tasks in different ways and to different levels. What is important is doing the best that *we* can, as 'Biblical success is making the most of what we have been given by God' (Greene 1997: 105). This is one of the lessons of the parable of the talents (Matthew 25:14–30). It helps us to avoid the dangers of creating a cult of excellence. In Plato's *The Republic*, special privileges and training were given to those who excelled, the élite upon whom special responsibilities were laid. Nietzsche carried the ethic of excellence to its extreme with his doctrine of the 'superman', the tradition within which some Fascist and racist movements are rooted. In an increasingly technological world, requiring highly skilled people and ever higher standards of quality, it is easy to place increasing emphasis on excellence. A Christian view of excellence is not at odds with highly skilled people who do things well. However, it holds that everyone should have the opportunity to shine, and that achievements are measured in relation to a person's capability and desire to serve, not only by the results of a task. We can all please God if we have worked to the best of our ability.

The quality of the work we do, then, is important because of whom we serve; we are to work conscientiously and well, as for God. But it must always be done with an understanding of what is required, and using time and resources well. Otherwise we will end up working all hours so that work becomes our god, as well as failing at other areas of our lives and losing the balance referred to in chapter 2. We need God's help to get this balance right. Sometimes it will be better to do well what is possible in the time, rather than try to do too much and fail; as described in chapter 3, this involves being able to say 'no'. There are times when it is right to go the 'extra mile', in line with Jesus' teaching about serving others (Matthew 5:41), again being careful to judge where the real need is; some organizations would have us go the extra mile *for them* all the time in pursuit of productivity and profit!

Doing our work well is our duty to the ultimate 'boss', and brings us satisfaction as we use our skills. It is also a powerful witness to the one we serve.

## Christian character

### A distinctive character

Using our skills to do a good job is one aspect of serving God in our work. Another is *how* we undertake our work. This brings us to *character.* One of the most distinctive contributions we bring to our work as Christians is ourselves, through our character. As well as our unique personalities, we bring the distinctive qualities of Christian character – those moral qualities that shine through what we do and are. The relationship between work and character is two-way:

- Character helps to shape the work we do and the way we do it; work is a major area of life in which our character is utilized. We are to 'Be holy', to 'Live such good lives', to 'shine like stars' in a hostile world (1 Peter 1:13–16; 2:11–12; Philippians 2:14–16), which includes the workplace.
- The work we do helps to build character. It is as we work with others, face challenges, undergo hardship, make decisions, strive to achieve and undertake actions, that we form good habits and build character (Romans 5:3–4). As E. F. Schumacher states: 'A person's work is undoubtedly one of the most formative influences on his character and personality' (1979: 3).

What is distinctive about Christian character? First, character is a crucial part of biblical (particularly New Testament) teaching. As Richard Higginson comments: 'when one reads the New Testament, the amount of ethical material which provides direction on specific issues is sparse compared with the great wealth of teaching which exhorts the disciples to adopt certain attitudes and cultivate certain qualities' (1986: 10). Secondly, Christian character reflects God's values. A model of character needs to be linked to a set of values so that the qualities pursued align with a particular view of the world. The ancient Greeks defined virtues to be cultivated and vices to be avoided in line with the values of heroic society – virtues such as courage, fidelity, friendship, even cunning, were important to them. Later, in the philosophical schemes of Plato and Aristotle, wisdom, self-discipline, justice and prudence were key virtues, aligned with their view of 'the good'. The qualities of Christian character are aligned to God's character and a biblical set of values; as God said to the Israelites: 'be holy, because I am holy' (Leviticus 11:45; cf. 1 Peter 1:15–16).

Many of the qualities which distinguish Christian character are distilled into a number of lists in the New Testament, principally Galatians 5:22–23; Ephesians 4:2–3; Philippians 4:8; Colossians 3:12–14; 1 Timothy 6:11; 2 Timothy 2:22; James 3:17–18; 2 Peter 1:5–9; and 1 Corinthians 13:4–8a. These form the Christian virtue-set, although 'qualities' may be a better term, since the history of the term 'virtue' associates it with the Greek understanding that they are possessions which people can acquire through their own merit, whereas Christians recognize these qualities as the 'fruit of the Spirit' (Galatians 5:22–23).

Christian love is paramount, and love, faith and hope are three qualities which above all should characterize a Christian (1 Corinthians 13:13; 1 Thessalonians 1:3). A range of other qualities is listed, many of which recur in different passages. A number reflect the outworking of love, such as kindness, gentleness, compassion and forgiveness. Patience and perseverance, together with hope, relate to handling difficulties and the future. Some, like wisdom, discernment, courage and obedience, are about judging and doing what is right. Trustworthiness, godliness, peace, self-control and righteousness are internal characteristics. Some qualities are not listed in the New Testament as such, but may be inferred from both Old and New Testament teaching, for example justice and openness to God. The variety of qualities listed suggests they are not exhaustive, but examples in line with the overall shape of Christian character (see diagram below). In some instances they are obviously directly related to the issues and problems being faced by the recipients of the particular letter; for instance, hope and self-control are stressed by Peter to a church under trial and persecution (1 Peter 1:13, 21; 5:8); love in all its aspects is expounded by Paul to a divided and quarrelsome church (1 Corinthians 13).

# New Testament passages describing qualities of Christian character

But the fruit of the Spirit is love, joy, peace, patience, kindness, goodness, faithfulness, gentleness and self-control (Galatians 5:22–23).

Be completely humble and gentle; be patient, bearing with one another in love. Make every effort to keep the unity of the Spirit through the bond of peace (Ephesians 4:2–3).

Finally, brothers, whatever is true, whatever is noble, whatever is right, whatever is pure, whatever is lovely, whatever is admirable – if anything is excellent or praiseworthy – think about such things (Philippians 4:8).

Therefore, as God's chosen people, holy and dearly loved, clothe yourselves with compassion, kindness, humility, gentleness and patience. Bear with each other and forgive whatever grievances you may have against one another. Forgive as the Lord forgave you. And over all these virtues put on love, which binds them all together in perfect unity (Colossians 3:12–14).

But you, man of God … pursue righteousness, godliness, faith, love, endurance and gentleness (1 Timothy 6:11).

Flee the evil desires of youth, and pursue righteousness, faith, love and peace, along with those who call on the Lord out of a pure heart (2 Timothy 2:22).

For this very reason, make every effort to add to your faith goodness; and to goodness, knowledge; and to knowledge, self-control; and to self-control, perseverance; and to perseverance, godliness; and to godliness, brotherly kindness, and to brotherly kindness, love. For if you possess these qualities in increasing measure, they will keep you from being ineffective and unproductive in your knowledge of our Lord Jesus Christ (2 Peter 1:5–8).

But the wisdom that comes from heaven is first of all pure; then peace-loving, considerate, submissive, full of mercy and good fruit, impartial and sincere. Peacemakers who sow in peace raise a harvest of righteousness (James 3:17–18).

Love is patient, love is kind. It does not envy, it does not boast, it is not proud. It is not rude, it is not self-seeking, it is not easily angered, it keeps no record of wrongs. Love does not delight in evil but rejoices with the truth. It always protects, always trusts, always hopes, always perseveres. Love never fails (1 Corinthians 13:4–8a).

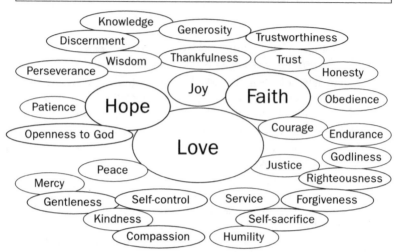

## Qualities of Christian character

Knowledge  Generosity  Trustworthiness

Discernment  Thankfulness  Trust

Wisdom  Honesty

Perseverance

Joy

Patience  **Hope**  **Faith**  Obedience

Openness to God  Courage  Endurance

**Love**

Godliness

Peace  Justice

Mercy  Righteousness

Gentleness  Self-control  Service  Forgiveness

Kindness  Self-sacrifice

Compassion  Humility

The qualities of Christian character are described as 'the *fruit* of the
Spirit', implying a unity of character. As Richard Higginson points out,
it 'suggests that they are inter-related, and that it is the Christian's
responsibility to "grow" them all' (1986: 11). The common themes
highlighted in the qualities that make up Christian character underline
this unity. Such unity is necessary if a person is to act consistently and
not be pulled in different directions. The importance of a unity of
virtues was emphasized by the Greek philosophers from Plato onwards,
and its significance grasped by both Augustine and Aquinas, who saw
love as the unifying virtue: 'And over all these virtues put on love,
which binds them all together in perfect unity' (Colossians 3:14).

The important point is that Christian character has a distinctive
direction and shape that are recognizable because they touch the image
of God in human beings. It is neither cloning nor social engineering,
and if it ever feels like this, it is unauthentic and misses the point.
Rather, it helps people to be more fully human and complete as they
move towards who God made them to be. This does not take away
individual personality; it enhances it, like polishing a tarnished coin,
bringing out the best and making it shine. But more than this, it adds
something as the Spirit of God enables and empowers growth in godly
character and subordination of ungodly behaviour: 'being a Christian
involves acceptance of a certain obligatory *shape* to one's life. Indi-

viduality is not extinguished when one becomes a follower of Jesus, but there is such a thing as a recognizable Christian character' (Higginson 1986: 11).

How do we grow in Christian character? We do so with God's help, through following the example of Jesus, learning from the Bible and the Christian community, and through our own volition as we put into practice the qualities that comprise Christian character.

### Fruit of the Spirit

'Fruit of the *Spirit*' underlines that the source of Christian character is the Spirit, and that it is he who helps us to cultivate its qualities. Since God is their source, they reflect God's own character; hence to possess and develop them we are exhorted to 'live by the Spirit' and 'to keep in step with the Spirit' (Galatians 5:16, 25).

But bad habits are hard to break; they are testament to the reality and power of human sinfulness. And, to be honest, we do not always desire Christian qualities, and even when we do, it is a struggle to develop them. It is here that 'the Spirit helps us in our weakness' (Romans 8:26). As we begin to live by the Spirit, he is able to lead us (Romans 8:14; Galatians 5:18), to help us align our desires with his (Romans 8:5), and to set us free from the pull of sinful desires as we give control of our minds and lives to him, which is true freedom to live as God intended (Romans 8:6, 9, 2). This is all part of the Spirit's sanctifying work in the lives of Christians. As Arthur F. Holmes describes it: 'In the Christian context moral development must therefore go hand in hand with spiritual development – what theologians speak of as sanctification – and the means of grace by which the Holy Spirit frees people from sin's bondage and produces a hunger for righteousness that God can fill' (1991: 68). The process is aptly summed up in 2 Corinthians 3:17–18, which speaks of Christ drawing back the veil between human beings and God, so that as people then turn to God they are free to develop their full potential in the likeness of Christ: 'Now the Lord is the Spirit, and where the Spirit of the Lord is, there is freedom. And we, who with unveiled faces all reflect the Lord's glory, are being transformed into his likeness with ever-increasing glory, which comes from the Lord, who is the Spirit.'

God's Spirit is at work within us always, but we can work with him as we make time to develop our relationship with him, our inner life, which, as Paul contends, requires the discipline of an athlete (1 Corinthians 9:24–27). Gordon MacDonald likens the growth of our inner life to a garden: 'When the inner garden is under cultivation and God's Spirit is present, harvests are regular events. The fruits? Things like courage, hope, love, endurance, joy and lots of peace. Unusual capacities for self-control, the ability to discern evil and to ferret out truth are also reaped' (1985: 158).

### Following Jesus

The title of the spiritual classic by Thomas à Kempis, *The Imitation of Christ*, emphasizes the importance of Jesus' life as an example for us. Indeed, Jesus encouraged people to follow him in renunciation (Mark 8:34) and in service (Mark 10:42–45), to name but two examples. Many of the themes taken up by Paul and other writers of the New Testament have their origin in the example and teaching of Jesus, made explicit in passages such as Philippians 2:5ff.: 'Your attitude should be the same as that of Christ Jesus ...', and in 2 Corinthians 10:1: 'By the meekness and gentleness of Christ, I appeal to you ...'As Holmes summarizes: 'As one fully human as well as fully divine Jesus is the perfect example: his moral identity was found in family and religious community in relation to the Father. And character like his is the goal' (1991: 71).

However, we must beware of merely 'copying', since with any role model we must also understand intent and motive, and the context within which actions were undertaken; the context of Jesus' life was his mission as Saviour of humankind. And we must be aware that Jesus did not encounter exactly the same situations that we will encounter, nor was everything about his character recorded. Hence our following of Christ needs to be informed by the whole of the biblical revelation defining Christian character.

### The Word

Following on from the last point, character is to be cultivated through teaching and study of the Bible. The Christian qualities listed in Colossians 3:12–14 are closely followed by the exhortation: 'Let the word of Christ dwell in you richly as you teach and admonish one another with all wisdom' (verse 16). The Bible records the stories that help to train our characters. In recounting the story of God's dealings, 'The Scriptures themselves school our affections by penetrating, as the apostle says, into the thoughts and *intentions* of the heart, the seat of the virtues. It is the primary means God uses in nurturing the virtuous fruit of his Spirit' (Holmes 1991: 67). As we immerse ourselves in the

Word, its values and teaching rub off on us and help to form our character in line with its teaching. As Jesus prayed for his disciples, 'Sanctify them by the truth; your word is truth' (John 17:17).

### In community

Fellowship, community and following the example of others are emphasized as the contexts in and through which teaching and character-building can occur (Acts 2:42–47). Paul encouraged Christians to imitate himself and others in learning to live the Christian life (1 Corinthians 4:16–17; 1 Thessalonians 1:6); clearly, mentoring relationships and role models can help character development.

The picture of the church as a body, with all its members interdependent, and all depending on Christ as its Head, emphasizes such a context for character growth and development (Ephesians 5:15–16). Stanley Hauerwas underlines how Christian convictions have a *narrative form* (a story) which constitute a tradition. This tradition helps to create a community which is instrumental in forming and nurturing Christian character (1984: 22, 62). As people who work 'in the world', we are bombarded with *its* values and influences on a daily basis; we need to immerse ourselves in the Christian community and its teaching, confirming our Christian values and refreshing our spirits so that we can remain in the world but 'not of the world' (John 17:13–19).

### Clothe yourselves ...

The Bible's description of these qualities as 'fruit' implies that they require cultivation through the way we choose to behave. Aristotle (1976: 91–92) saw that the cultivation of virtue came through the habitual practice of particular behaviours; one brave deed does not make a brave person, but if we keep doing brave deeds we shall eventually become brave. As Arthur Holmes states: 'the fact remains that habitual behaviours do nurture moral dispositions, and dispositions are what virtue is about' (1991: 62). And such practice needs to be by deliberate choice if it is to result in developing a settled part of a person's character; we need to make 'choices that are repeated until they become habitual, until one is no longer inclined otherwise' (Holmes 1991: 62). Biblical passages on character capture the respons-ibility of the individual deliberately and habitually to practise the qualities mentioned, through phrases such as 'clothe yourselves', 'make every effort', 'pursue', 'think about such things'. They list corresponding vices that are to be 'put off' or 'put to death', or from which one is to 'flee'.

Work is one of the environments in which we utilize and build character. We have to make decisions, overcome difficulties, work with and lead other people, meet requirements, and, on top of all this, to do it more quickly, more cheaply and with fewer resources than before. The analogy of the refiner's fire (Psalm 66:10; Isaiah 48:10), whereby God tests and strengthens us through problems and challenges (work is full of these!), thereby orienting us towards himself, includes our growth in character.

## Character and work

Important teaching on work in the New Testament is found in a group of passages called the 'house-tables' (*Haustafeln,* after Luther). These teach the good ordering of various relationships within the family or household. They deal with the attitudes and duties of Christian workers and their bosses by describing what is required of slaves and of slave-owners (Colossians 3:22 – 4:1; Ephesians 6:5–9; 1 Timothy 6:1–2; Titus 2:9–10; 1 Peter 2:18–25). However, slavery in both the Old and New Testaments was domestic rather than the criminal slavery of the galleys or mines. Alan Richardson suggests that the Greek *doulos,* usually translated 'slave', 'servant' or 'bond-servant', is best translated 'worker', even though this term does not denote the slave's mandatory tie to occupation or employer: '*douloi* were the workers who performed the daily toil of the household, the farm and the workshop in the ancient world; they were pre-eminently the labouring classes' (Richardson 1963: 39). Slaves could rise to high positions of responsibility and were often treated with respect and affection as members of the family. While there is no direct criticism of slavery in the New Testament, the implications of Christian teaching on social relationships were beginning to be articulated (e.g. Galatians 3:28; James 2:1–13).

These passages provide helpful guidance on the proper attitude of slaves (workers) to masters (bosses), wives to husbands, husbands to wives, and children to parents. They are based on the truth that Christian workers perform their service to Christ himself, which provides the motivation for honest and conscientious work. Even when their masters are not Christians, they are still to treat them with godly respect (1 Peter 2:18). The writers of 1 Peter, 1 Timothy and Titus are particularly concerned with the impression given to the outside world; they do not want Christianity to be charged with causing rebelliousness. In his first letter, Peter is most explicit that workers are to endure injustice and suffer patiently as a way of imitating Christ; the Suffering Servant of Isaiah 53 is held up as an example for Christian workers to follow (1 Peter 2:21–24). Workers are to be dutiful, obedient and respectful to their masters, thus commending the truth of Christianity by their faithful and honest service. Tasks are to be done well, whether or not this attracts earthly reward and recognition.

The house-tables differ from other such codes found outside the New Testament in that Christian masters are to treat slaves with justice and kindness, as they have a Master in heaven who is also their slaves' master (Colossians 4:1). In the society of the day, the house-tables created a new attitude towards daily work: 'A Christian's daily work is primarily something rendered to the Lord and not to men. It is the fulfilment of a duty, and its aim is not reward or profit but the glory of Christ' (Richardson 1963: 42). In modern society, workers are not bound to masters through ownership, as in slavery, but usually to employers through voluntary contracts. Nevertheless, the fact that they are work relationships means that the underlying principles of the house-tables remain valid.

Several of the lists of virtues and vices found in the New Testament are included under the fabric of the house-tables. For example, the house-tables of Colossians 3:18 – 4:1 are preceded by encouragement to Christians to 'clothe' themselves with Christian qualities, and rid themselves of their 'earthly nature' (Colossians 3:1–17). Similarly, the house-tables of Titus 2:2–10 are intertwined with and preceded by instruction on the qualities necessary for Christian living. The house-tables of Ephesians 5:22 – 6:9 occur between passages which encourage Christians to 'live a life of love' and 'Put on the full armour of God' (Ephesians 5:1 and 6:11), again emphasizing the connection between Christian duties (including work) and the character needed to perform them aright.

In this way, the New Testament establishes a link between work and character. In work we are to serve Christ. To serve him best we need to grow more like him and espouse his character in all our activity, which specifically includes our work.

### Self-realization or self-sacrifice?

A criticism of the idea of developing our own qualities of character is that it can lead to an unhealthy preoccupation with self. This in turn can lead to pride in our own ability, and to the false assumption that we can become good or be justified before God through our own achievements. Whereas Aristotle held that habitual behaviour is in a person's power (1976: 91), Christianity emphasizes grace and the need for God's help. To a certain extent our character is shaped by choosing to behave in a certain way, but such behaviour requires both God's help and his forgiveness because of our sinfulness and fallibility.

Christianity emphasizes self-sacrifice, not self-realization; humility and the self-sacrificial desire to forget oneself and serve others are central to this. The Christian goal of serving God and others gives the proper context for developing qualities of character, so that they are tools to achieve this goal. As Christ described, it is only by losing ourselves in love for God and others that we find true life in God (Matthew 16:24–25). Hence, paradoxically, the qualities of Christian character grow in us most when we are concentrating not on ourselves but on serving God and others. This also helps us to look outwards; Jesus' exhortation to be 'the salt of the earth' and 'the light of the world' (Matthew 5:13–14) denotes people whose lives, through the goodness of their character and actions, both penetrate and stand out in the world around them. 'The non-Christian can ignore almost every direct communication of the gospel. But he cannot ignore you wandering around filled with the fruit of the Spirit (Gal 5:22–23)' (Greene 1997: 57–58).

## The salt of the earth

Jesus said, 'You are the salt of the earth … You are the light of the world' (Matthew 5:13–14). His dual metaphor is a powerful reminder of our Christian responsibility to the world in which we live. It counters the view that the world and its structures are totally corrupt and beyond redemption, with Christian withdrawal being the only option. Being 'salt and light' to the world also runs counter to complete identification with the world and all its ways. The gospel inspires both evangelism and social involvement. We are in the world and, like Jesus, we are to engage with the world and at the same time be distinctive.

### *To purify, preserve and give flavour*
Salt in the ancient world symbolized that which purified, preserved and gave flavour. As an ingredient it performs these tasks by becoming an

integral part of that upon which it acts. However, it does this without losing its distinctive flavour; in fact, it imparts this to the whole. In the rabbinical tradition salt was used as a metaphor for wisdom (cf. Colossians 4:6). In using this metaphor, Jesus was saying that we as his followers are to keep the world wholesome, our presence having a distinctive effect upon society. We are not to lose this impact by losing our saltiness (distinctiveness), otherwise we will lose our usefulness.

Being salt in the world of work speaks of working shoulder to shoulder with colleagues of other persuasions, of being committed to the enterprise of work, of playing a full and integral part in the work of our world. Involvement is important because it is a way of witnessing to our faith. And since work is important to God, God would have us influence what is done and how it is done. However, being present as salt implies that we should engage in our work in the same way as we engage in our worship in church – as followers of Christ – hence bringing the values and virtues of his kingdom with us. We do not leave the distinctive characteristics of our Christian life outside the workplace, but allow them to affect the way we work, the way we use power, the way we lead and serve. This amounts to a willingness to *involve* ourselves in the world of work, and thus to influence it for God by our presence. It is not to attempt to Christianize society, nor is it a utopian idea that the whole world of work can be transformed into the kingdom of God. Rather, it is to bring the kingdom of God into work through the lives of Christians in whom God rules, and, like salt, to infuse it with God's wisdom, love and justice, and thereby with God's help to redeem some part of it for him.

Through work, we share in creative partnership with God, and share in the sufferings of Christ in the context of a fallen world. In both of these, we can be said to share in God's redemption of the world. We can be more effective in this by deliberately giving our work over to God, and by working towards his sovereignty within the context of our work environment or enterprise. As Derek Tasker writes, the Christian 'is concerned not only with offering his own work to God but with claiming the enterprise itself for God, in doing all he can to see that the principles on which it is organized conform more and more to what God wants' (1960: 60). This is achieved through the example of distinctive Christian character, the proficiency of the work done, the influence wielded through work roles, and explicit witness to Christ.

One of the nicest compliments I have been paid came from one of my colleagues, Daphne, who said, 'People respect you because they respect your values and know that they can trust you.' I couldn't remember what I had done specifically to deserve this, and quickly thought of times when I had not lived up to it, but this was her impression. We often perform the role of 'salt' without realizing it as we go about our work as Christians.

### Being involved

Is there a biblical basis for such involvement? Yes; first, through recognizing that God is God of all life, secular and sacred. In fact, what we term 'sacred' is authentic and acceptable before God only if it is related to and worked out in the whole of life, otherwise it is merely hypocrisy (Isaiah 1:10–17; Amos 5:21–24; James 1:27; 2:17–18). While the Bible emphasizes a God of the covenant, first made with Abraham and Israel, then in Christ with the church, he remains the God of the whole of creation. And just as he promised to bless all the families of the earth through Abraham, that promise continues through Abraham's spiritual descendants, the church. Being the God of creation, he is concerned that the life of the communities in which we live is characterized by justice (Psalm 146:5–9; Amos 5:24). Such justice is a virtue expected of his followers, but also of all people, nations and the social structures that make them up. Before Amos brought God's judgment on Judah and Israel, he pronounced it on all the surrounding nations (Amos 1:3 – 2:3). As John Stott states, such passages make it clear 'that God hates injustice and oppression *everywhere*, and that he loves and promotes justice *everywhere*' (1999: 22). Our concern, therefore, needs to be as broad as God's.

A second reason for involvement is a biblical view of humankind which recognizes human beings as created in God's image, uniquely valued by God, and with the potential to love him and grow more like him (Genesis 1:26–27; 9:6; James 3:9). People are not just souls to be saved, or just bodies that need care, but a unity of both; they need to be treated as whole beings so as to bring them to wholeness. Through our involvement in work, we serve those for whom Christ died, and participate in drawing them towards him.

The example of Christ is also a powerful argument for our involvement in the world. In addition to proclaiming the good news and opening up a way back to God through his sacrifice on the cross, Jesus fully entered our world, serving those with whom he had contact irrespective of their background, class or status. 'For if the Christian mission is to be modelled on Christ's mission, it will surely involve for us, as it did for him, an entering into other people's worlds' (Stott 1999: 26).

The doctrine of salvation is often reduced to conversion, or to access to heaven as a result of being saved from the consequences of sin. Salvation includes these, but, biblically speaking, it is more. It is the blessing of God's rule in individuals' lives and in their communities – the coming of the kingdom of God (Isaiah 52:7). In Jesus, the kingdom of God broke into history, confronting evil and bringing wholeness to people and communities. Through us who belong to God's kingdom, his rule can exist in the work we do, and can influence for good the enterprises to which we give our energy.

On the one hand, Christians are called out of the world to be a holy people belonging to God (1 Peter 2:9–12), aliens and strangers to the world. On the other hand, they are sent into the world to serve and to witness, and to be good citizens in it (1 Peter 2:13–17). Just as salt is radically different from decay, Christians are to be in the world but not of it (John 17:13–18; 1 John 2:15–17); like salt, we are to penetrate the world with God's kingdom through our lives and work.

## The light of the world

### *To bring light*

Jesus told his disciples they were to be 'the light of the world'; as well as taking over Israel's role as the world's saviour, they were also to take over its mission as 'a light for the Gentiles' (Isaiah 42:6; 49:6; Romans 2:19). This is the task of Yahweh's Servant, as a way of bringing to fulfilment God's glorification in the messianic era. The mantle was taken up by Jesus, who, in John's words, came as the 'true light that gives light to every man' (John 1:9), and said of himself, 'I am the light of the world. Whoever follows me will never walk in darkness, but will have the light of life' (John 8:12). This was the role given to the disciples of Jesus and is to be taken up by the church (Philippians 2:15; 2 Corinthians 4:6). As we, as Jesus' followers, let our light shine through good deeds (Matthew 5:16; 1 Peter 2:12), others will pay attention and give glory to God.

In the context of work, being God's light means glorifying him through the work we do, the way we work (character), and the way we relate to others in our work. Thus people can see God at work in us and give him glory (1 Peter 2:12). This underlies the advice of the 'house-tables' for slaves and masters (Ephesians 6:5–9; Colossians 3:22–25); in our work we are serving God, and by doing it conscientiously and well we enable others to perceive God's light and glorify him.

## *Sharing good news*

Alongside good deeds as a way of letting God's light shine, we may also include sharing the gospel. Paul makes this connection when, with reference to preaching, he speaks of 'the light of the gospel' (2 Corinthians 4:4–6). In Philippians 2:14–16, Christians are urged to 'shine like stars' through their blameless life and through holding out the 'word of life'.

Work provides occasions and opportunities to share the gospel in an explicit way. In fact, the workplace, where many of us spend a good proportion of our time, offers the natural environment for us to witness to our faith. It must be said, though, that in secular employment we are paid to work, not to preach, and that work should not be seen solely as a means to witnessing if the role of work in God's creation is not to be denigrated. Having guarded against these dangers, however (and not using them as an excuse for inactivity), it is clear that for many of us work is our principal contact with the world outside family and church. As such it provides our main interaction with non-Christians. Many churches tie themselves in knots in their efforts to reach out to the non-Christian world around them, straining to make contacts that are often forced and unnatural, while failing to recognize the most natural of their members' contacts through work. As Mark Greene writes: 'The workplace is, day in, day out, the one place where non-Christians can see the difference that being a Christian makes – the one place where Christian and non-Christian face the same stresses, may have the same boss, may be rebuked for similar failures, praised for similar successes, are subject to the same structural dynamics, to the same corporate culture, the same food, the same gossip …' (1997: 15). Greene goes on to point out that in the workplace we already have common ground and have built bridges and developed relationships. For many of us, it is our natural and most obvious mission field.

Peter's advice to Christians witnessing in situations where persecution was possible is particularly applicable to the work situation, for this is where many Christians are most immersed in the world, most vulnerable yet also most influential: 'Always be prepared to give an answer to everyone who asks you to give the reason for the hope that you have' (1 Peter 3:15). This approach acknowledges the obligation to the employer (to work, not to preach), and recognizes that those with whom we work are not voluntary attenders at a church service or rally. We must take care not to take advantage of a potentially captive audience without their consent (our work team, subordinates, etc.), otherwise we may soon find ourselves having strained relations with the people with whom we have to work each day, or worse, being left to work alone.

Continued contact gives the opportunity for friendships to grow, for respect to be earned, and for the light of the gospel to shine through naturally. (I explore some of work's potential for relationships in chapter 7.) Peter goes on to say that we are to give our response 'with gentleness and respect, keeping a clear conscience …' (1 Peter 3:15–16). It is such gentleness and respect that opened the way for Jesus' conversations with many, and which should characterize our sharing of the gospel with work colleagues. Paul expressed it similarly: 'Let your conversation be always full of grace, seasoned with salt, so that you may know how to answer everyone' (Colossians 4:6).

We need to be true to our beliefs and openly share our faith when the time is right, always listening so that we meet the person at his or her point of need. Some of the most fruitful conversations I have had at work have been when a colleague has noticed the way I have gone about a task or handled a situation and wanted to know more about the values that I hold. One colleague of mine does not have to advertise the fact that he is a Christian; he is respected because of his integrity and trustworthiness (and because he is good at his job); people know that he is someone they can go to for support or advice. I have another friend, Caroline, whose warm and outgoing personality enables her to engage people readily at their point of need, and quite naturally to share with them how God can make a difference. She does this as opportunities arise and as the Lord leads, and with such gentleness and respect that people do not take offence but are drawn towards God.

Sharing good news can involve:

- giving a Christian perspective on a topical issue (from ethics at work to the latest trouble-spot in the world);
- listening to someone who has a personal problem and wants to talk;
- giving someone a Christian book relevant to his or her situation;
- admitting an error, apologizing, making sure the right person gets the credit;
- sharing the gospel with someone;

- going about our work in ways that display the fruit of the Spirit: love and concern for others, patience with someone new to the job, fair treatment, peace amid pressure, etc.

But there are times when, despite all the right motives, we get it wrong. A manager I once worked for many years ago expressed his Christian convictions over lunch to the team, who had little choice but to listen. He meant well. Later, though he shared with me how good it had been to witness, they told me how they greatly resented being force-fed. I gave a friend a booklet on Christian relationships when she had just had a relationship breakdown. It seemed a good idea at the time, but for her it was the wrong time and it took a while before she talked openly with me again. On other occasions I have been drawn into group discussions on topics of morality, the sexual behaviour of celebrities, or someone's view of the church, and ended up fighting the wrong battle on the wrong battleground. 'Don't have anything to do with foolish and stupid arguments,' Paul advised (2 Timothy 2:23). And there are times when I have said nothing in the face of an opportunity that begged for someone to explain how God could help, or failed to respond adequately to someone who asked to know more about Christ, or even sidestepped a genuine invitation to give a Christian view on an issue.

But, believe it or not, God can turn even our poor attempts (or lack of them) to his glory, and somehow shine through despite us. So notching up what may appear to be failed attempts or no-shows in our witnessing should not deter us, but should prompt us to 'make the most of every opportunity' (Colossians 4:5). When I look back at my witness at college, I do not feel very good about it. I was articulate in the Christian Union and my life was full of church activities, but among my college friends I think I appeared unfriendly and uninvolved. However, a few years later, Tony, my closest friend at college, became a Christian. Although I had nothing to do with this directly, I like to think that God used my presence at college as part of the process. God uses different people and events to draw people to himself. As Paul said, 'I planted the seed, Apollos watered it, but God made it grow' (1 Corinthians 3:6). It is God who converts, by his grace working in people's hearts. We, as God's servants and fellow-workers, just need to be available to play the part he gives us in the process. God, through his Spirit, enables us to be both courageous and bold, as he did with the apostles (Acts 4), and also promises to help us, when in difficulty, with the words to say (Luke 12:11–12).

## Light that exposes

Light guides and shows the way. It also illuminates and exposes. Jesus' light shines in the darkness of a sinful world (John 1:5), a light that will one day expose all that is hidden in the darkness (1 Corinthians 4:5). We are to live as 'children of the light', which means lives of goodness, righteousness and truth (Ephesians 5:8–10). In order to walk in the light, Paul urges: 'Have nothing to do with the fruitless deeds of darkness, but rather expose them' (Ephesians 5:11). There are times in our work when a stand has to be made, when we are confronted by blatant wrongdoing or are asked to take part in something dishonest. We have to uphold the light of God's righteousness and refuse; this is a form of exposing wrong. Sometimes it is also appropriate more publicly to expose what is going on. Care must be taken in public exposure since this can become 'tale-telling' for wrong motives. If there is a way of exposing wrong that enables those involved to put it right first, this is often the best course of action, as widespread exposure can easily injure people out of all proportion to the wrong they have done. The gravity of the situation is often a good guide. If someone has borrowed company office equipment, perhaps meaning to replace it, a challenge may be sufficient to restore them to good practice and to get them to replenish what has been used. The person who has been deliberately siphoning off the organization's funds into a personal account needs to be exposed to those in authority inside the organization. Normally, only when internal processes are exhausted should external exposure be considered.

There had been a mistake on the salary sheets for the pay review; one of the managers had got more money for his team than he should have had. I worried about it all evening. If I left it, only he and I would know. I reasoned that the manager had some anomalously low salaries in his team anyway and the extra money would help, and there was no question of him gaining personally. But I couldn't sleep before I had resolved to expose the mistake. The manager thought me naïve, and retained the money to allocate to his team, saying, 'Everyone else gains by such mistakes; it's swings and roundabouts.' On that occasion my intervention did not change the situation. But I had done what I felt to be right and had a clear conscience; and I had placed a stake in the ground that would influence the administration of pay policy in the future.

Being God's light in work means looking at our world of work objectively, even prophetically, and exposing and challenging its shortcomings. But this is best done from a position of involvement (of being both salt and light), not detachment, which can so easily become pious and hypocritical criticism. In practice, this means being willing and able to step back from our work and to be candid about its motives, processes and products, and to be able to do the same with regard to the whole of our enterprise, company, organization and industry. This is not disloyalty, but a healthy process of analysis that prevents our being lulled into a complete identification with our work or our employer that can lead us into error. Instead we remain involved but distinctive.

## The action column

1. What is your attitude to the work you do? Is it done to the best of your ability? Can you offer it as worship to God?
2. Pray that God's character may shine through you as you work, and that your work, through its challenges, will further develop in you the fruit of the Spirit.
3. Is there an area in work where your involvement would make a real difference for good?
4. Is there a colleague with whom you have the opportunity to share the gospel? Is there an issue upon which you should make a stand?

CHAPTER 5

# What gets you out of bed in the morning?

*Staying motivated*

## Understanding what makes you tick

*Hot buttons*

Someone in an interview asked me what my ideal job would be. I outlined the type of role that would satisfy my professional interests, and went on to specify what was important to me: doing something worthwhile, having the space to be creative, being able to learn some new skills, being respected for my contribution, playing a role in a team. When I have asked such questions of other people the answers have varied, either absolutely or in the priorities placed on the different elements. Their replies have included:

- 'I like being listened to and knowing that my contribution is valued.'
- 'I want to be recognized and rewarded for what I do.'
- 'Relationships are very important to me; I work best when I know I am accepted as part of the team.'
- 'Working for an inspiring boss.'
- 'Having career prospects, going as far as I can.'
- 'Earning a good salary.'
- 'Having a job that really interests me.'
- 'I like to be constantly challenged; that brings out the best in me.'
- 'I want the security of regular work and the benefits of being with a large company.'
- 'Being a consultant, I can choose the work I want to do and decide how I spend my time.'
- 'I need to feel I am treated fairly and with respect.'

73

- 'Now I'm working for a solar-energy company, its great because I really believe in what I'm doing. My kids think I'm helping to save the planet!'
- 'I like to be kept busy. If there is not enough to do my motivation goes down.'

People perceive a variety of purposes in the work they do and have a variety of needs to be met, aspirations to be fulfilled and values to be upheld. As a friend put it as we discussed changes to the company's promotion and reward structure: 'Everyone has their "hot buttons"; you just need to press the right ones.' Motivation is about the ways we go about satisfying these needs and aspirations, and the behaviours we use. It is also about emotion, since to be motivated is to feel strongly enough about something that it moves us into action.

During a planning meeting when the organization I work for was in the middle of momentous change, the human-resources managers moaned about the effect of the impending upheaval, the uncertainty, the redundancies, more work demanded from already stressed people, and the dark shadow of an industry moving into rough seas. Steve saw it differently: 'We are part of the largest industrial merger on the planet, we have done it in record time, we are ahead of the pack; there's lots more to do but it's challenging and exciting stuff. I don't know about you, but it's what gets me out of bed in the morning.'

Understanding what motivates is particularly pertinent to a Christian book on work, since any description of the motivation to work (or to do anything else) is closely linked to the view we hold of human nature, and of work itself. Christianity has some clear statements on both of these. The link between motivation and views on human nature and work becomes apparent if we look at some of the approaches to motivation which have found their way into the workplace. Motivation is a subject that organizations wrestle with; they surmise that if their staff are well motivated they will perform better and the company will benefit. Many theories have been put forward and practices adopted; some of the most common are described below.

### Approaches to motivation

'*You can get people to do anything if you pay them enough.*' This underlies the approach Henry Ford put into practice with his assembly line. In much factory work which followed, tasks were fragmented to gain efficiencies, the control of tasks was given to supervisors, and people were made subservient to machines. The notion is that however boring or soul-destroying the work, people can be motivated to do it for reward, and incentivized to higher performance by greater reward.

Implicit in such an approach to motivation and behaviour is a particular view of human nature: that people are inherently lazy and therefore need external incentives, and that because their goals are contrary to those of the organization, they need to be held to the task by tight controls (usually autocratic management). People work best if they are told clearly what to do, and work harder if promised material rewards. Despite the development of more sophisticated theories of motivation, many organizations still use this approach as one way of motivating people.

Each of us has needs, from the necessities of life to the desire for fulfilment. Some emphasize that it is our *greatest needs* that motivate us. The psychologist Abraham Maslow (1954) devised a 'hierarchy of needs' which has been applied to motivation at work. The theory suggests that individuals have a set of needs arranged in a loose hierarchy from physiological at the bottom through safety, social needs and self-esteem to self-actualization at the top. Our primary need is to obtain food to survive. Once this need is satisfied, we require satisfaction of needs further up the hierarchy to motivate us. For Maslow, self-actualization meant reaching our full potential.

Frederick Herzberg (1968) also proposed a needs-based approach to motivation. His research suggested that the factors causing satisfaction in the workplace were largely separate and distinct from those causing dissatisfaction; what causes satisfaction does not cause dissatisfaction if it is not present, and *vice versa*. Instead of viewing human needs as a continuum, he suggested that there are two sets of factors relevant to motivating people which can pull in opposite directions:

- Hygiene factors: these do not motivate but if they are not met in a satisfactory way they have the power to demotivate (e.g. working conditions, supervision, salary, job security, status, interpersonal relations).
- Motivators: factors such as the work itself, responsibility, recognition, sense of achievement, advancement, possibility of growth – these are able to motivate people, providing the hygiene factors are taken care of.

In Herzberg's view, motivators are related to what a person does (the task); they are intrinsic to the work itself. Hygiene factors are related to the context or environment in which a person does the job, and can be satisfied by regular care and maintenance. Herzberg linked the hygiene factors to man's 'Animal-Adam nature, which is concerned with avoidance of pain stemming from the environment, and for man the psychological environment is the major source of this pain.' However, in order to be happy, people need some psychological growth, and this is achieved through 'man's Human-Abraham nature, which is concerned with approaching self-fulfilment or psychological growth through the accomplishment of tasks' (1968: 76).

Some people are motivated by *the need to achieve*. David McClelland (in Statt 1994: 283) argued that people with a high need for achievement are motivated in situations with:

- moderately risky tasks (low-risk tasks would be unchallenging; high-risk tasks would be avoided due to fear of failure);
- feedback on their performance; and
- acknowledgment of individual responsibility.

Meeting our needs is one factor that motivates us to action. However, from a Christian viewpoint, on its own it does not take enough account of concepts such as serving and self-sacrifice; people can be motivated to meet others' needs, and by aims and values that transcend individual fulfilment. Such theories also emphasize the self apart from God, as if fulfilment can be reached through meeting physiological and/or psychological needs.

Regarding reward as the prime motivator for work takes too pessimistic a view of human nature and fails to take account of humankind's potential as people made in God's image. However, motivation based on the need to be fulfilled can take an unrealistically optimistic picture of human nature, ignoring the fall. Herzberg's two opposing sets of needs (animal versus psychological growth) based on his interpretation of two strands of thought on the nature of humankind in the Old Testament, tends to emphasize the dualism between soul and body of Greek thought. Christianity recognizes the conflict between humankind's sinful nature and the image of God within, but does not equate this with the division of bodily and psychological needs; rather, we are integrated beings with a range of needs which our work can help us to meet.

Working with others can help to make work enjoyable and satisfying, and some take the view that *people's behaviour is primarily motivated by their social needs*. This approach was in part a response to industrialization, when, for many, the intrinsic meaning of work was lost, leading them to find greater meaning in social relationships at work. This approach saw some resurgence in the 1990s through increased emphasis on teamwork, although this was largely driven by organizations seeing potential for competitive advantage and greater productivity through teams rather than by a desire to meet social needs.

In concentrating on social needs, this approach pays little attention to the intrinsic value of work or to the importance of letting people use their gifts, grow and develop. It can encourage a paternalistic management style, and in some large organizations has led to a psychological contract characterized by loyalty in exchange for security: 'Do as we say and we will look after you.' However, social needs are certainly a factor in motivation; a Christian account recognizes that people have social needs, and that work is something to be done *with* and *for* others.

People are also motivated by *how much they want something, and their expectancy of achieving it*. People will not be motivated by the prospect of what is unimportant to them. But if they are to be motivated by what is more important to them, it must appear achievable. Whereas needs theories of motivation are concerned with the *content* of motivation, the expectancy approach looks at the *process* of motivation: how people decide which behaviours to engage in.

However, people do not always behave in the calculative and rational ways that expectancy theory predicts. Nor do they focus only on the extrinsic outcomes, such as reward or promotion, that this approach tends to concentrate on. As Statt states, 'the *intrinsic* motivation to be found in achieving something because it is enjoyable to do so for its own sake is not usually found in expectancy theory' (Statt 1994: 287).

Perceiving *a sense of justice and fairness* is another factor in motivation. People who feel underpaid or under-promoted see this as inequitable and are motivated to do something about it. They are unlikely to work harder; they may go on strike, lobby their boss or use representative channels. People do not generally have the same problem if they are overpaid!

For the Christian, seeing justice done at work is important and is a factor in motivation. It is linked to upholding biblical values and to the desire to serve others in and through work. However, its focus is justice for all, not just for self.

It has been argued 'that having a (conscious) specific goal or purpose in mind that one was trying to accomplish was the most important factor in explaining motivation' (Statt 1994: 289). Using *goals to motivate* is based on the premise that intention is important in understanding motivational behaviour, and has been taken up by industry through initiatives such as 'Management by Objectives'. It emphasizes self-control and taking responsibility for one's own work and, as Statt points out (1994: 289–290), works best when the goals set are specific and difficult, and when feedback on progress is given.

Clearly, goals are a factor in motivation. But not all goals are easily articulated or measurable (e.g. quality, or how a task is done), and a person can be set conflicting goals (e.g. quantity versus quality). Sometimes concentrating on a goal (e.g. reducing hospital waiting-lists) can detract from the task in hand (i.e. caring for sick people).

These theories have influenced the way organizations and individuals think about motivation. Iain Maitland (1995: 4) lists what he thinks needs to be done in practice for people to be motivated in their work:

- being a good leader;
- working as a team;
- improving jobs;
- developing people;
- paying staff;
- providing a safe and healthy workplace.

Certainly all of these play a part. For some, their work is intrinsically satisfying and therefore motivating. For others, it is the pay (or what it can buy) that seems to be the principal motivation. When the job itself is not satisfying, then pay or environmental factors often become more important. For others, altruistic factors are supreme – what is being achieved by the job is what provides the prime motivation. How does being a Christian affect motivation?

## All called to serve, all unique

### Work and its purposes

The theories and practice described above all yield insights into motivation and certainly capture aspects that we can all relate to. For the Christian, the motivation to work also relates to a Christian view of work. According to the Bible, work (which I describe as *purposeful activity*) fulfils a number of purposes:

- *Sustenance.* We work to secure food, clothing, shelter and a decent way of life for ourselves and our dependants through responsible use of the earth's resources (Genesis 1:28; 2:15; 2 Thessalonians 3:10, 12). A fundamental motivation to work is the necessity to provide for and improve life, which is not to be confused with greed or the lust for material wealth.

- *Satisfaction.* Through work, we should be able to use and develop our gifts, and thereby find satisfaction (Ecclesiastes 3:13). People, made in God's image, are by nature active and creative, and as these attributes are engaged, we find satisfaction. This is a key motivator intrinsic to work itself, although it needs to be distinguished from the desire solely for self-fulfilment or vain ambition.
- *Service to others.* As we support the enterprises of our community, society and the world at large, we render service to and with others. Part of the Christian calling is to look to the interests of others, and to work with others willingly (Philippians 2:4; 1 Peter 4:10).
- *Service to God.* Ultimately, our work is service to God, done for his glory and offered as worship to him (Colossians 3:23).

Each of these provides legitimate motivation for our work, but the overarching one is serving God, which makes the Christian motivation to work distinctive: 'For the Christian, the motivation to work is to honour and worship God who, from the very beginning, created men and women as workers like himself' (Westcott 1996: 94). Within this service, we work to support ourselves and our dependants, to serve others and to find satisfaction as we use and develop our gifts.

### Fallen but with potential

A Christian view of human nature also underlies how we understand motivation. People are made in the image of God, are loved by him, and have value, identity and esteem because of this, irrespective of the work they do. They are endowed with gifts and aptitudes which reflect God's image, and which, when used, bring glory to him and satisfaction to themselves. Hence, people are best motivated when treated with dignity and respect, as unique individuals capable of creative, even remarkable, actions.

While the Bible places humankind 'a little lower than the heavenly beings' (Psalm 8:5) in terms of value to God and potential to be like him, it is bluntly realistic about the fallen nature we all share, which manifests itself in sin, selfishness and rebellion against God. Given this, it is not difficult to understand our susceptibility to be motivated by purely material things: greed, the lust for power, vain ambition and the like. However, in Christ, we can work as God intended, motivated by the desire to serve him, within which all the other aspects of motivation correctly take their place. Being redeemed by him helps us also to bring the work we do under his redemption.

We are all uniquely different in the talents we possess, in what we are capable of, in our interests and the things we excel in and enjoy. It follows that, even given the same overall aim (to serve), different things will motivate us. Two people in the same type of job will find different elements motivating. People with the same background and education will look for different things in their work. Such variations in motivation depend on

- personality: the way we are;
- interests: what fascinates or excites us;
- age and experience: what we find motivating in our twenties (e.g. new career challenges, travel) may change as we get older (e.g. job security, choice);
- skills, abilities and aptitudes: what we are good at or could be good at.

A Christian motivational framework for work, then, is clear about work's ultimate purpose, is realistic about human nature, and recognizes that we are all uniquely different. We can apply this to ourselves by understanding the balance appropriate for us at any one time and, within the elements of this framework, to understand what it is that we find motivating. For example, in your current circumstances and stage of life, is it earning enough to support your dependants that is paramount, or doing something that interests you, or working in a supporting environment? To find fulfilment, is it using your technical skills that is most important to you, or managing activities and people, or progressing your professional abilities?

In relation to *the job itself*, do you prefer routine or variability, short tasks or large projects, being reactive or being proactive? In relation to *the job's outcomes*, do you prefer customer service to producing things, and direct service (e.g. voluntary sector) or indirect (industry)? With regard to *relationships*, do you prefer to work in a team or mostly on your own, to be directed or to be autonomous? In your *work environment*, do you prefer a formal or a casual ethos, regular hours, indoors or outdoors?

## What keeps you motivated?

Let's look more closely at the elements which most people find motivating and which align with a Christian view of the motivation to work.

```
┌─────────────────────────────────────────────┐
│             Staying motivated                 │
└─────────────────────────────────────────────┘
```

### The job's outcomes
· Worthwhile work
· Not just a cog

### The job itself
· Interesting work
· Room for development
· Goals and challenges

### Relationships
· Good leadership
· Respect and recognition
· Part of the team

### Work setting
· Honest treatment
· Fair pay, good conditions
· Security

### Worthwhile work

To know that our work has a worthy purpose – that it provides goods and services in an honest way, thereby serving others and ultimately God – is an important motivation. I work for an oil company and have at times wondered if I should be using my skills more directly for God. I remember a rousing talk by a previous chairman, as the company relaunched itself after a difficult period in 1992. He said something like this: 'We find oil. We dig it out of the ground. We refine it into products and energy and chemicals. It's not very glamorous, but if we can provide good products and make an honest margin, that's a good way to earn a living.' He went on to emphasize performance, reputation and teamwork, and the company re-created itself. It was motivational because his message was honest and straightforward, and reminded us all that we were embarked on a worthy enterprise.

Being part of a worthwhile enterprise means that during the difficult or boring aspects of your job (all jobs, even the most exciting, have these), there is a reason to keep at it. This is not to condone mindless, boring work, but it does help us when we know we are in the right job. In the Old Testament, the rebuilding of Jerusalem's walls as the exiles began to return was a difficult and dangerous task. Despite ridicule and opposition, Nehemiah and his fellow-Jews continued: 'So we rebuilt the wall till all of it reached half its height, for the people worked with all their heart' (Nehemiah 4:6). They were motivated to continue because they were convinced of the worthiness of their task.

Ivor, a Christian prison officer, said that what motivated him most in his work was being involved in helping prisoners get back into society. He told me this was one of the reasons he never took promotion; he saw it as more worthwhile to continue to work with the prisoners.

## Not just a cog

Knowing that you are part of something bigger and that your contribution has an impact, however small, is motivating. After a member of the business's executive committee had visited, Daphne made a point of telling me how well it had gone. 'He spent half an hour with *me*. He listened to what I had to say, and later in his talk to the staff he referred to a couple of the points I had made.' Not only was this good leadership, but it helped Daphne to see how her role fitted in and influenced the business. The film industry recognizes the contribution of its people by listing *all* the crew – the lighting assistant, and the lighting assistant's assistant, and so on.

Understanding how one's job fits into a larger purpose is particularly helpful when undertaking the more tedious parts of a role. To know how your job contributes to the whole affirms the worth of your work and contributes to your self-esteem. Too often, the less glamorous roles are overlooked as powerful executives or superstars, entrepreneurs or managers, or even machines, take the limelight. In writing about the roles people play in the church, Paul turns such a notion on its head: 'The eye cannot say to the hand, "I don't need you!" And the head cannot say to the feet, "I don't need you!" On the contrary, those parts of the body that seem to be weaker are indispensable, and the parts that we think are less honourable we treat with special honour' (1 Corinthians 12:21–23). The same is true in work; each contribution is important because it is undertaken by a human being who adds some skill and value to the task. Treat people as registered numbers, human resources or cogs, and they are likely to behave like inanimate objects. Treat them as intelligent and creative individuals with something to offer, and they will more often than not be motivated to do a good job.

## Interesting work

It is difficult to be motivated to do repetitive, boring or mindless tasks. The more a job uses and develops our skills, and gives us satisfaction through doing it, the more motivated we will be. Some people have the opportunity to learn the subject they love, and then to practise it as a job. Professions such as medicine, law, teaching, engineering, the arts and sport offer this. Many of us get as close as we can to our interests; if satisfaction is a legitimate purpose of work, it is right to choose work that interests us.

But what about those who have little interest in their job, or who have lost the interest they first had, or who have outgrown the job? If you are in this position, think about the following ways of making your job more interesting or investigate them with your boss or organization:

- Ask for more challenging tasks, or take on more responsibility (sometimes called job enrichment), aiming to match personal growth with growth in the job.
- Increase variety by including more aspects in the job, or undertaking more parts of a process.
- Try to see a job through from start to finish. Being responsible for the whole task means that you take greater ownership and feel greater satisfaction on completion.
- Learn to do a variety of tasks and rotate them with others.
- Challenge yourself to learn a new skill or further develop an existing skill.
- When a job is of little or no interest, and there are no ways of making it so, then you have to ask the question, 'Is this the job God wants me in?' Chapter 8 suggests some ways of checking this.

Usually, what interests us is also what we do well. We tend to gravitate towards what we can do well because it allows us to express our skills, find greatest satisfaction and serve best. This is often evident in the way we manage our time; we can usually find time to do things we are good at and enjoy, though this is not always good time management, since we leave the less attractive tasks.

## Room for development

Most people are motivated by knowing that the job they do has prospects, that it is leading somewhere – towards more responsibility, higher skills, greater impact or a particular role. For the Christian, this should not be 'vain ambition' in pursuit of status or power, but the desire to use gifts and serve better. God has given us gifts and aptitudes and expects us to use and develop them. As the parable of the talents makes clear with respect to the kingdom of God, if we are given much, much will be expected from us (Matthew 25:14–30). The same is true in all spheres of life.

Being able to look ahead is consistent with the biblical concept of having hope for the future, which helps us to stay motivated in the present and draws us on towards what lies ahead. It is one of the ways God fulfils his plans for us (Jeremiah 29:10–14). It is also consistent with an open and enquiring approach to learning new skills, so necessary in the changing world of work (chapter 6).

But you might say, 'I'm satisfied in my job', or 'I find room for development in other areas of my life.' This is good; for some, factors outside work offer development enough, while others have reached a stage in life when they are not looking for extra responsibility.

Many organizations now expect people to play an active part in their own development through constructing development plans and making clear their career aspirations and training needs. In part, this reflects the changing nature of the employment relationship between organizations and their employees (as described in chapter 7); formerly, only a small proportion of staff deemed to have high potential had a career path planned by the organization. With the support of one's boss, taking the initiative and starting to plan one's own development can be very empowering.

## Goals and challenges

Paul used the concept of a goal or target to draw people along in the Christian life: 'Forgetting what is behind and straining towards what is ahead, I press on towards the goal to win the prize for which God has called me heavenwards in Christ Jesus' (Philippians 3:13–14). Likewise, to have targets and goals at work which give us something to aim at and which stretch us and bring out the best in us, can be very motivating. There is nothing like a tight deadline to meet (as experienced in completing this book, for example!) or a tough financial target to shift us into a higher gear; we often perform well and enjoy a sense of achievement afterwards. If no goals are set, it is good to set your own. This is particularly effective for those unpopular tasks such as filing or, at home, cleaning.

Goals and targets work only if we have some say in setting them (or at least if we accept them), if they are achievable, and if the goalposts are not continually moved. Impossible targets can put us under unfair pressure. Failure can cause the ploy to backfire and demotivate us. If targets are repeatedly changed, we may pull out all the stops once or twice, but if we feel we are being abused, we become resentful and dig in our heels.

Tackling challenges and overcoming difficulties seem to bring out the best in people. Although they are not always welcome at the time, there is something about human nature that rises to a challenge. Christianity adds a further dimension. The writer to the Hebrews speaks of life as a race: 'let us run with perseverance the race marked out for us' (Hebrews 12:1). By fixing our eyes on Jesus and considering how he endured opposition, we 'will not grow weary and lose heart' (Hebrews 12:3). God helps us to face all life's challenges and to overcome its difficulties.

## Good leadership

Having a boss who leads well, inspires you, delegates, empowers you, supports and trains you, and gives you responsibility and the space to exercise your gifts, can make all the difference. Joshua took command of the Israelites with the exhortation, 'Be strong and courageous' (Joshua 1:6), and the people responded to his leadership, committing themselves to go wherever he sent them (Joshua 1:16). The Bible has many examples of good leadership as a key factor in the motivation of others to undertake challenging tasks. Chapter 10 explores the importance of leadership in work; one of a leader's key roles is motivating others so that they work with commitment rather than compliance, because they respect and trust the leader and understand and believe in the task.

One of the most motivating things leaders can do is to have a high expectation of their staff, since this demonstrates belief and trust in them and has a huge impact on their self-esteem and confidence: 'The more you expect of people, the more they will give, as long as you support them' (Heller 1998: 30). God expected a lot of Moses and gave him the support he needed to accomplish the task (Exodus 3 – 4). Jesus expected a lot of Peter in reinstating him to lead the first church (John 21:15–19), and of the disciples in commissioning them to spread the gospel (Matthew 28:16–20); with the support of the Holy Spirit they went on to fulfil what was asked of them. People raise their game when a lot is expected of them, provided they have the support they need.

### *Respect and recognition*

Being appreciated for who we *are,* as well as for our work contribution, is an important component in motivation. 'Recognition in this context implies respect, and there is no more powerful motivator than that' (Statt 1994: 297). To know that we are respected and that our work is recognized and appreciated builds self-esteem and creates the desire to contribute more. In the matter of sharing the faith, Peter advised Christians to treat people with 'gentleness and respect' (1 Peter 3:16), because this how we demonstrate Christ's love for them, and we ought to treat people similarly in work.

Clare told me that it was personal, positive feedback that motivated her most in her work as a pharmacist. She said that such affirmation, although infrequently given, kept her going for a long time, because it recognized that she was doing something useful and using her professional skills to good effect. When a colleague told her, 'People really like working with you because you have such a calming influence when everyone else is panicking,' she was delighted. Those few words cost nothing but meant much.

Recognition can take many forms: a simple 'thank you', taking an interest in someone's work, praise for a task well done, or a public acknowledgment. Recognition can also be marked by reward, such as a gift, a pay increase, a bonus or a promotion. This is not to encourage people to work for praise or reward (which can easily pander to vanity, greed or materialism), but rather to recognize appropriately the work people do and to show that it is appreciated. 'They cost you nothing, but praise and recognition based upon performance are the oxygen of the human spirit' (Adair 1997: 26).

Closely related to recognition is encouragement, which can have a big impact on motivation, particularly when we are facing challenging or difficult tasks. The encouragement given by Barnabas to other Christians, including Paul, is noted in Acts 11:22–26. Paul himself used his missionary journeys and his letters to encourage people in their Christian lives. Encouragement provides mutual benefit because, as Paul found in encouraging others, we ourselves are encouraged by their enhanced motivation and their growth (1 Thessalonians 3:6–13).

All of these – respect, recognition, affirmation, praise and encouragement – are ways of showing a genuine appreciation for others and a concern for their well-being and success in work. They are ways of treating people as unique and valuable in their own right because they are human, and of affirming them in the role they are undertaking in their work.

### Part of the team

To be part of the team, work group or task force, and to be accepted and to have a role to play, can be tremendously positive experiences. When a team operates well, with members playing complementary roles, all pulling in the same direction towards a shared goal, supporting each other and recognizing each other's contributions, getting results and achieving the task, it is highly satisfying as well as enjoyable. This is because work is a community task – to be done with and for others. Sports teams often capture this spirit well; the members are truly interdependent. A soccer team cannot rely on its forwards only; if it is to win, it needs the support of its mid-fielders and its defenders, and a good goalkeeper. Being part of the team motivates all the members to do their best. They don't want to let the team down; they want the best for the other team members, and realize that they all need each other.

Paul's analogy of the church as a body, with each part accepted by the others and fulfilling its unique function (1 Corinthians 12:12–31), affirms the importance of working together. God has arranged creation in wonderful diversity. As complementary functions and skills are brought together, as in a body, the whole is more effective than the parts, and cannot function fully (if at all) if one part is missing. Experiencing the outcome of such team work is uplifting. Being part of the team motivates us because we can get a better result, and because, as social beings, it is good to work together with others. In his letters, Paul encourages people to work together to make this a reality (Philippians 2:1–2; 4:2–3; 1 Corinthians 3:1–9; Ephesians 4:15–16).

Team spirit can be enhanced by celebrating key milestones or achievements. The Bible encourages God's people to celebrate significant events in their history, focusing in the New Testament on the life, death and resurrection of Jesus. As work is part of a Christian's service and worship to God, then celebrating its achievements is a good and motivating thing to do.

*Honest treatment*

Some organizations make promises they cannot keep, or imply that the needs of the individual and of the organization are the same, which they are not (few work organizations are set up primarily for the benefit of their employees). People become cynical if their organization says one thing and does another, or treats them in a patronizing, unjust or dishonest way. God abhors dishonesty (Proverbs 11:3), and opposes those who perpetrate injustice (Amos 2:6–7; 8:4–6). Christians will want to work in an environment where people are treated fairly and honestly, and to be part of a culture where people are not blamed for mistakes, or discriminated against for being different. Before any race-relations legislation or diversity initiatives, Paul articulated the oneness of Christians in Christ irrespective of their religious or ethnic origin, status or sex (Galatians 3:28). Underlying this is the principle that all people are to be treated with dignity and respect because they have been created in God's image and are loved by him, with no room for discrimination or favouritism.

*Fair pay, good conditions*

Linked to honest treatment is fair pay. The Bible upholds the right of fair reward for work done (see chapter 11); it is only just that employers, clients and customers should meet their obligations to those who performed the work. As Herzberg suggested (and as described earlier), without fair reward people quickly become demotivated. In the biblical framework, fair reward can also be a motivator – but not by pandering to greed or materialism; rather, fair pay is the just reward for work well done, and also a way of showing appreciation and of recognizing particular effort or achievement.

People also have the right to safe and healthy working conditions. Life is precious and infinitely more valuable than company profits; it should never knowingly be jeopardized for lack of safety precautions.

Flexibility of working arrangements may also be a key motivational factor for those who have young children to care for or other commitments to balance.

*Security*

'It will be hard – if not virtually impossible – to motivate someone who believes that his or her job could end at any time' (Maitland 1995: 22). The Bible makes many references to security, with God being the ultimate source of security both now and for eternity (e.g. Psalm 18:2; Matthew 6:25–34, John 3:16). This points to security as an important human need; we like to feel that the relationships we enter into and the enterprises to which we give our energy have some longevity, that we can be part of them, help them grow and share in their outcome. Granted, the security of a 'job for life' is largely gone in today's fast-changing work environment. However, having *some* security of work is a basic human need on many counts, the most pressing of which is to pay the bills.

Organizations which treat people as a totally flexible resource, to be turned on and off like a power supply, cannot expect those same individuals to be highly motivated to contribute to the future of that organization. While people are contracted to perform certain duties and work certain hours, a relationship with an employer is more than this; it includes being part of an enterprise and sharing in its fruits (1 Timothy 5:18; based on Deuteronomy 25:4), and requires a degree of mutual trust (explored in chapter 7). For such trust to be built requires mutual delivery of obligations, which in turn requires some continuity of relationship and some security.

## What if you are demotivated?

### Getting going again

What about the times when you feel totally demotivated in your work? Maybe you are in a boring dead-end job, or just don't enjoy your work as you used to. Perhaps you have been under pressure and it has all got too much, or, at the opposite extreme, you have not had enough to do. A change of boss or working in a new team has not worked out well, or the organization has merged and its ethos is now very different. Perhaps there has been a disagreement; bad relationships at work can be demotivating, as well as a source of stress. Perhaps you have put off a difficult task which now seems insurmountable, and it is frightening to think about it.

Whatever the cause, it becomes difficult to get out of bed in the morning.

Here are some steps to help you get going again:

- Discover why you feel demotivated. For example, has something gone wrong at work, or is it time for a change of role or job?
- Make what changes you can within the situation. There are always some factors in it that lie within your control or

influence, and a change in one of them could make a difference.

- Depending on the issue, decide who can best support or advise, and ask for their help.
- Try to see God's purpose in and beyond your situation.

## The action column

1. Think about the things that get you out of bed in the morning. Where do they fit in a Christian framework for understanding work and motivation? Are your priorities correct?
2. What are the things that are most important to you in a job? What is it that most motivates you in your work? If this element is missing or poorly represented, think of ways of redressing the balance.
3. What elements of your job demotivate you? What can you do to change them?

# CHAPTER 6

# Riding the rollercoaster

*Coping with change at work*

## Change – the name of the game?

*At times exciting, at times frightening*

I rode a rollercoaster in Florida, reputedly one of the biggest in the world. The slow, nail-biting climb up the ratcheted slope at the beginning of the ride was full of anticipation, uncertainty and a degree of fear. Then it was a fast and furious experience. If we weren't hurtling vertically downwards, we were hanging from our seats in one of seven loop-the-loops, or corkscrewing with our legs flying, or plunging through a tunnel only to be spun round and sent whirling again. It was at times exciting, at times frightening.

For many, the rapid process of change thrust upon them in the course of their work is like riding a rollercoaster. If it's not spinning upwards, it's coming down, sometimes crashing down. Periods of uncertainty are followed by rapid change – reorganization, redundancy, re-engineering – leaving employees reeling, while those who are made redundant face further uncertainty. Self-employment is no more certain, since demand for products or services can vary dramatically, and a small business can be squeezed by large organizations for which it is a supplier, a contractor or a consultant. During 1998, the fall in the oil price led many oil companies to cut costs, resulting in much less use of travel services, and a lot of management and training consultants struggling to find other work.

Like riding a rollercoaster, the more times you go round, the less frightening it may be (or perhaps the more anaesthetized you become). But change remains an unsettling experience. The transition we undergo when change occurs starts with an 'ending' as we suffer the loss of the 'old', and it ends with a 'beginning' as we grasp the new (Bridges 1991: 3–6). And we have to adapt to the new; a new role, new ways of doing things, a new boss, a new job, or perhaps no job at all, which means facing an array of new and often demanding experiences. We have to cope with the loss *and* find the energy and ability to handle the new. But it can also yield more, since, with change, 'Work can become an opportunity for self-expression, personal as well as professional development, and excitement' (Hardingham 1992: 2). This is because change brings fresh possibilities, some of which we do not always see at first. God, through Isaiah, reminded the exiled people of Israel: 'See, I am doing a new thing! Now it springs up; do you not perceive it?' (Isaiah 43:19). Even if the change is less than desirable (your job gets smaller due to an industrial takeover, or as a consultant you lose a major client, or you are made redundant), good can come out of it because 'we know that in all things God works for the good of those who love him, who have been called according to his purpose' (Romans 8:28). This means not that the change will be easy, but that we can rely on God to help us through it.

The Bible does not deal specifically with changes in work. Ways of earning a living in Bible times – farming, fishing, craftsmanship, soldiering – did not undergo the drastic changes we associate with work today. Most people would normally have continued in the type of work that fell to them, or perhaps was chosen by them, for a lifetime. However, the Bible does recount episodes of change which affected the way of life of individuals and communities, including their work. One major episode of change in the Old Testament was the exodus from Egypt.

The people of Israel embarked on a remarkable journey of change when God announced to Moses that he had 'come down to rescue them from the hand of the Egyptians and to bring them up out of that land into a good and spacious land, a land flowing with milk and honey …' (Exodus 3:8). This was a change for the good; from the misery and suffering of slavery and oppression to freedom, living as God's people in a land he had promised them. Initially, the elders and the people accepted it as such (Exodus 4:29–31), but, despite a remarkable deliverance from Egypt, the crossing of the sea, and God's direct guidance, with the Egyptians in hot pursuit they soon lost heart: 'Didn't we say to you in Egypt, "Leave us alone; let us serve the Egyptians"? It would have been better for us to serve the Egyptians than to die in the desert!' (Exodus 14:12). And later, when they were hungry, they grumbled: 'If only we had died by the LORD's hand in Egypt! There we sat round pots of meat and ate all the food we wanted ...' (Exodus 16:3). They found themselves harking back to what they had lost, forgetting the bad things they had also left behind.

But at other times, seeing God's power at work, they were full of awe and trust and praise, recognizing they were involved in something remarkable and exciting (Exodus 14:31; 15:1–21). Then came a long period of wandering in the wilderness. The old had gone, but the new had not yet fully arrived, so there was lots of ambiguity and uncertainty, and the opportunity (or necessity) to get ready for the new. Graphically, the old generation had to die off before the new could arrive. The last stage of the change was the conquest of Canaan – the grasping of the new, which was really the beginning of the next story.

### What is driving the changes in work?

My father worked on the railway for thirty-seven years, and, for many of his generation, working in one industry, one profession or one company for a lifetime was commonplace. Now, changes in job, location, company or career are the norm. My first ten years at work. were fairly stable, but in the last ten years, although I have worked with the same organization, I have changed role seven times, moved office location six times, had three jobs disappear while I was the incumbent, been through three major periods of redundancy and experienced two industrial mergers.

What lies behind the ever-increasing pace of change in work? Organizations, facing ever fiercer competition and uncertain economic conditions, are having to react fast – to refocus, reorganize, merge, demerge. Small companies are being squeezed harder and harder. The self-employed are having to become more flexible. In the past, many professions and organizations offered a career for life; now people may have to retrain several times. The so-called 'psychological contract' – the unwritten understanding between individuals and organizations which traded loyalty for security – is changing, since many of the old certainties have gone.

What are the underlying factors driving the changes happening to work?

*New technology* has reshaped many industries and organizations in recent years, causing jobs to change or disappear, and creating new jobs in other sectors. Past advances in technology have caused shifts in the way people have been employed (e.g. the Industrial Revolution). The current era, variously called the 'second industrial revolution', the 'micro-electronics revolution', or the 'information-technology revolution', is based on the computer. As Miroslav Volf states: 'At the root of this transformation, which might be the most momentous of all technological transformations so far in human history, lies the computer chip' (1991: 33). In some manufacturing industries, computers now control or undertake (through robotics) much of the work. In the growing service sector (which includes finance, leisure, education and health), information is handled by computers. It is disputed whether a net increase or decrease in jobs will result, but the speed of change means that old jobs are lost before new jobs have been created, or that people do not have the skills required by the new jobs or do not live in the regions where they are available.

*Increased global competition* has forced organizations to streamline and cut costs to survive. Competition from the newly industrializing countries is causing the decline of much traditional industry and manufacturing, and hastening the shift towards the service sector. Work is moved to where it can be done most efficiently. For example, a large proportion of the sports trainers sold in the West are made in the Far East, where manufacturing labour is cheaper. The table shows how the proportions of people employed in different sectors changed in the UK during the twentieth century.

| Year | Agriculture | Industry (mostly manufacturing) | Services |
|------|-------------|--------------------------------|----------|
| 1901 | 13.0% | 43.9% | 43.1% |
| 1961 | 3.7% | 48.4% | 47.9% |
| 1995 | 2.1% | 28.7% | 69.2% |

(Organization for Economic Co-operation and Development 1994)

Globally, economic and political liberation has opened up new markets, but 'As nations emerge into the global market, they rapidly acquire the investment in knowledge, skills and technology to enable them to compete successfully with mature economies that have higher labour costs' (Herriot et al. 1998: 15). And within national economies, deregulation in sectors ranging from finance to utilities has increased competition in markets previously restricted to particular organizations or professions. In the UK, British Gas, a former nationalized monopoly, now has to compete with oil and electricity companies to sell its gas. In the public sector, market forces have been introduced through competitive tendering, market testing and outsourcing (Kessler & Undy 1996: 23), and pressure increased by growing customer awareness and citizens' charters.

In the UK, these pressures have resulted in shifts in employment from the manufacturing to the service sector, from large to medium and small organizations, and from manual to managerial, professional and technical occupations.

## How have organizations responded?

Organizations are under pressure to cut costs, to innovate and to be more productive. This requires both structures and people to be more flexible, as well as to cost less. A plethora of new terms describe the way organizations have responded; this is where the rollercoaster ride goes into a spin!

- *Delayering:* organizational pyramids have been 'flattened' by removing middle-management layers, making them more flexible and responsive.
- *Devolving* of authority from the centre to business units which are given considerable discretion to respond to their own markets, circumstances and needs.
- *Downsizing:* the overall reduction of jobs, which has particularly affected the manufacturing, utilities, retail and government sectors.
- *Flexible contracts:* these are designed to match available labour with demand more efficiently, and to save on certain costs incurred by employing 'permanent' staff. 'If current trends continue, more than half of the working population [in the UK] will very soon be on some form of part-time or flexible contract' (Herriot et al. 1998: 36).
- *Outsourcing:* 'non-core' activities are 'contracted out' to individuals or agencies who work only when needed, so that costs are reduced. Tenders for the best deal can be invited from a range of suppliers.
- *Process re-engineering:* the way work is done is 'redesigned' to enhance productivity, thereby reducing costs per unit of production. Productivity has continued to increase, but so has the average number of hours worked, so that the UK now has the dubious honour of the longest working hours in Europe (Herriot et al. 1998: 37). UK males work an average of 45.4 hours per week (cf. the EU norm of 41.1), while UK females work an average of 40.4 hours per week (cf. the EU norm of 38.9).

The extent and speed of change in an organization will depend on its history and culture, and its particular circumstances, markets and customers. Different approaches to change are shown in the diagram below.

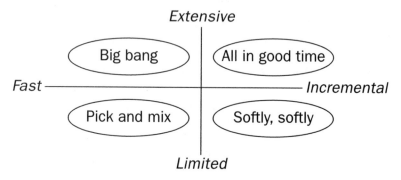

(after Kessler and Undy, 1996: 28)

When a business is taken over, or a new 'charismatic' leader takes control, change can feel like the 'big bang' – fast and far-reaching.

When an organization embarks on a change in strategy or culture, but like a large ship it takes time to turn itself around and move in the new direction, change can be slow and incremental.

Some organizations have core strengths which they want to keep, but some practices they know they must change, and so take a 'pick and mix' approach.

The 'softly, softly' approach, in which limited change is introduced incrementally, is a luxury few organizations can afford these days.

### What does change mean for the individual?

Workplace change cannot take place without affecting people. In fact, as some organizations recognize, unless they pay attention to their staff, such change cannot succeed. 'An effective change process needs to focus simultaneously on the company's "hardware" – its business configuration and organization structure – and on its "software" – the motivations, values, and commitments of the company's employees' (Ghoshal & Bartlett 1996: 26).

Downsizing, delayering and outsourcing may result in changes in or the disappearance of some people's roles. The move to more autonomous structures may increase their span of responsibility, and the hours they have to work. The trend to outsource has led to a rapid rise in self-employment, part-time, fixed-term and temporary employment. This may have presented some with new opportunities to enter the job market, and, at the highly skilled consultancy end, jobs can be well paid. For others it may have meant a less secure, less regular and lower-paid job. Those who remain in the 'core' of an organization also face a new and less certain future. The changes may not be reflected in their contracts, but expectations and commitments are certainly being reshaped, generally with more empowerment but less security.

Another outcome of advances in new technology and of the shift to the service sector is a demand for *higher skills*. In manufacturing jobs, roles are changing from that of operator to that of overseer, and in the growing service sector, people with professional and technical skills – 'knowledge workers' – are in great demand. 'Focused intelligence, the ability to acquire and apply knowledge and know-how, is the new source of wealth' (Handy 1994: 23). Those who can acquire new and higher skills may find their work more rewarding and fulfilling. Those who cannot are likely to lose out.

Change is never comfortable. 'The metaphor of a caterpillar transforming into a butterfly may be romantic, but the experience is an unpleasant one for the caterpillar. In the process of transformation, it goes blind, its legs fall off and its body is torn apart, as beautiful wings emerge. Similarly, the transformation from a hierarchical bureaucracy to a flexible, self-regenerating company will be painful and requires the enormous courage of its leaders' (Ghoshal & Bartlett 1996: 35). Such changes in organizations and work also require enormous fortitude and flexibility of all those who are affected by them.

## Change and changelessness

### What to change, what to keep the same?

Looking for a more interesting place to work? Change Management Consultants ... You would team with some of the most successful organizations – those seeking sustainable profound change, exploring new markets, leading their industries and creating their futures ... You won't have routine days ... You'll work in dynamic, intellectually stimulating teams, helping to make the changes essential to a client's success. The nature and complexity of our projects will stretch your analytical skills to the point that will push you to get the very best out of yourself.

This was one of several such advertisements in the Appointments section of an edition of *The Sunday Times*, which also featured an MA in Change Management from a UK university. This just illustrates how extensive and widespread the changes happening in work today are. What is a biblical response to this?

Much change is the result of humankind's creativity – that God-given ability to use intellect and skills to make and adapt things, to learn from mistakes, to build and link knowledge. Such creativity is a key aspect of work and, linked to the desire to improve life, has brought many beneficial changes: medicines, domestic appliances that reduce drudgery, machines such as computers which help people to share knowledge and express their creative gifts, and much more. However, creativity can be harnessed to both good and bad ends. God's creativity – his work – brought about change: a world out of nothing, a world that was 'very good'. Some elements in that world awaited human intervention (i.e. change); for instance, the land needed cultivation. But other elements were to be protected and cherished. So there is a place for change and for changelessness: 'Life and hope are to be found in the fusion of change and sameness, in getting the balance right, in changing the right things and keeping other things the same' (Hardingham 1992: 12). As Richard Higginson states: 'Discernment is needed to distinguish change which is vital and necessary from change which is trivial and faddish' (1996: 83).

## Change and stability, growth and consistency

The world features both change and changelessness. Every day is different and the world is constantly changing, but regular patterns are built into it which reassure us of its stability – the cycle of day and night, and the laws of nature, for example. God's command to human beings to subdue the earth through working it and taking care of it (Genesis 1:28; 2:15) was a command both to bring order to it and to change it. 'In fact, we human beings are outstanding as a species for our ability to impose order on an unstructured and constantly changing world' (Hardingham 1992: 13). We human beings, too, are a mixture of the changing and the stable: we grow and learn, develop skills and interests, encounter various stages of life, have likes and dislikes, personality traits, relationships which we cherish, and values and beliefs.

The Bible encourages change for positive ends, such as justice and peace, righteousness and love (e.g. Amos 5:24), within both individual lives and the community. The Old Testament emphasizes the need for God's people to renew their covenant with him, to change their ways and to return to him as a nation.

The message of the New Testament is that God changes individual lives by challenging people to turn to him and follow him. This radical change in our position before God is likened by Jesus to being 'born again' (John 3:3). But the change does not stop there, since, by his Spirit, God helps us to become more like him, building Christian character (Matthew 18:3; 2 Corinthians 3:18). The Christian life becomes one of change through growth.

The Bible also makes it clear that not all the change we encounter will be comfortable (1 Peter 4:12–13); Christians are not immune from the pressures of life, although God helps us to face them (Philippians 4:12–13). Change which is evil needs to be resisted; that which is dubious or may lead to harm needs to be challenged, and where possible influenced so that it will bring good. Calls for change need to be critically examined, distinguishing change which is negative or for change's sake from change which is good or necessary.

Some things are changeless: God's Word, his standards, promises and character (Psalm 100:5; Hebrews 13:8). Many elements of our life on earth are subject to change, but our fundamental needs, despite increased sophistication, do not change: the need for food, clothing and shelter; the need to be loved, valued and respected; the need to create, achieve, and be satisfied; and the need to belong. Work plays a part in meeting these needs.

### Towards the good life?

*The Good Life* was a sitcom that portrayed Tom and Barbara Good opting out of suburban life with all its trappings and pressures in order to live a simpler life of self-sufficiency under their own control, according to need rather than greed. Living more simply within their suburban setting does not prove as easy as the ideal sounds, but they rediscover joy in some of the simpler things of life. Their neighbours Jerry and Margot look on in a derogatory and patronizing way, but often find themselves envying the less cluttered lives of their impoverished friends.

*The Good Life* amusingly challenged what modern society tells us the good life should be – a world where technological wizardry will meet all our needs and bring wealth and happiness in its wake. Well, we know that happiness does not reside in material things, however smart, and that such a utopia is constantly frustrated by our wrongdoing and by the fact that technology can be put to evil as well as good uses. But, being an outcome of our God-given creativity, technology cannot simply be ignored; while we can live more simply, we cannot re-create the lifestyle of a bygone age. Besides, few in the industrialized world would want to return to the drudgery of washing clothes by hand, and automated production has eliminated much mundane, dirty or dangerous work. As Peter Mayhew states: 'All realists on both sides of industry know, in fact, that the technological revolution has to go forward for the benefit of the whole community, including all those who work in it' (1985: 96).

However, there are times when we feel that our lives are ruled by the things human beings have created, rather than the other way round. Machine-minding is a soul-destroying job, but, more subtly, we can become dominated by the technological gadgets many of us use every day. The laptop computer is an example. It can be an excellent tool for balancing work and home better. Instead of staying late, it enables us get home to the family, and work when it suits us. We can use travelling time to keep up or catch up, or work from home, thus avoiding having to commute. But it can also increase the pressure to work more hours, since the office effectively goes where we go. The boundaries of home life and work can become blurred; the organization has you twenty-four hours a day.

Our God-given creativity, which gives rise to technology, carries with it a deeper danger. It inspires us to achieve more than is necessary for survival, 'for it is also the transformation of desire, of thought, of will, of spirit, into substantial embodiments of culture' (Houston 1979: 160). Unless we acknowledge God as its source and use it to serve him, this drive can easily engender self-sufficiency and pride in what we achieve. As the story of the Tower of Babel shows (Genesis 11:1–9), if by our own achievements we try to rival God, the edifice (or technology) we create will be our downfall. The creativity we are gifted with can be seduced by the lust for power, by greed, by the pursuit of fame and by selfish ambition, so that it is divorced from its source and from its true end – to reveal God's image and glory in us (1 Corinthians 10:31).

The more inventive and apparently transcendent we become (genetics is not far from cloning human beings), the greater the danger is. 'For it is the essence of *technē* to extend the powers available to man, as an axe is to man's hand, or a computer to his brain, or an organization to his presence. This reinforces his attitude that, given the right tools ... man can do anything and everything' (Houston 1979: 161). As James Houston continues, this can lead us to think that the only value needed is technical efficiency, eliminating the need for man as a moral person.

Similarly, science may be pursued for questionable ends. Once undertaken for the Creator's sake – to illuminate, describe, understand, protect and harness the wonders of his world – it is now too often used to exploit the world or to create things which destroy it. Science divorced from the context of a world created and loved by God becomes a secular search to explain and exploit. But, used correctly, it can express our God-given creativity and help us to order and look after the world's resources more responsibly.

Miroslav Volf gives some helpful criteria by which to evaluate technology (1991: 182–183): it should not become an object of worship or self-aggrandizement; destroy non-human creation; promote social disintegration or dominion; or use people as a 'means', hindering their self-directedness or development.

In addition, technology needs to be matched by continual learning so that people stay in control. It should be designed to safeguard and promote freedom and creativity, and where possible kept to a 'human scale', as advocated by E. F. Schumacher in his book *Small is Beautiful* (1974). Human-scale technology emphasizes tools rather than machines, and fosters simplicity, capital cheapness and non-violence to nature. Information technology is now facilitating the restructuring of work into smaller units, as networking replaces cumbersome hierarchical structures. This, together with the eradication of many of the most boring jobs by the use of robotics, proves that technology can be part of the answer to bad work.

How do we ensure that technology is our tool and not our taskmaster? First, we must acknowledge God as Creator and as the source of our creativity, and seek to develop and use technology which honours him (Psalm 95:6). Secondly, our values must guide us to create and use technology in good ways and for good ends, establishing guidelines and boundaries for its use. (The Nuclear Non-Proliferation Treaty is an example of a deliberate limiting of the development of a particular technology.) Thirdly, we should not forget the often simple, unchanging pleasures of life such as friendship and fun, a sunset, a fireside conversation, a walk in the country – and God's love (Psalm 106:1). Finally, we can say 'no' to technology that we believe is wrong or harmful. The fact that we have invented it does not mean we have to use it.

# Handling change

## *The impact of change upon us*

A number of factors affect the impact change makes on us and the ease or difficulty with which we handle it.

- *Our personality:* some people find change invigorating and tend to welcome it. Others prefer stability and view change as unsettling and disruptive.
- *The desirability of the change:* if we view a particular change as positive, we will find it easier to accept.
- *The measure of control we have:* it is easier to come to terms with a change we have instigated or over which we have some control than with a change that is merely 'done to us'.
- *The number of change events:* if several changes are happening simultaneously or in quick succession, our ability to handle them will be stretched.
- *Duration:* if the change is prolonged, we wonder if things will ever settle.

As we have already noted, all change includes some loss, and the pain varies in accordance with the importance to us of what we have lost. The process of undergoing change is thus similar to the grieving process that follows a bereavement or other major loss. The *transition curve* described in the diagram shows a number of recognized phases including shock, discounting (the way we may try to ignore or minimize the situation), anxiety and sadness, anger and despondency, then gradual acceptance and internalization (when we fully accept the new situation). This process is not always linear; people can revisit phases, or sometimes get stuck and therefore struggle to come to terms with the change. I met a person who had been made redundant years before, but was still bitter and angry about it. Another was resentful because, much earlier in her career, she did not get the promotion she sought.

Transitions involve fundamental emotions such as fear, anxiety, sadness and anger, as well as excitement and joy. Each of these needs to be handled and expressed if we are to move through the transition.

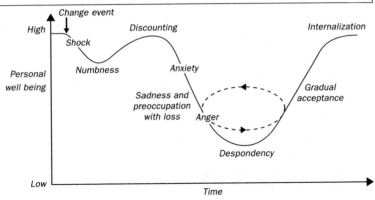

## Change – the transition curve

(after Hopson et al, 1992, reproduced in Jones 1995: 50)

Suppressing them can do harm, as can prolonged periods of change, since emotions such as fear and anxiety put our bodies on 'alert', which is tiring and stressful over time.

### Approaches to handling change

There are a number of approaches to handling change. First, we can *ignore* it and assume (or hope) that it will go away. This works if we rightly judged that the change was a flash in the pan or of less consequence than current practice. But where the approaching change is more fundamental or has obvious benefits, ignoring it will only put off the day of reckoning, and is tantamount to burying one's head in the sand. Some organizations have tried to ignore impending change and have paid the price by losing market share or going out of business.

Secondly, we might *oppose* change. This is the right thing to do when the change is evil, will lead to evil, or on balance will do more harm than good. The prophets opposed moral decay when it was not fashionable to do so (Jeremiah 3; Amos 4). Jesus challenged the money-changers in the temple: '"It is written," he said to them, "'My house will be called a house of prayer,' but you are making it a 'den of robbers'"' (Matthew 21:13). Paul challenged those who confused new Christians by altering the message of the gospel (Galatians 1:6–10). But resisting change because it is uncomfortable (there are jobs at stake) or inconvenient ('We have always done it like this') can be futile when change is inevitable (the organization will cease to exist if it does not cut jobs) and out of our control (as when a whole industry is in terminal decline so that its workers need to learn to do something else). In fact, resistance can use up valuable energy that could be used to face up to the change and the future.

Thirdly, *accepting* change can be the right course of action when we are convinced it is for the good, or when we judge that it is the lesser of two evils. Changes in working practices (employees becoming multi-skilled, employers granting flexible working options) may be necessary to compete or to keep skilled staff. But an unquestioning acceptance of change – 'what will be, will be' – can be an abdication of responsibility. Sometimes it is appropriate to challenge, or at least to question, the proposed change.

Finally, we can *embrace* change. This is often the most positive response to the changes happening in work, since many of these changes are coming at us and have to be dealt with; they will not go away if we ignore them. Some are too important to accept without question, some too inevitable to resist.

When the merger of our company with another was announced as the largest industrial merger of all time, we knew that big changes would ensue. Just after the announcement, a manager likened the impending change to being chased: if you run to meet your assailant and put your arms around him, it is much harder for him to hit you. If you move towards change and embrace it, it is less likely to surprise you and to do you harm.

The most positive approach to the major changes happening in work is to face them and become involved with them, hoping to harness them for good. Such an approach can make us partakers in change, even makers of change, rather than people upon whom change is thrust. Whether we think it appropriate to resist, postpone or accept a change, if we get involved in it we are better able to influence change and manage its effects upon us.

When will it all end? It will not, since the drivers of this change show no signs of faltering. Change is endemic to human creativity, and work is one of the arenas in which it displays its wares. Recognizing this, Charles Handy suggests we should anticipate the next change by preparing for it while things are going well: 'The Sigmoid Curve sums up the story of life itself. We start slowly, experimentally and falteringly, we wax and then we wane' (Handy 1994: 50). His point is that as organizations, and individuals, we should start the next upward curve just before the present one reaches its peak, so that we have the time, energy and resources to get through the difficult stages of the subsequent curve. Otherwise, we will be caught facing disaster and will be less able to make the necessary changes.

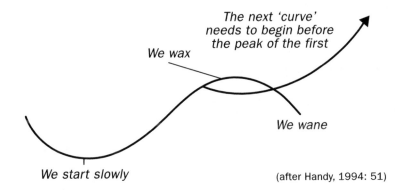

## The Sigmoid Curve

The next 'curve'
needs to begin before
the peak of the first

We wax

We wane

We start slowly

(after Handy, 1994: 51)

### *Ways of influencing change*

Since much change is the result of creativity, one of the best ways to influence change is to discover ways of being creative with it. To do this, we need to identify where we have the freedom to operate, and the points at which we can exert some influence. When a large change happens, those directing the change (in an organization, usually the senior managers) do not have all the answers, nor can they predict all the consequences of the changes they initiate. There is room for ideas and solutions and, when change has started, lots of scope for finding ways of implementing it to best advantage. At times of change, the ensuing uncertainty may bring a period when work is slack, which again gives an opportunity to make an impact on change.

Many people think that only those in senior positions, those who have direct power, are able to effect change. In reality, only a few people have unfettered power – all bosses report to or are accountable to someone – and even those with power cannot achieve change solely by telling the workforce that it is going to happen. This can set direction and elicit compliance, but to make change enduring and to win commitment requires the use of *influence*. We bring influence to bear in a number of ways. Sometimes influencing is regarded in a negative way because it implies getting people to do something they do not want to do. Being persuaded to buy something we don't want through a 'hard selling' technique, for instance, is not a pleasant experience. When influence is applied to bring about something for one's own gain or to forward a particular issue in an underhand way, it is manipulative. But there are good and legitimate ways to influence people towards what we think is a good idea or the best way forward, and there are biblical examples of doing it well:

- *By putting forward a good case*, based on knowledge of the issues, thought-through proposals and innovative ideas. Those who come to the table with something to offer are often influential. This involves being prepared, and understanding what is important to those whom we seek to influence. Paul and Barnabas brought a convincing case to the apostles in Jerusalem concerning the acceptance of Gentile Christians and influenced future policy (Acts 15:12–21).

- *By credibility* based on respected skills and experience, and a track record of giving sound advice in the past. Just as Pharaoh looked to Joseph because there was 'no-one so discerning and wise' as he (Genesis 41:39–40), people look to those who know what they are talking about.

- *By personal character and example*, being honest, trustworthy and open. People listen to those whom they trust, and who show a good way ahead by example (1 Peter 2:12).

- *By timely interventions.* There is 'a time to be silent and a time to speak' (Ecclesiastes 3:7). Trying to influence a situation too early in the process may mean that your voice is not heard; too late, and your view may be seen as irrelevant. The best time to influence is often close to the time when decisions are to be made.

- *By picking the right battles.* We waste our energies trying to influence issues where the outcome is unlikely to change, unless it is a matter of principle upon which we feel we must take a stand. When Paul deemed the situation in a city to be beyond change at that time, he would leave (e.g. Acts 17), yet he stood firm on certain issues of principle (e.g. opposing Peter, Galatians 2:11).

- *Through relationships* – not the 'old-boy network', which is based on favours reciprocated within a privileged inner circle, but by utilizing our working relationships in an open way to achieve what is best, both within and beyond our closest circle. As Paul did, we can appeal to people when we have an interest in common with them (1 Corinthians 1:10).

- *By being passionate but open to influence ourselves.* If we care about an issue we will be enthusiastic and committed to it, which can help to convince others. However, if we are unwilling to be influenced differently, people will suspect us of having our own fixed and fully worked out views and may question our motives. Why should we expect to influence others if we are closed to their views? As James instructed, we 'should be quick to listen, slow to speak and slow to become angry' (James 1:19).
- *By effective conversation.* We are much more likely to influence people if we listen to their views and show how our proposals will affect them and relate to their needs. The way we communicate can be crucial; if we do so aggressively, arrogantly or argumentatively, we are likely to build resistance. As Paul wrote to Timothy, 'the Lord's servant must not quarrel; instead, he must be kind to everyone' (2 Timothy 2:24). We need to be clear, succinct and relevant to those we are addressing, using illustrations and examples to illuminate our point. If our conversation is 'always full of grace', we are more likely to win people over (Colossians 4:6).

## Practical steps for handling change

Below are some steps for handling change that we encounter in work. If we believe we are in the work God has for us, our role is to be 'salt and light', influencing the change for good even if we may not fully support every aspect of it.

*Face change and help to shape it.* With God's help, we can face change and influence it for good. Those who ignore impending change are like the people of Jeremiah's day who did not listen to his warnings and were then surprised when they were swept away in defeat and exile (Jeremiah 25). Facing change will mean acknowledging the losses as well as the benefits that it brings; grief as well as joy can accompany change. The disciples experienced both with the changes brought about by Jesus' death and resurrection. Facing up to the change was a trying experience, as Peter found in his clumsy attempt to defend Jesus, and then in his denials. But with God's help, he embraced the changes that led to the fledgling church (Acts 1:15ff.). Making the effort to understand the need for change will help us to face it better, and influencing its direction will help us to accept it.

*Grieve the loss, then let go.* As human beings, when we experience loss we need to come to terms with it through expressing our grief before we can move on. Jesus said: 'Blessed are those who mourn, for they will be comforted' (Matthew 5:4). The loss experienced through redundancy and some of the ways the Christian faith can help us deal with it are addressed in chapter 9. The grief we experience, often evident through expressions of denial, anger, sadness or depression, should not be confused with low morale. The reaction is usually to the loss, not the new things brought about by change.

*Keep going in between times.* During the time of uncertainty when we know that the old is going but the new has not fully come, we need to hold on to the certainties of God (his character, word, promises; 1 Peter 1:25) and all that he has given us (the love of our families, the world in which we live), *not* the past. It is strange how, when change comes, the past can suddenly appear as a golden age because of its familiarity and comfort. The Bible shows us that we are to learn from the past by recalling the key lessons of history and of God's deliverance, but not to live in it. Rather, we can move on because our lives are based on changeless realities which remain with us despite change: 'The LORD is my rock, my fortress and my deliverer; my God is my rock, in whom I take refuge' (Psalm 18:2). We need to ride the change with perseverance and patience, recognizing that it will not all be sorted out straight away.

*Look forward.* 'Forget the former things; do not dwell on the past. See, I am doing a new thing! Now it springs up; do you not perceive it?' This was God's message through Isaiah to his people in exile (43:18–19). We are to look for the new opportunities brought about by change. In the case in point, God was indicating to the people of Israel that they would return from exile; a new start was possible, but they had to understand it and grasp it. In the New Testament, the persecution which followed Stephen's death scattered the church. Despite the apparent disaster, good came of the change since 'Those who had been scattered preached the word wherever they went' (Acts 8:4). When change occurs, instead of trying to hold on to the past, we are to look for the new opportunities it brings (there is often a silver lining, even when the change is formidable) and grasp the future. This requires both faith and courage.

*Be full of hope.* It is common to feel hurt during change because of what we lose. While it is necessary to acknowledge the loss and grieve, some get stuck in a negative frame of mind, resenting the change, and forever holding a grudge against those they think are responsible for it. The hope we have in God helps to counter such attitudes. Whatever the change, God is with us and gives us hope for what lies ahead. We can choose the attitude we adopt when change occurs: if we choose to be hopeful, we are far more likely to have an effect on the change and to locate the good in it rather than be swamped by it. 'Be strong and take heart, all you who hope in the LORD' (Psalm 31:24).

*In God's hands.* Much change is driven by factors beyond our direct control and thrust upon us. However, ultimately it is God who is in control, and his will cannot be thwarted. Looking for his plan in what is happening will help us to make sense of the change and to see our role in it. Whether we feel we can guide the change or not, we can trust: 'But I trust in you, O LORD; I say, "You are my God." My times are in your hands' (Psalm 31:14–15).

## Leadership and change

One of the key tasks of leadership is to lead change. Leadership involves helping people to move to something new, initiated sometimes by the leader, sometimes by the organization. In chapter 10, I outline the key functions of leadership, which include bringing vision and direction, and motivating people towards a goal. In times of change, such functions are crucial. When the first major redundancy round in the organization I work for occurred in 1992, the job cuts and organizational change were so drastic that it felt as if the company was in free fall, and no-one seemed able to predict, let alone manage, the consequences. But there was one senior manager who had a vision of what the organization needed to become, and his articulation of this vision helped to keep the company and the employees on track.

Here are some key points to put into practice when leading people through change.

- *Communicate:* explain the need for change, keep people informed, be open and honest. During the changes of the exodus, Moses communicated regularly with the Israelites about what was happening (Exodus 14:13).
- *Involve and consult,* so that people can contribute to shaping the change; they will then be more committed to it. This shows respect for them and for what they think; some good changes

are met with resistance because no-one bothered to consult those affected. Joshua won the commitment of Israel by consulting on the crucial issue: 'choose for yourselves this day whom you will serve' (Joshua 24:15).

- *Allow people to express their loss* and to celebrate the good things of the past. Be sensitive to people's feelings: 'Rejoice with those who rejoice; mourn with those who mourn' (Romans 12:15).
- Before the new has come, *inject as much certainty as possible*, and protect people from further change while they are vulnerable. During the exodus, Moses needed to reassure people that necessities (food, water) would continue, despite traumatic change.
- *Listen, but don't be deflected* from change that is necessary; the uncomfortable nature of change means there will be opposition. Paul stood up to those who wanted to force Gentile Christians to follow Jewish customs (Galatians 2), and in so doing brought about change in the church so that Gentile Christians were accepted; this required courage and perseverance.

## The action column

1. Think about the changes that have happened in your industry and your work. How has your organization responded? How has it affected you?
2. Of the changes affecting your work, decide which are good and need to be encouraged, which are not good and need to be resisted or influenced, and which are probably inevitable and therefore need to be harnessed for good.
3. Are you making the best use of technology to help you manage your work, or is it driving you to work harder and longer? Devise ways to make it your tool, not your taskmaster.
4. Where are you on the 'transition curve' of handling the major changes affecting your work? What steps can you take to help you to move through the transition?

# CHAPTER 7

# It takes two to tango

## Working at relationships

## Relationships

*Can't live with them, can't live without them*

We need to live and work in relationship with others, and yet, as individuals and communities, we find this difficult to do. Like porcupines on a cold night, we huddle together for warmth, but have to move apart because we get spiked. But the need to relate remains, because the doctrine of the Trinity reveals a God in relationship, and this is how he has made us, in his image. The God who made humankind is a God who wishes to have a relationship with his creatures and who, through Christ, has gone to enormous lengths to make it possible. And he wishes us to live in relationship with each other because 'It is not good for man to be alone' (Genesis 2:18). Our in-built desire and need to relate to others draw us together in friendships and personal relationships, in organizations and teams, in communities and societies. Yet our fallen nature – our tendency to be selfish and to do wrong – works in the opposite direction and spoils the relationships we so much need. It mars our relationship with God, as Adam and Eve's fall so graphically portrays (Genesis 3).

Undergirding a Christian understanding of relationships are the twin pillars of love and trust. Love is the fundamental motivation to form relationships. Love in the Christian sense is sacrificial, it reaches out before there is love in return (Ephesians 2:4–5) and is unconditional. It is the opposite of selfishness, being focused on what we can give rather than what we can get. It affects the way we relate to friends and others with whom we have personal relationships, and the way we relate to those we don't know through care and compassion. It influences our relationships in our community and in organizations. Trust is the belief that another will fulfil his or her obligations to us, and the means by which relationships grow and flourish. The biblical concept of covenant – comprising promises and mutual obligations – is built on the pillars of love and trust.

## The problems with relationships

If relationships are based on taking rather than giving, they soon collapse. Yet this is characteristic of many relationships today. Prenuptial agreements typify the desire to take rather than to give, and express a lack of trust in what should be the closest human relationship of all, that of husband and wife. In the City, a person's word used to be enough. Now, deals have to be underpinned by long, watertight legal contracts with get-out clauses and financial penalties should one of the signatories get a better offer. Selfishness and greed are the main causes.

Then there is the effect of the urban society in which most of us live; the 'megacity', as Michael Schluter and David Lee term modern life in their influential book *The R Factor*. They differentiate between relationships where people encounter (meet) each other and those which are contingent, and make the point that although we live on top of each other, we do not relate. 'Anyone who has travelled on the London Underground at rush hour will have noticed the extraordinary ability of Westerners to ignore each other even in situations of extreme physical intimacy. This deliberate refraining from encounter is one of the most striking features of the modern city' (1993: 15). One of the reasons for this is that 'we find ourselves scattered too far and moving too fast to maintain a strong base of encounter relationships' (1993: 13). The mobility demanded of people for work reasons (either because their organization requires them to relocate, or because they have to move to get a job) may yield employment or a good career step, but it can also disrupt relationships in the family, with friends and within the community. It carries with it other consequences; children's friendships and education are disrupted, extended-family members are not within easy reach.

Technology offers some help; when away on business we can communicate with the family via phone or e-mail. But it can also reduce the amount of quality time we have for relationships, because it enables us (and tempts us) to do more, making life faster and more complex. And the danger is that we use non-contact forms of communication even when people are sitting nearby, rather than talk to them face to face. Technology also affects our leisure; while computer games and other forms of virtual reality can be fun, they can also be the 'ultimate denial of encounter' (Schluter & Lee 1993: 33).

## As you would wish to be treated

### *The greatest commandment*

The central and most powerful theme of the New Testament is love – the love God has for his creation (John 3:16) and the love he wishes his human creatures to have for him and for each other. This is a biblical theme, its development evident in the covenant theology of the Old Testament where God makes possible a loving reciprocal relationship with his people. Jesus, in his response to the question 'Teacher, which is the greatest commandment in the law?' (Matthew 22:36) combined Deuteronomy 6:5 and Leviticus 19:18, bringing together love of God and of neighbour: '"Love the Lord your God with all your heart and with all your soul and with all your mind." This is the first and great commandment. And the second is like it: "Love your neighbour as yourself." All the Law and the Prophets hang on these two commandments' (Matthew 22:37–40).

Jesus made it clear that love was to be the hallmark of his followers (John 13:34–35). Correspondingly, it was recognized by Paul as the most important quality of Christian character (1 Corinthians 13:13), binding the other qualities together (Colossians 3:14) and helping people to build the community of the church (Ephesians 4:15–16). Christian love is not confined to the circle of believers; it is to be extended to our neighbours, which, as Jesus made clear, includes anyone who needs our help (Luke 10:30–37), and also to our enemies (Matthew 5:43-45; Romans 12:14). Christian love – God's love at work in us – is shown to be authentic by the actions it inspires (John 13:9–12; 1 John 3:18). As Christians, we are 'to consider how we may spur one another towards love and good deeds' (Hebrews 10:24).

### *Charity starts at work*

How does the love at work in us show itself in our work? Principally, by spurring us to want the best for others. Writing of *agapē*, C. S. Lewis states: 'Divine Gift-love – Love Himself working in man – is wholly disinterested and desires what is simply best for the beloved' (1963: 117). As such, it drives acts of appreciation and self-sacrifice, reconciliation and forgiveness, kindness and compassion. In a working world often characterized by self-seeking ambition and individualism, competition and confrontation, Christian love is distinctive indeed.

*Appreciation.* There are lots of ways of appreciating others for who they are as well as for what they contribute. (I have mentioned such appreciation as a key aspect of motivation in chapter 5.) Christians should appreciate others not primarily to motivate them (though this is an outcome), but because of their intrinsic worth as people. Because Christian love 'always protects, always trusts, always hopes, always perseveres' (1 Corinthians 13:7), it makes our appreciation of people practical: doing things for their benefit, being willing to empower them, expecting the best of them. Mark Greene gives some good examples of expressing such appreciative Christian love in relationships at work: 'A thank-you note. An apology for a sharp word ... A note of encouragement in someone's top drawer. A flower. A Polo mint. The offer of a cup of coffee,' and so on (1997: 56). As he points out, these can pave the way for explicit witness when the time is right.

When I was at a particularly low point, with my job disappearing and no sign of another on the horizon, a Christian friend at work said, 'I would rather have you as our personnel manager than anyone else, a thousand times more than anyone else.' Just when I felt rejected by everyone, someone showed me I was appreciated, and it meant the world.

*Self-sacrifice.* Christian love is not self-seeking (1 Corinthians 13:5), but self-sacrificing in working towards the success of others and of the enterprise. This may mean standing aside for someone more capable to take a particular role, or giving time to coach and train others without concern that their skill may one day exceed our own. It means being willing to share opportunities for desirable tasks, delegating to the benefit of others, and making sure credit is given to all who have contributed to a project. It means taking responsibility for our own mistakes, and at times for the mistakes of those for whom we are responsible. Where mistakes mean inconvenience to customers or clients, it may involve saying 'I'm sorry' on behalf of the organization. Such action can redeem the situation through self-sacrificially 'taking the blame vicariously' (Higginson 1993: 141).

An extreme example of self-sacrifice is to resign on a matter of principle. This should never be done lightly. As Richard Higginson points out, in most situations 'the appropriate response for a Christian faced by dubious demands at work will be to stick it out, argue the case for a different way of proceeding and be patient' (1993: 148). When the organization is intent on a direction that is patently immoral, or when a particular action or decision is deliberately evil or unjust, however, resignation becomes a serious consideration.

Self-sacrifice does not mean neglecting our own opportunities, development, or the balance between life and work, but holding these alongside the well-being of others. Truly to love others as ourselves means recognizing their aspirations and rights to opportunities, and being prepared to help them to achieve them. Where love for others and a proper self-love are in conflict, we are to respond in a loving way, seeking God's guidance to balance aright our concern for others and our responsibilities to ourselves and our dependants.

*Reconciliation.* As Christians, we have a 'ministry of reconciliation' (2 Corinthians 5:18) in calling others to be reconciled to God. But the concept of reconciliation is wider and extends to other situations of conflict, including work. As Jesus demonstrated, this is often most powerfully done through example and self-sacrifice: inspiring people to see the other view, looking for justice to be done, treating the claims and needs of others seriously. This is the role of the 'peacemaker' given prominence by Jesus (Matthew 5:9). James defines heavenly wisdom as peace-loving, and then goes on to state that 'Peacemakers who sow in peace raise a harvest of righteousness' (James 3:17–18). So we are to be peacemakers in the world of work.

When I began working in personnel, I soon realized that handling conflict and controversy was part of the territory: a disputed pay rise, a case of sexual harassment, competition by two managers to recruit the same person, complaints about an autocratic boss, a disciplinary hearing, firing someone for misusing the internet, a personality conflict tearing a team apart. Sometimes these seemed insurmountable, intractable issues, but I came to see that there was always a way forward, and it was usually the path of reconciliation. I have prayed on numerous occasions, 'Lord, show me how to sort this out.' It usually begins with helping one party to see the other's point of view, or getting them to reflect on their own contribution to the issue.

Once I was called in to help a manager and one of his team members to resolve a disputed appraisal rating. For the team member it was a matter of principle that the good rating for his past year's work should be recorded; he had since been promoted and given a nominal rating at the new grade. His boss did not want to lose face by having to change the rating *and* show a higher distribution than other teams. The boss did not intend to give way. The employee was about to invoke the company grievance procedure. We talked. With the assistance of another manager, I got the boss to see the demotivational effect of what he was doing, and its perceived unfairness. I got the employee to refrain from using the grievance procedure; in this instance, it would have done him more harm than good. In the end, we recorded two appraisal ratings, one for the past performance at the previous grade, and one for the time in the new grade; the situation was resolved.

*Forgiveness.* In the increasingly competitive environment of work, the unforgiving ethos of 'one mistake and you are out' is becoming more common. By contrast, Christian love is ready to forgive wrongs as well as mistakes (Colossians 3:13). As Christians we are to seek to build people up again rather than knock them down when they have failed at a task. We can demonstrate such an attitude through appreciating people's strengths, as well as helping them where they are weak or lacking in skills or experience. It means not continually judging people on past failures, but trusting and supporting them in the future, and seeking to find the best use for their skills.

As a personnel manager attending staff-development sessions, I have sometimes found myself challenging managers who had a preconceived and often prejudiced view of certain employees. Perhaps they had met the person five years ago when he was inexperienced, and had since written him off. Because she had not impressed the management team in a five-minute presentation, she could not be any good. Because the project had failed, this person could not be assigned a responsible role again. We need to think back to the times we have been given a second chance, or a little more time to finish the job, or when we were listened to when we explained why we could not complete a task. The simple spirit of forgiveness can turn mistakes into learning, false starts into experience, potential failures into confident success stories.

*Kindness.* 'Love is patient and kind,' so our response to an employee learning a new job, or someone struggling with a work task, should reassure, protect and encourage him or her. Kindness can turn a potential nightmare into a manageable new experience. Just as the psalmist credits God with lifting a person 'out of the slimy pit, out of the mud and mire' (Psalm 40:2), so we can lift people up through our kindness. Kindness manifests itself through a concern for and understanding of others, and a gentleness in the way we treat them. It puts aside thoughts of status and what others might think, and mediates the fragrance of Christian love through its gentle, personal touch. Jesus' kindness brought grace to those with whom he came into contact, and drew people to him (e.g. Mark 10:13–16; Luke 7:36–50).

*Compassion.* Jesus' response to those in need was compassion. He changed his schedule so that their needs could be met (e.g. Matthew 14:13–14; Mark 1:40–42). The story of the good Samaritan (Luke 10:30–37) illustrates how compassion goes beyond sympathy to determined action. Correspondingly, Thomas Aquinas described compassion as 'heartfelt identification with another's distress, driving us to do what we can to help'. With regard to outward activity, it is 'the Christian's whole rule of life' (1991: 360)

In the voluntary sector, compassion provides a key motivation for work, since the principal purpose of the enterprise is action on behalf of the poor, oppressed or disadvantaged. In all types of work, however, Christians are called to be compassionate to those in need. This may mean supporting a colleague at a time of personal tragedy or disappointment, or helping someone to cope with the loss experienced through redundancy. It is the opposite of gloating over another person's downfall because it creates an opportunity for ourselves, or 'passing by on the other side' because stopping to help will hinder our own work schedule or performance. Whereas we have a responsibility to perform our work tasks, compassion may at times overrule if there is an urgent need to be met; tasks and hours can (and normally should) be made up, but a person in danger or distress needs our help immediately.

Sue provided personnel support for the pilot-plant team, and, when they were told their jobs were to disappear, she spent many hours working on their behalf despite her own job uncertainty. Because Sue knew them well, she understood what they were going through, and recognized that it would not be easy for them to find jobs inside or outside the company. While it was part of her job to help, Sue's compassionate approach led her to listen more patiently, visit the plant more often and go to greater lengths in helping them to adjust to the new reality and start seeking other jobs. Sympathy is patronizing; empathy shows understanding; compassion rolls up its sleeves and gets its hands dirty alongside those in need.

### In this together

A plaque my parents had on their bedroom wall read: 'A life without friends is like a garden without flowers.' Sadly, friendship today often seems to be put in the 'take it or leave it' category. It is neglected because we haven't got the time. It often seems eclipsed by the individualism and materialism which permeate our society. It is made more difficult by work patterns which result in commuting long distances, working long hours, or continually uprooting and moving to another part of the country or overseas. This is in sharp contrast to the classical tradition and to the biblical record: 'To the Ancients, Friendship seemed the happiest and most fully human of all loves; the crown of life and the school of virtue' (Lewis 1963: 55).

The context for friendship is some shared focus, activity or cause, but also a liking for the other person described 'as a reciprocal good will founded in sentiment or choice' (Meilaender, in Macquarrie & Childress 1986: 240–241). As C. S. Lewis described, it differs from affection or erotic love since 'Lovers are normally face to face, absorbed in each other; Friends, side by side, absorbed in some common interest' (1963: 58).

In the Bible, perhaps the most quoted example of friendship is that of David and Jonathan, where Jonathan is said to have loved David as he loved himself (1 Samuel 18:1; 20:17). Their relationship was clearly reciprocal (2 Samuel 1:26), and exemplified by noble and loyal acts on both sides. They are described as being 'one in spirit' (1 Samuel 18:1), their friendship being based on the shared focus of their faith in God and their understanding of his purposes (to put David on the throne despite the fact that Jonathan was Saul's heir), coupled with their respect for each other.

'A friend loves at all times' (Proverbs 17:17); a true friend still accepts us when we fail. There are times when everything seems to be going wrong and we need someone to stand by us and show us loyalty. 'A man of many companions may come to ruin, but there is a friend who sticks closer than a brother' (Proverbs 18:24).

Jesus worked with the twelve disciples, but seems to have had particularly close friendships with Peter, James and John, sharing with them some of the significant moments of his ministry (Matthew 17:1–13). John recognized this in referring to himself as 'the disciple whom Jesus loved' (John 13:23; 19:26; 21:20). Lazarus and his sisters Mary and Martha were also portrayed as close friends of Jesus (John 11:5, 11, 36). Jesus endorsed the importance of friends in his statement that the greatest example of love is to lay down one's life for one's friends (John 15:13). Jesus called his disciples his friends, their shared focus being the Father's business (John 15:15). While Paul exhorts his Christian readers to love one another deeply, and speaks of his love for all his Christian brothers (e.g. Philippians 4:1), he also refers with particular affection to individuals who were his friends (e.g. Romans 16:3ff.). Christian friendship has the potential to be especially strong because of the deep focus we share in Christ, together with the love God puts in our hearts for others.

Making and enjoying friendships is part of the way God has made us. And he himself invites us into the most important friendship of all: to be his friend (John 15:13, 15). Thomas Aquinas made much of this astonishing fact in his understanding of divine love: 'Charity is friendship between God and man based on sharing eternal happiness' (1991: 352). As Wadell comments on Aquinas: 'We are called through love to be for God who God has always been for us, a friend, a source of happiness and delight, one who is key to the other person's joy' (1992: 64).

Friends offer a listening ear and a shoulder to cry on in the knowledge that we will not be rejected. When facing taxing decisions or traumatic circumstances such as deciding on a job (discussed in chapter 8), or redundancy (discussed in chapter 9), we look to friends to offer advice and support. Friends can act as role models and mentors, helping us to learn and develop, and as a deep influence on the building of our character (chapter 4). Friendship is used by God for the good of us all: 'It is the instrument by which God reveals to each the beauties of all the others' (Lewis 1963: 83).

During a demanding phase of reorganizing and redundancy in which Roy and I were immersed for four months, frequently shuttling between London and Chicago, our friendship kept us going. And when the time came to think about our own futures, I found I could express to Roy my thoughts and my anger as well as my dreams, and he understood. Because of our shared experience under pressure, and the fact that we shared the same Christian faith, we could help each other to give thought in a Christian way to the work we were doing and to our own situations.

Certainly, a life full of friends is like a garden with beautiful flowers.

## Working at friendships

Work is a fertile environment in which friendships can grow and thrive because it is where we focus on similar activities or have common goals, and where co-operation and mutual trust are often required. Friendships are a source of job satisfaction; they enrich work and workers alike. Those whose main work activity is changed through retirement or redundancy often comment that what they most miss is the company of work friends.

Not all shared activities result in friendship; there may be too great a difference in outlook, interest or personality for this to develop. Nevertheless, as Christians at work, wherever possible we are to seek to transform our colleagues, companions, fellow-pupils and so on, into friends. Jesus' transformation of his relationship with his disciples from that of teacher to that of close friend is an example (John 15:12–15). In such friendships, we are to demonstrate the acceptance, trust and loyalty commensurate with promoting the well-being of others. How does this transformation happen? Alistair Ross, in his book *Understanding Friends*, includes a helpful chapter entitled 'Making friends' (1993: 27–47). He describes how we are to find common ground and create the opportunities for friendships to start, and to build and maintain friendships through listening, giving clear signals, and respecting other people's boundaries. He also mentions the necessity to take risky steps of commitment if trust is to develop: 'Trust is a necessary part of any relationship. No matter how we met our friend, how many common interests we have, or how skilled our listening has become, a point comes where we need to commit ourselves to sharing something of the real "you" or "me" with the other person' (1993: 43). Such self-disclosure can be difficult because it makes us vulnerable, but it leads to the acceptance and understanding characteristic of deep friendship.

I spent two years working in a great team. It was well balanced in terms of personality types and the roles we liked to play; we knew, because we had analysed ourselves using Myers-Briggs personality typing and the Belbin team-roles model. Daphne was practical and had a lovely interactive style. Tara was good at assimilating new ideas as well as being sensitive to people's feelings. Sue had a caring spirit and a huge capacity for hard work. Cath had an eye for detail and precision. Ian displayed a quiet, unassuming professionalism and an ability to coach others. Carly had a talent for presenting to others. Fiona could handle difficult situations with a deft touch. I possessed the dubious skill of balancing lots of plates, often precariously. The head of the organization came to one of our team meetings and said, 'Your team members really listen to each other and support each other.' Another manager remarked, 'Why can't I get my engineers to work together like your team?' I think the fact that we had developed good friendships and liked one another was more important in our becoming a high-performing team than its balanced profile. We did not always agree, but our loyalty and mutual respect meant that we worked through issues and presented a united front. As well as enhancing what we achieved, it was both satisfying and fun.

Friendships at work carry dangers. We can be led astray by 'friends' who conspire to skive or otherwise neglect their work. As with youngsters who get in with a bad crowd, friendships can become a school of vice. Many an extramarital relationship started as a work friendship. One overseas office I visited a number of times in the early 1980s had been damaged by several extramarital affairs, which had left a number of bitter partners and split families. Such dangers occur when the focus of the friendship shifts from the shared activity of work to a shared activity that is unhelpful, wrong or liable to lead to wrongdoing. Inward-looking, exclusive friendships can lead to favouritism, and the old-boy network can conflict with the just aims of many equal-opportunities initiatives.

Healthy friendships, however, bring out the best in people. At work, it can make all the difference to share a common interest with another, enjoying both the activity and the friendship. Paul and I have undertaken some challenging work together over the years, sometimes in testing and dangerous situations. We were visiting Jakarta when riots erupted in 1996; we delivered training in Nigeria when it was under military rule; we worked together in war-torn Angola. I would not have liked to have undertaken those tasks on my own. They would have been manageable with a colleague; sharing them with a friend made them positive and worthwhile experiences.

## What's in a contract?

### More than words

I remember the day I signed my first employment contract. Smiling, the personnel officer asked, 'Salary enough for you?' After the meagre sustenance of student life, it felt like a fortune. The contract specified 7.25 hours a day, four weeks' leave, one month's notice period. But at the time I knew it went further than that. This was a multinational company that I expected to give me interesting tasks, career prospects and job security. At my interview, someone had said, 'This is a good company to work for. They look after you.' And I came to learn that the company expected more of me than was specified in the written contract; as well as competence to do my job, they expected willingness to put in more hours when the pressure was on, commitment to the task and loyalty in the face of other offers.

The employment relationship is usually defined in terms of a formal contract. This is important for clarifying obligations and for ensuring that obligations are honoured. But, important as formal agreements are, there is more to relationships between organizations and their employees. The wider 'psychological contract' comprises a set of unwritten expectations based on a relationship of mutual trust, which are important for the well-being of individuals and of the organization. In part, this reflects our human need to relate to others, to belong, to be fulfilled, to feel secure. Those who run organizations recognize that if they have their employees' commitment as well as consent, the results are likely to be better. So working is not just about contracting labour, goods and services for pay, but also about *hearts and minds*.

The written contract specifies the nature of the job, the expected standard of performance, the pay, hours, notice period and so on. But the organization will also expect employees to be competent, conscientious and well motivated. A growing requirement in many organizations concerns behaviours and ways of working which align with the organization's culture (such as open thinking, networking, team working). While these are normally outside of employment contracts, they are often codified in objective-setting, development and appraisal systems. As David Statt points out, organizations 'always demand loyalty of their members as their side of the psychological contract' (1994: 39). In a world of ever fiercer competition, loyalty (in the form of commitment to delivering tasks, coping with increasing demands, working long hours and doing more with less) becomes more and more important to organizations. Individuals' expectations of the organization include job security, career prospects, a sense of belonging, fair treatment and respect. So, the employment relationship is *more than words*.

## Change in the air

Research commissioned by the Institute of Personnel and Development (Kessler & Undy 1996) cited evidence of the changing nature of employment relationships. They examined the psychological contract in terms of the individual and informal dimensions of the employment relationship (as contrasting with the collective and formal dimensions): 'The concept focuses attention on the way in which employees and management come together at the workplace with certain assumptions and expectations about what each has to offer and is willing to deliver' (1996: viii). The main conclusion was that employees think that while they are keeping their side of the psychological contract, management are reneging on theirs. This lack of reciprocity was felt in three areas. First, *job attachment:* employees' commitment to a long-term job or career is not matched by some management views that it is no longer possible to offer job security or a 'job for life'. Secondly, *loyalty and trust:* while employees display relatively high degrees of loyalty to their organizations, the level of their trust in management to keep its promises is markedly lower. Thirdly, *involvement:* there is a marked gap between employees' desire for involvement across a range of work issues and the extent to which they perceive themselves to be involved.

Kessler and Undy explained the dilemma: 'Employees' trust and identification with the organization are predicated upon reciprocity and yet managerial inability to control the external environment which threatens employment raises questions about their ability to deliver their side of the psychological contract. This in turn raises questions about organizations' ability to achieve key objectives related to product and service delivery' (1996: x). In short, although organizations still need their people to be loyal and committed (to work as if they will stay for ever), they are finding themselves less able to reciprocate loyalty through job security and career prospects. Organizations therefore often try to change expectations rather than meet them. This leads to culture-change initiatives which focus on the needs of customers and of the business, and on greater flexibility in the workforce.

A further study by the IPD just a year later painted a less gloomy picture: 'The traditional psychological contract, built around job security and a career, is still alive and surprisingly well. This is what most employees still seek and what many believe their employer still tries to provide. A clear manifestation of this is that most people expect to stay with their present employer for the next five years and most hope to be promoted in that time' (Guest et al. 1996: 1). Why the difference? Probably because in this survey respondents felt more secure; the low levels of trust in the previous survey were linked to employees' experience of redundancy. This reinforces the need for security, part of an ongoing commitment that cuts both ways, as an important element of the psychological contract. The later survey did note a significant minority for whom the psychological contract was not in good repair; these tended to be less educated workers who were more likely to have experienced redundancy and were more likely to experience it again. It described the content of the psychological contract as a perception of fairness, a sense that the implicit deal is being sufficiently delivered, and trust that promises will continue to be kept and obligations met (Guest et al. 1996: 5).

## Redressing the balance?

The changes in work now render some elements of psychological contracts less valid because they cannot be delivered. However, organizations still need to have committed employees, and employees still need some security and a sense of belonging, and to be treated with respect. David Statt argues that the specifics of the psychological contract may change as individual and organizational needs change, but that the underlying need for a relationship of loyalty and respect remains constant. He comments that individual expectations 'can usually be boiled down to being taken seriously and treated with respect' (1994: 39). In recessionary periods, organizations have the advantage in determining the terms of this new psychological contract. As many forms of work become more highly skilled and intelligence-based, however, much more of what is important to an organization will be in the brains of its employees, and, since 'Intelligence is a leaky form of property' (Handy 1994: 24), the balance may shift in favour of employees, at least for those who are more highly skilled.

But the current reality for many is that the employment contract seems to be moving out of balance, as indicated in the diagram below. In order to maintain the commitment of their employees, what can employers offer to meet the need for job-security, belonging and career prospects, given the uncertainties of the world of work? Some options are job-security guarantees; a 'no enforced redundancy' policy; preferential treatment for former employees when new opportunities arise; changes which are designed, implemented and operated with people in mind; and skills training and retraining. It is becoming more common for the term 'contract' to be used in various less formal ways. For example, 'performance contracts' between organizations and their managers comprise a set of agreed targets, and are a way of aligning individual and organizational goals and of gaining commitment. 'Learning contracts' or 'personal development plans' are usually agreed between an individual and his or her boss, both of whom commit themselves to learning or development plans which will benefit the organization and the individual. The trend is to focus more on the commitment between individuals, their mutual needs, and their personal responsibilities in meeting their respective parts of the 'contract'.

## How the psychological contract is changing

How should we respond when an employer can no longer fulfil some key aspects of the 'psychological contract' which we thought was in place, yet still requires our commitment and loyalty, and in fact is demanding more of us than ever before? Given that some aspects of the psychological contract touch fundamental aspects of our humanity – ongoing relationships, mutual commitment, security – are there any biblical principles to guide us?

## Learning from the Bible

### Covenant relationships

The Bible has much to say about relationships. Its pages tell of relationships between individuals, groups and nations, and between people and God. The principles it teaches can guide our thinking about the way we relate to the organizations that employ us through contracts, formal and informal. A key biblical concept is that of the *covenant*. 'Covenant' refers to a certain kind of social relationship, or to the transaction that brings it about. It is 'a binding, enduring relationship of mutual loyalty' (Allen, in Macquarrie & Childress 1986: 136) which can come about through explicit, reciprocated promises (as in marriage), or where people entrust themselves to one another and accept one another's trust implicitly. A covenant is morally binding, and places obligations upon the parties who give and receive trust.

In the Old Testament, God initiated (not negotiated) covenants with his people, and showed himself to be sure, steadfast and faithful in them. Obligations on the people with whom the covenant was made are laid out sometimes explicitly (e.g. Genesis 17; Exodus 34) and sometimes implicitly (e.g. Genesis 9). In all cases, faithfulness was required. Obedience to obligations was not to be viewed as a painstaking task grudgingly undertaken, but as a loving response to a gracious God who had initiated a relationship with his people (Exodus 34:6–7). Correspondingly, in Deuteronomy, God's covenant is described as a 'covenant of love' (Deuteronomy 7:7–12). The prophets hoped for a covenant of true faithfulness on Israel's part. Hosea pictured Israel's breaking of the covenant as a wife's prostitution, and God as wooing Israel back (Hosea 2:14–15; 3:1). Following disaster and exile, the hope of a new covenant was expressed in Isaiah's Servant Songs (e.g. Isaiah 42:1–4; 52:13 – 53:12), and in the promise of a covenant written on people's hearts (Jeremiah 31:31–34; Ezekiel 36:24–28).

In the New Testament, Jesus was seen as the fulfilment of God's promises to Israel (2 Corinthians 1:19–20). The 'suffering servant' image from the Old Testament was used to give a new insight into God's nature and purposes. Whereas the old covenant exposed people's sin and their inability to fulfil their obligations under it, the new covenant, through Christ's sacrificial death, brought forgiveness of sins upon repentance. Their lives were then to be characterized by faithfulness to this covenant through allegiance to Christ and growth in holiness.

Covenants and contracts share some features, but differ in that covenants strongly affirm the relationship between the parties, rather than just focusing on the stipulations. They stress mutual faithfulness and trust, rather than what each party can gain from the other. Can this help us with the implicit obligations of psychological contracts? How can these be honoured, or reshaped so that they still meet the needs of individuals and of the organization? As the existence of psychological contracts shows, people desire more in a work relationship with an organization than the obligatory clauses of a written employment contract, and so does the organization. The biblical notion of covenant is not wholly applicable to employee–employer relationships since its purpose is a permanent relationship of mutual benefit founded on love and faithfulness, rather than the exchange of labour for reward. However, there are some principles in the idea of covenant, such as faithfulness and mutual trust, which are good foundations for reshaping the implicit obligations of psychological contracts and putting the 'R' back into employment relationships.

## Trust and trustworthiness

### *The need for trust*

The existence of an employment relationship which goes beyond a written contract presupposes a degree of *trust*. Formal employment contracts stipulate certain duties and rights, but in order to enable the collaboration that efficient work requires, and to foster the commitment that makes it productive and enjoyable, an informal understanding based on trust is required. But this trust is being eroded in the workplace as organizations have difficulty in keeping their side of the bargain.

As already noted, trust is about believing that others will meet their side of an agreement and fulfil their obligations and responsibilities, which may have been stated explicitly or implicitly. Along with this goes the confidence that the other party will not try to deceive you by dishonesty or by being 'economical with the truth', is not out to harm you, and can deliver what his or her role, qualifications and experience suggest. Trust in the Christian sense goes beyond a calculated mutuality to having the other party's interests at heart, and so works for their good. Between individuals, it is the necessary basis of any good relationship.

It is often our personal experience of people that leads us to trust them and to see them as trustworthy; they have met their obligations in the past. Their reputation, or what other people have told us about them, can also engender our trust. In organizations, trust in senior management or in the organization as a whole can be low because of perceived reneging on what has been promised. In some large organizations the perception has changed from 'This is a good company, they will look after you', to 'You've got to look out for yourself. Don't believe anything they say because it will have changed by next week.'

Nevertheless, trust often exists between colleagues, within teams, or with immediate line managers 'who consistently fulfil their obligations to the work group, or who repeatedly demonstrate their capacity to tackle difficult problems and succeed' (Herriot et al. 1998: 43). At this level, too, people are more able to make commitments that are within their power to keep, and the personal relationships exist within which trust can thrive.

### In God we trust

Love 'always trusts' (1 Corinthians 13:7). As people motivated by love, we should be characterized by a willingness to take things on trust, and to put trust in others. We trust God for daily provision and for our eternal salvation. We trust other Christians because they are growing closer to God. We desire to trust others because it is a way of affirming their worth as people, just as God trusts us.

Trust is an expression of confidence in or reliance upon another. It carries certain expectations: that the person trusted will do what he or she says, undertake his or her role, act morally, and so on. It also has beneficial effects on the person trusted: 'Sometimes acts of trust may be "therapeutic" and even "redemptive" to the trustee, contributing significantly to his or her moral development (e.g., parents trusting their children)' (Macquarrie & Childress 1986: 633). But trust must be given appropriately; trusting people with something beyond their power or skill to deliver may result in harm to them as well as in failure of the task. We may trust children to do an errand at the local shops, but we would be foolish and irresponsible to trust them to rewire the house. It is important that the person bestowing trust is realistic and gives the necessary support. Jesus equipped his disciples (through delegated authority and instruction, Luke 9:1–6) and supported them (through listening and coaching, Luke 10:17–24) in the tasks with which he entrusted them.

Trust is particularly important in the following situations:

*For building relationships.* Trust expresses our respect and confidence, not only in colleagues' competence, but also in them as people. Relationships are stronger when trust is mutual.

*In teams.* Team members must trust each other to perform their allotted roles and should be acknowledged and respected for doing so. Team-working is required in many areas of work, as no one individual has the whole range of skills necessary for the overall task. Hence, trust is not optional but necessary if the work is to be done. Take building a house: the plumber and electrician rely on the builders to construct the basic structure; the roofer relies on the carpenter for the timbers; the decorator on the plasterer for the walls and ceilings. In some teams interdependence is even more marked, and may even involve putting one's life in a colleague's hands (as in the emergency services or the military).

*As a redemptive tool.* Following a failure, being trusted again can save someone from a stunted future. Where possible, turning failure into a learning experience can rebuild self-assurance and give them the skill and experience to cope in future. An apocryphal story makes this point. An employee who had made a serious mistake, costing his company £10,000, expected to lose his job. His boss, however, responded: 'Having just spent £10,000 on your training, you don't expect me to let you go now, do you?' Jesus' reinstatement of Peter, following the apostle's public and heart-rending failure (cf. Luke 22:31–34, 54–62 with John 21:15–19), is perhaps an example of trust at its most redemptive. This is trust going the extra mile, taking a calculated risk based on the principle that some learning has occurred. It requires a degree of forgiveness, not necessarily of wrongdoing (although this may be the case), but of failure: 'Look, it's all right to make a mistake. It happens to all of us. Let's put it down to experience.'

*In rebuilding relationships.* Following traumatic times in a company (such as a period of unexpected redundancies), mistrust is common. Promises may have been broken, expectations dashed, careers cut short. If the situation is not managed well, the mistrust deepens. But trust can be restored by communicating openly and honestly; by the appropriate disclosure of information; by making realistic commitments; and by following through on what is said. Let's explore each of these.

### Open, honest communication

Employees need their managers to communicate openly and honestly if they are to believe what they say. Openness and honesty characterize trustworthy people. 'A wicked messenger falls into trouble, but a trust-worthy envoy brings healing' (Proverbs 13:17). God is trustworthy (2 Samuel 7:28; Psalm 19:7; 119:86; 1 Timothy 1:15; 4:9; Titus 1:9; 3:8), and we should make trustworthiness our aim. Trustworthiness presupposes the integrity and wholeness characteristic of a rounded Christian character. It involves guarding that which is entrusted to us, be it undertaking a task, keeping a confidence, or proving reliable in some delegated area. Despite difficulty or opposition, trustworthy people will not willingly or knowingly betray the trust placed in them. They mean what they say, and do it, not occasionally but repeatedly. Trustworthi-ness is demonstrated through honesty, commitment and consistency.

Richard Higginson cites honesty as a key attribute in his discussion of integrity: 'Honesty breeds an atmosphere of trust' (1993: 212). Honesty means being truthful in what we say or imply, and not willingly or knowingly deceiving or telling untruths. It is a fundamental quality of Christian character and is grounded in the commandment, 'You shall not give false testimony against your neighbour' (Deuteronomy 5:20). The New Testament places great importance on making known the truth (the gospel we are to proclaim is called 'the word of truth', Ephesians 1:13), and on being truthful (2 Corinthians 6:7).

Ephesians 4:15 refers to 'speaking the truth in love'. This means exercising honesty with sensitivity and discretion. Being 'totally' honest (expressing all there is to say) about someone or something is not always the best way of dealing with our own frustration or of helping someone to correct an error.

## Disclosure of information

In keeping with open and honest communication, it is right to keep people informed about things that affect them. Withholding information can be as deceitful as a lie if it is something that people ought to know; for instance, key facts that affect their future. However, there are occasions when it is legitimate and not deceitful to keep quiet about something. As the writer of Ecclesiastes wrote, there is 'a time to be silent and a time to speak' (Ecclesiastes 3:7). It might be something personal told you in confidence by a colleague, or it might be the quarterly results of your company which have yet to be announced. In both cases, you have a responsibility to keep the confidence entrusted to you. In relation to an individual, this is out of respect for their dignity as a person, and also out of loyalty and commitment to him or her as someone who values you enough to share information with you. Releasing confidential information belonging to the organization for which you work, as well as betraying trust, and breaking the confidentiality clause in your contract, may also infringe the property rights of the organization.

When an organization is considering a major change such as an acquisition or a redundancy programme, there are usually good business reasons not to disclose information until an appropriate time. This may mean keeping silent, or declining to comment, or divulging only what is necessary at that time. Similarly, an employee contemplating a change of job has a right to keep his or her own counsel. This is not dishonest; it becomes so only if silence becomes deceit, or if disclosure is withheld at the appropriate time – when decisions have been made and set in motion, or even before this stage so that consultation and discussion can occur.

But there are occasions when disclosure of information normally regarded as confidential may be appropriate. For example, there may be instances when information entrusted to us exposes a great evil and it becomes right (or at least the lesser of two evils) to make it more widely known. When I worked as a personnel officer, I used to assure those who came to see me of complete confidence, but added the caveat, ' ... unless you tell me you are going to kill someone'. To betray trust and inform the appropriate authorities in order to prevent a greater calamity would normally be the most responsible course of action if all other reasonable measures (such as dialogue with the individual, internal procedures) have been exhausted.

### Realistic commitments

When we make commitments we pledge ourselves to implement what we have agreed to or what is expected of us. Such an attitude should characterize all we do, holding us to the task despite obstacles or discouragement. If we have said we will assist a colleague, or have agreed to meet him or her, or promised to provide information, we will not renege on that commitment, even if barriers appear. Commitments vary in their magnitude, but whatever the commitment, we should aim to honour it. This means that we should not commit to what we cannot deliver. Sometimes, due to changed circumstances, it may not be possible to meet a commitment. We should be honest and open when this happens (rather than making excuses or hoping that no-one notices), talk the situation through and agree on a revised course of action in line with the new circumstances.

Don offered a job to an experienced human-resources manager from the US. The job was to be for at least three years, and on this basis the manager uprooted his family, got a house and arranged schooling. The day his wife arrived in the UK, it was announced that the chief executive would be leaving and that the company would be reorganized. The job changed, and later it all but disappeared. Expatriates were being sent home to save money, and recent appointments were being reversed. But Don bucked the pressure of repatriation and found a different way to utilize the manager's talents. The assignment was fruitful for several years, and Don had been faithful to his commitment.

A promise is a specific type of commitment, 'a self-imposed obligation' in which people 'bind themselves to actions in the future' (Macquarrie & Childress 1986: 505). Jewish and Christian morality is rooted in the biblical conception of a God who makes promises and lives up to those promises. He acts with fidelity in his covenants, demonstrating his faithfulness and trustworthiness and giving a firm foundation for trust and hope in him. 'Know therefore that the LORD your God is God; he is the faithful God, keeping his covenant of love to a thousand generations of those who love him and keep his commands' (Deuteronomy 7:9). God's promise to the house of David is that he will not remove his love, 'nor will I ever betray my faithfulness. I will not violate my covenant or alter what my lips have uttered' (Psalm 89:33–34).

Christians regard promises as binding because honesty obliges them to keep their word. Any commitment, particularly a promise, creates expectation and trust on the part of others. Commitment has an important role to play in contracts, and therefore in the business world: 'Many interpreters hold that promise-keeping is the key moral ingredient in contracts, which play an important role in modern societies' (Macquarrie & Childress 1986: 506). Written, legally watertight contracts are now ubiquitous in almost all areas of business. While there are good reasons for this (the increased complexity of business, clarity and fairness to employees, employers and third parties), there is also the underlying notion that trustworthiness can no longer be taken for granted. To the contrary, Christians are to be characterized by keeping their commitments.

### Following through

The Bible portrays God as consistent: 'The LORD is good and his love endures for ever; his faithfulness continues through all generations' (Psalm 100:5). Consistency means repeatedly applying the same standards, being predictable on fundamental issues of right and wrong, having a constant direction and being reliable. Richard Higginson cites consistency as an ingredient of integrity, and as being particularly important for those in business leadership: 'Whereas a leader who makes arbitrary decisions spreads confusion and even fear among the ranks, the person who is consistent has a reassuring effect upon his or her staff' (1993: 216).

# Reshaping employment relationships

## *Demonstrating faithfulness and flexibility*

When change happens at work, organizations are held by law to the obligations of formal employment contracts, and are required to make additional provisions if redundancies are involved (including opportunity for consultation between staff and management, and time off for people to attend interviews).

But what of the less tangible obligations of employment relationships in situations of change? An organization may no longer be able to promise long-term security or career development, but it can demonstrate faithfulness in other ways. When redundancy threatens, it can make every effort to keep employees in jobs where there is meaningful work to be done, or where there is a good possibility of such work emerging in the future. It can help employees to keep their skills up to date and to add new ones, so that however the job situation turns out within the organization, they have some transferable skills to enhance future employment prospects. Where redundancy is the only option, the organization can ensure that people are treated with care. and respect, so that they can say, 'It was a shock to be made redundant, but the company did well by me.'

Employees may also need to recast their relationship with the organization. This is not an easy transition to make. 'For employees reared in a culture of employment by others, employment in large or small secure firms offering long-term, regular, even life-long opportunities of the use of skills, development of career and steady progress towards rewarding pensionable retirement, the new era may indeed be traumatic' (Ormiston & Ross 1990: viii). However, the transition can be successfully made. A research scientist I knew was downcast as redundancies hit and his expectation of a long-term career evaporated. However, a few months later, he was still employed, and was delighted at the prospect of working against a single year's funding. He had adjusted to the new reality and was still committed to his work, but more prepared to leave when he or the organization chose.

As employees we will still give our commitment and work conscientiously, but, like the organization, we will retain the right to be more flexible in relation to future opportunities, whatever they may be. Peter Herriot and his colleagues (1998: 102) offer a model of career contracting which recognizes the rights and needs of both sides of the employment relationship. Although not all work situations lend themselves to individual negotiation, the principle of being able to contract a fair deal is important.

We will need to ensure that our portfolio of skills is continually updated, so that we are ready to move on at our own volition or if redundancy strikes. As one manager commented, it means carrying an up-to-date CV in one's briefcase. Working with our employer to increase what Alison Hardingham terms our 'ability security' by learning new skills, undergoing new experiences and changing jobs, is one way of keeping work skills up to date. This is in employees' control more than job security ever was: 'Whereas job security implies "I'll work hard for you if you'll look after me", ability security implies "I'll increase your marketability if you'll increase mine"' (Hardingham 1992: 107).

More varied and mobile careers, with perhaps periods of employment, self-employment and unemployment, may become commonplace. For people who can offer a product or service to a range of clients, Charles Handy's notion of a 'portfolio career' can be helpful. Here full-time employment is exchanged for more independence, arising either from choice or through being forced into it by redundancy. What we sell is our product or service, not our time, so that 'What matters now is *how* we use our time, not *how much* of that time we use' (Handy 1994: 177). As Handy points out, knowledge workers (professionals) can develop a portfolio career, as can those who make or fix things (such as plumbers and builders) and those he terms the 'new fixers', such as brokers, travel agents and estate agents (1994: 176–177). This way of working gives greater freedom, since we become 'self-managers of our own assets' (Handy 1996: 28), but it has its own pressures, notably the need to attract and maintain sufficient work to earn a living – something that those who are self-employed or who run their own businesses know only too well.

When all is said and done, it is unrealistic for employers to expect employees to give the unerring commitment necessary for organizations to survive in today's globally competitive world without some recognition of the need for security of employment. This may not be the 'job for life' of a few years ago, but employers must make a serious attempt to create a future for those whose commitment is needed for the venture. This is only just, and expresses the mutual faithfulness necessary for a positive relationship. It is also common sense. People need some security of livelihood, enjoy the sense of belonging that work often brings, and will be more committed to the venture and enjoy more job satisfaction when they perceive their employment relationship positively. While the connection between these factors and the results of the business is not easy to establish, it is widely held that committed employees aligned with the aims of the business will make it more successful, not less.

Trust and faithfulness are necessary on both sides. To maintain a balance in the employment relationship, organizations need to make some attempt in the area of job security, and to help employees in other ways (e.g. to become more versatile). On the employees' side, there is the need to be more flexible, not blindly loyal to benevolent institutions that no longer exist, but faithful in meeting requirements, doing what is reasonable, and working well with honesty, consistency and commitment.

## The action column

1. Think how you can demonstrate Christian love in your work relationships.
2. What is it you value about the friendships you have at work? How can you deepen them, as well as widen the circle of people you would call your work friends?
3. What expectations do you have of your employer? How can you work towards a relationship of mutual trust and commitment?
4. How are you responding to the changes happening in work which may affect the way you earn a living?

# CHAPTER 8

# Is the world my oyster?

## Finding the right job

## Which job?

### Looking for guidance

Decisions about our careers will affect many aspects of our lives. Whether it is planning a career path, deciding whether to answer an advertisement, accepting a first job or changing job or career, it is no less taxing a decision. When my aunt asked me, 'What would you like to do when you grow up?' I said (of course), 'A train driver.' She smiled, but her interest, like that of so many aunts and grandparents, points to the significance of the question. Our answer determines how we will spend a good proportion of our waking hours and so how we will use the time and abilities given us by God.

But how much choice do I have? In times of high unemployment, the choice may seem very limited. Isn't it just a question of getting what work is available? Doesn't it depend on where I live or the opportunities open to me? It can be confusing working out what God's will is and how it fits with what I want to do, and with what seems possible. Does God have a particular 'calling' for me to follow, or is it up to me? Such questions can be perplexing. It is tempting to leave it to God to sort it all out; doesn't he have a plan for my life, anyway?

A friend had decided to leave a job in which he was unhappy, and make a new start. He had been offered two opportunities, both commensurate with his skills and interests, but they would lead in very different directions. He had written two replies – both affirmative – and had sealed and stamped them, but had posted neither. We sat in McDonalds discussing the advantages and disadvantages of each, trying to weigh up which would be best and to discern God's guidance. I did not envy him, holding these two letters, undecided, and with deadlines approaching. In the end, he posted one and binned the other. I can't remember what swung the argument, but it seemed a fraught way to choose.

When I have faced such last-minute dilemmas myself, it has often been because I have missed some 'pointers' on the way. Although God expects us to take responsibility in making decisions about our future, he does also offer us help. The Bible teaches that God guides in life's decisions, and this is borne out in the experience of many Christians. He helps us choose work that is both in line with his purposes and good for us. A Christian approach to finding the right job looks for God's guidance as well as taking account of the gifts he has given us and the opportunities available. It considers our responsibility to support dependants and to serve God and others, as well as our career aspirations.

### Called to a vocation?

'That's definitely his vocation,' a friend said of someone who was training for ministry in the church. It is often said of missionaries, and of those who have become teachers, doctors or nurses. This can make the rest of us feel that our chosen careers are second-class. Is having a 'vocation' limited to a few people who are called to do something special, or do we all have a vocation? Are vocations limited to certain professions?

The term 'vocation' is generally used simply to mean 'associated with a particular career', where people undertake vocational training and National Vocational Qualifications leading to particular jobs, in contrast to a more general and academic education. Some university courses are regarded as vocational since they lead to specific professions; for example, pharmacy and the law. It is also used to single out particular jobs as callings, such as medicine, nursing, teaching or Christian ministry. These professions usually require special inclination or devotion, and may be referred to as someone's life's work.

But, in its original biblical sense, 'vocation' does not refer to earthly professions (as the Reformers held of its use in 1 Corinthians 7:20) but to God's personal calling of people to himself. As Derek Tasker comments in his book on vocation and work: 'vocation is first and foremost God's personal call to each of us as individuals to "follow Him," to "be with Him"' (1960: 11). Within this calling, which is common to all Christians, God calls people to serve him through what they are and do. Steve Walton, in his book *A Call to Live* (1994), shows how the biblical account of vocation in fact comprises four types of calling.

- We are called to *belong*. As described above, this is the calling to follow Christ, to become a Christian. As Paul addressed the Roman Christians: 'And you also are among those who are called to belong to Jesus Christ' (Romans 1:6).

- We are called to *be* – to 'be holy' (1 Peter 1:15), to 'be saints' (Romans 1:7). This refers to our becoming more like Christ, to 'being transformed into his likeness' (2 Corinthians 3:18) in deeds and character.

- We are called to *let God be God*. We are to trust that God has a plan of which we are a part and which he will see through to completion (Romans 8:29–30).

- We are called to *do*. This is the call to particular tasks or roles in which we serve God. Paul was 'called to be an apostle' (Romans 1:1). As Steve Walton points out, however, 'call' and work 'are never identified as the same thing in the New Testament' (1994: 25). We cannot simply equate work with this understanding of vocation, since work is not the whole of life, but one element of it.

The Reformers were right to affirm everyday work as an appropriate way to please God, and to acknowledge that God does have specific jobs, careers, tasks and activities for Christians to undertake within their overall calling to him. 'He [God] calls us not only to be new men and new women in Christ but also to be co-workers with Him in making a new world. *He calls us*, in short, *to a ministry*' (Tasker 1960: 11). This is not restricted to ministry in the church or caring professions; 'we are called to exercise our ministry at every point of life' (Tasker 1960: 12). Our whole lives become an offering to him, and this gives significance to all the activities in which we partake, including the work we choose.

As Christians, we are 'called' in the biblical sense, first to belong to God, then to become more like him, to trust him, and to serve him. This includes our work, for which God has gifted us. While some devote themselves to a life's work, or follow single professions, others serve in a variety of ways. Some have high-profile roles or jobs that directly serve the needy; others serve through the ordinary tasks that ensure that society can function. All of us are required to use our work as part of the way we serve God within our overall calling as Christians. An important aspect of rendering this service is finding the right job.

In what we are called to do, secular work can be just as valid a calling as 'full-time' Christian work, and working in a factory or in business just as valid as one of the traditional professions, if this is where God wants us to serve him.

## Dreams, glass ceilings and brick walls

### Dare to dream

'What would you choose to do if you could have the job you really wanted?' my boss asked. I couldn't remember being asked that since I was a youngster. Was it a trick question? I was usually too busy with the daily pressures of work to step back and take a more objective view of my situation and think about what I would really like to do. My sense of duty meant that I generally accepted tasks that might not be much fun but that needed doing. However, I soon found myself talking with enthusiasm about some things that I aspired to, and I started to create a picture of what the future might be. My boss helped me to articulate these goals and then said, 'Let's look at how we can move you towards them.'

The Bible is full of stories of people with a vision, an aspiration to achieve something they held to be important. For Abraham, it was the promise of founding a nation. For Moses, it was leading God's people to the promised land. David longed to build the temple, and Gideon to rid the land of his enemies. In the New Testament, Peter was commissioned to found the church, and Paul was sent out to spread the gospel. Some received their vision directly from God, others in less direct ways. Recognizing it as God's purpose, they held on to it and with God's help moved towards it. They had a dream and they dared to believe it.

God has things for each of us to achieve in line with his purposes, and our work is one of the principal ways we do this. It is good to dream, to aspire to do things beyond ourselves and to identify ways of moving towards them. Some lose sight of their dreams and, pummelled by the harshness of life, discouraged by others or disappointed by failure, they give them up. Others' dreams become fantasies to escape from real life, and cause frustration because they are forever elusive. Certainly, some of our dreams need refocusing, often through the advice of others and the recognition of some boundaries (see below). But for most of us it is rekindling that is needed rather than damping down. Many of the glass ceilings we come up against can be broken through, and many of the brick walls scaled. The apostle Paul reminded Timothy 'to fan into flame the gift of God' given him for the work he had to do (2 Timothy 1:6). When did you last think through what you would like God to help you to do with your life? When did you last let yourself dream?

Childhood dreams often espouse, quite unconsciously, the characteristic of hope since they focus on what can be rather than on present obstacles. Hope is fundamental to the Christian life (1 Corinthians 13:13; Romans 15:13). It is the virtue that keeps us going when all seems lost (Isaiah 40:29–31), the element of Christian character that helps us hold on to our vision until it is fulfilled. Christian hope is an overall hope, within which all the other hopes in life align and derive their meaning. Such hope is not the hesitant 'I hope so' of modern usage, but the assured expectation that what God has promised will come to pass (Hebrews 10:23). Speaking of the certainty of God's promises, the writer to the Hebrews states: 'We have this hope as an anchor for the soul, firm and secure' (6:19). And when we have a vision of what God would have us do, we can move towards it with hope.

## Is the world my oyster?

A fitness coach told us that we could make our bodies whatever we wanted them to be. I felt sceptical. In one sense he was right; through good training techniques, some discipline and a little sweat, we could build biceps or slim thighs. But we could not change our height from five feet to six feet, or change our build from large to petite. The same is true of some of our basic aptitudes for the jobs we may want to do. It is essential to dream, to have aspirations and set goals, but how can we avoid delusion and the frustration which destroys dreams, and along with them our confidence? Where should we direct our aspirations? Isn't the world our oyster after all?

We can turn our hand to learning new skills, but there are some limitations. This can sound restrictive, but in reality is a liberating truth because it helps us to focus our aspirations on what is truly possible and best for us, and can direct our search. As the theologian Karl Barth observes, the limits God places on individuals do not belittle them but distinguish them from others and give them their individual identity. 'His limiting is His definite, concrete and specific affirmation. The man who is limited by Him is the man who is loved by Him' (1961: 568). God understands the limits he places on us and therefore does not ask us to perform outside of these.

What are the limits or boundaries to our choosing, and how can our awareness of them help us to find the right job?

## A place in history

It was not the 'done thing' in my family to go away to university. I owe a great deal to my parents; their honest and conscientious approach to work, their concern to do a good job, and their careful use of the fruits of work have had a lasting effect. But going away to college was not part of their experience. After all, they were coping with a war at the age kids of my generation went off to study. Undertaking a degree at all was expanding the boundaries of what was expected, without leaving home as well. But the teachers could not persuade me to do that; why would I want to leave unless I was getting married? My parents willingly supported me at college, but I soon found that it was difficult to get the best out of university life commuting from home. I survived, and was later able to experience life away. My 'place in history' – my background and expectations and the experiences that had influenced me – had affected the opportunities I was willing to consider and the decisions I made. This was not necessarily negative, or outside of God's purposes for me; but recognizing that fact has helped me to understand the route by which I have come, and has assisted me in making subsequent decisions.

Each of us is born at a certain time, in a particular place. We have parents we cannot choose, and an education which, at least initially, we have little control over. The attitudes nurtured in us and the opportunities we are willing to consider influence the work we choose. If we feel disadvantaged by these attitudes and expectations, we can reflect that they are not insurmountable; God has often done mighty things through the lowly. Our background does, however, help to explain the situations we find ourselves in, and understanding this can prevent us from feeling envious or blaming ourselves when we don't match the achievements of others. We are called to be who we can be. In a discussion of freedom and the paradox of accepting the unwanted situations we find ourselves in, Bishop Stephen Neill wrote: 'Within the limits of the given material a great variety of choice is open to us, but there are certain unalterable structures of our life; if we resent these or kick against them, we merely reduce our capacity to make the best of what may in itself be a rather unpromising situation' (1984: 23). The key is serving God to our best ability in each situation, including those over which we have little control.

We should not view our 'place in history' negatively or in a deterministic way as if we were merely the product of our situation. Rather, it is a starting-point. We are wise to acknowledge its impact on our lives, but each of us bears the responsibility for what we will make of it.

## Skills, abilities and aptitudes

I liked Phil's straightforward approach to life. He could say things that others found difficult, or just didn't dare to say. He had moved from a scientific role into safety training. I was a little surprised when he asked me about a general personnel role. I had not seen him in this light, but thought that if this was what he really wanted to do, why not? However, feedback from others suggested that his rather direct (to some, blunt) approach might not be appropriate in delicate counselling situations or in giving advice to managers. No doubt he could have developed his counselling skills and adapted his approach. But in the end we could not find him a personnel role and he moved from safety into general training. He blossomed; his direct style and natural confidence in front of people were enhanced in a role that utilized what he did best.

The aptitudes and talents which characterize us, and the skills and abilities which we possess or are able to develop, open up for us many opportunities and also place boundaries around our choosing. Long ago, Plato stated that 'no two of us are born exactly alike. We have different natural aptitudes, which fit us for different jobs' (1974: 118). These include our personal aptitudes, our gifts and inclinations; what we are naturally good at, the things we can do that no-one else can, the things we prefer. Isabel Myers, one of the developers of the Myers-Briggs Indicator (1980), shows a correlation between personality type and the occupations people prefer; the way we *are* affects what we will be good at and what we will enjoy. Within the boundaries of our skills and abilities there is room for great movement, but there are things that we will never be able to do, and others that would merely frustrate us were we to attempt them. It is better to keep our dreams tied to reality if we want to find satisfaction in the work we choose.

## Honouring to God?

A further limit a Christian will want to impose is whether or not the work is honouring to God. Can the work being considered be done as service, indeed as worship to God? At the extreme, some 'occupations' can be ruled out immediately, as they are explicitly contrary to God's values. A further consideration is the structural context of the work. While a particular job may be perfectly acceptable, its context may render it dishonouring to God; for example, it may involve oppression of others, or irresponsible pollution of the environment. Most other types of work can be honouring to God providing certain general criteria are met; as Tasker states, 'any work which is necessary to a right re-ordering of the world God has made and the redemption of which He seeks, or to the legitimate human needs of His family all over the world, is work pleasing to Him, work we can offer to Him' (1960: 30).

I have described how background, skills and abilities and the desire to do work honouring to God can set some helpful boundaries for our search to find the right job. These are very broad boundaries, and within them is a huge range of possibilities open to us precisely because of the persons we are, our skills and our desire to serve God.

## Choosing and God's will

### *A mixture of divine and human responsibility*

'We are not going to use contraceptives when we are married. If God doesn't want us to have children, then he will prevent it,' the young woman asserted. It was one of those interesting discussions that teenagers have. While not wanting to deny God the power to do anything, I couldn't help thinking that this approach was flawed. It sounded devout, but it seemed to me a way of abdicating responsibility to God in an area where God has given us the understanding to make such decisions (especially since we know where babies come from!). My wife, Clare, still smiles when she recalls my response: 'If you point a loaded gun at your head and pull the trigger, will God stop the bullet?' I did not believe we could get off the hook that easily.

God has blessed us with the intelligence, freedom and responsibility to make decisions and accept their consequences, and this includes making decisions about our work. However, for the Christian, choosing and God's will should be closely related. As Peter Adam expresses in a booklet on guidance: 'The mixture of divine and human responsibility for our life with God is a creative and productive tension which allows "God to be God" and also calls on human beings to exercise their full responsibility as people made in God's image' (1988: 13). As we walk by the Spirit, our choosing and God's purposes will coalesce. As we base our lives on his priorities and grow more like him in character, we intuitively make choices in line with his will, and with 'the mind of Christ' which we have through his Spirit, who dwells within us (1 Corinthians 2:16). In many day-to-day decisions we act within the responsibility delegated to us by God without need of particular guidance; our character, knowledge of biblical principles and God-given rationality help to direct our decisions in ways that are pleasing to God. In these situations God is guiding all the time (Romans 8:28). Sometimes we will know God's very particular guidance; often this will confirm the direction of our choosing, but sometimes it will surprise us and prompt us to venture in a different direction.

## A plan for my life, or free choice?

Does God have a particular kind of work for each person to do? At one end of the spectrum is the view that everything is predestined and that people follow in detail the individual plan God has for their lives. This view emphasizes God's sovereignty, but carries the danger of allowing people to opt out of making decisions (and the responsibility for them), as they accept any situation as the will of God. At the other extreme is the notion that people have totally free choice and are to use the skills bestowed on them in the way that seems best to them, limited only by opportunity and circumstances. This view, which emphasizes individual responsibility, can give the impression that God is remote or disinterested, and that people do not need to consult him. However, 'even if God did have a perfect plan for everyone's life he would have to change it continually because of our constant rebellion and apathy with regards to doing his Will' (Adam 1988: 10). The Bible urges Christians to follow Christ and to live a holy life of love and obedience to God's standards. But we can be more specific than this, since God has an overall sovereign will with purposes that cannot be thwarted ('The LORD reigns,' Psalm 96:10). And the outworking of his will must involve human actions because of the authority God has delegated to humankind in creation.

Since work has the potential to be of great service to God and to others (and therefore to serve or hinder his overall purposes), it is reasonable to suggest that God's purpose will usually be specific to the job done, and to some (perhaps many) of the actions performed in it. This is not at odds with human choice, since our choosing does not put us outside the sphere of God's overall will and sovereignty. In fact, even though God allows people their choice, he retains, according to Karl

Barth, 'the first and the last word', as their choice is 'thickly surrounded by pure presuppositions and conditions' (including the limits outlined above) over which God has control (1961: 632, 631). 'The truth is that for all its independence and responsibility human choice takes place within the area and framework of the divine choice, counsel and decision, so that man's decisions as such are comprehended within the decree and fulfilment of the will of God' (1961: 633).

We do have a choice about how we use our God-given skills and abilities, but alongside this God guides us in ways that both fulfil his purposes and are best for us. God's plan can involve both a broad range of opportunity and, at times, very specific actions or tasks. Through foolishness or miscalculation, poor judgment or unwise counsel, we can make the wrong choice, fall into sin, or take less than the best path, but we cannot 'step out of reach of the will and plan of God' (Barth 1961: 633). God's overall purposes will be achieved, since he is sovereign: 'Many are the plans in a man's heart, but it is the LORD's purpose that prevails' (Proverbs 19:21).

## Going about choosing

### Questions to consider

We may be faced with an array of job opportunities in line with our aspirations and within the boundaries set out above, but how do we go about making the correct choice? 'If you live in a society where there is only one job available for you, then you are grateful for it and there is not much room for exercising choice. If you live in a society where you have the privilege of choosing between many different jobs in many different places, then you are under increased pressure to "get your Guidance right"' (Adam 1988: 14). The Bible describes work as a means of providing sustenance, but also of yielding satisfaction, serving others and glorifying God. Considering questions which relate to these purposes together with some biblical tools and elements of our Christian character can help us in our choice.

*Is this work a good way for me to serve and glorify God?* Many types of work can be used to serve God and share in his creativity. However, in a world where many tasks have to remain undone, is this particular work a good way for me to serve and glorify him?

*Is this work a good way for me to serve others?* Whereas most jobs serve others directly or indirectly by providing goods or services, Christians will want to be sure that their work uses their skills to serve in the best possible way. This does not mean that we should all work in the caring professions, but it should make us more discerning in choosing work, preferring jobs the results of which are truly needed and enrich life.

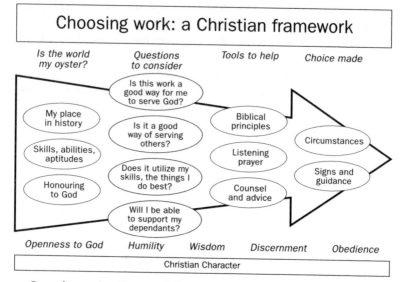

Does this work utilize my skills and abilities? My daughter Alison said, 'I don't know what job to do when I grow up.'

I found myself replying, 'Think about what interests you and what you are good at or could be good at. Then you'll find a job you'll enjoy.'

She thought she would be good at being a teacher, a tennis player and a doctor. At the age of six, it did not seem appropriate to ask her to refine her choice further!

My son David, when he was about the same age, came up with a neat way of handling the dilemma of multiple interests: 'I'll be a policeman in the morning, a roadworks man in the afternoon, and an ambulance man at night time.'

Ideally, a person's job is 'what he [or she] can do best' (Tasker 1960: 28); this is what each of us is motivated to do, enjoys and finds satisfying. The parable of the talents (Matthew 25:14–30) teaches that people should not ignore their gifts; in fact, they will be held accountable for the way they have used them. Paul teaches that we have varied gifts and abilities which are all to be used (1 Corinthians 12:14–31; Ephesians 4:11–13).

Skills, abilities and the things that interest us can change. Skills can be applied in different ways, transferred to other jobs or temporarily set aside. Natural gifts can be developed. New interests can be cultivated. God may lead us in unexpected ways through his Spirit, help us develop additional skills or empower us for particular tasks. The Bible gives examples of people whose aptitudes and skills were expanded for work that God wanted done (e.g. Moses, Exodus 3:11–12; Gideon, Judges 6:15–16). We need to take seriously what we can do for God, and the more we use our skills the greater our motivation will be.

*Can I support my dependants?* When looking at job advertisements, it is tempting to use the salary range as the first filter, rejecting many jobs because they do not pay enough. Certainly, work is the principal way we provide for our needs, support our dependants and improve our living conditions. When work is in short supply, or in environments or sectors where work is poorly paid, being able to support our dependants can justifiably become a paramount factor. But we must beware the materialistic pressure which suggests that remuneration should dominate our choice of work. Raising children, study and voluntary work remain meaningful forms of work where there are other means of support.

### Tools to help

Within a Christian framework for choosing work, there are some tools to help. Not all these pointers need to be used in all cases, but often their interplay and alignment confirm the direction we should take.

*Biblical principles.* Biblical principles help us to discern right from wrong, and sharpen out judgment in choosing between various 'good' paths (Psalm 119:105; Hebrews 4:12). Although the Bible does not directly deal with many of the choices and decisions we face regarding work, a Christian sense of values guides us, 'and this we acquire only as our thinking is increasingly moulded by the Bible' (Barclay 1978: 15). We use our minds to weigh up options against biblical norms, at the same time allowing the Holy Spirit to speak to us through 'the sword of the Spirit, which is the word of God' (Ephesians 6:17). But guidance (or justification) for choices should not be sought by picking verses out of context, or by treating the Bible like a horoscope. Passages need to be understood in their context and the principles they teach us applied to the issues we face.

*Listening prayer.* Listening prayer helps us to align our wills with God's, to clarify the issues on our hearts, and to give God the opportunity to speak (Psalms 40; 55; Isaiah 30:21; Romans 8:26–27). Many Christians experience an 'inner witness' when they believe that

God is guiding them in a particular way. The prophet Isaiah told the people of Israel that when they cried for help God would be gracious and answer them: 'Whether you turn to the right or to the left, your ears will hear a voice behind you, saying, "This is the way; walk in it"' (Isaiah 30:21). However, we need to be careful of the subjectivity of our own feelings (it is not difficult to 'feel led' to do something we really desire!), so this kind of guidance needs to be tested against the other 'tools'. And in order to hear God, we must be prepared to listen, which means spending time waiting before him in prayer (Philippians 4:6; Psalm 37:7).

*Circumstances.* Circumstances can bring opportunities to our attention, or rule out certain choices. Sometimes an opportunity arises that so obviously matches our skills that perhaps we should look to see if there are any reasons to reject it, rather than seeking reasons to accept. Sometimes a need that we have the ability to do something about presents itself so obviously that we can do nothing but help. Often, we can test circumstances by 'pushing the door'; if it opens, this is not necessarily the right job, but we may be encouraged to consider the option more seriously. If it closes, this can be a useful way of ruling out an option, at least on that occasion (sometimes perseverance is called for, and the door opens at a later stage). On his missionary journeys, Paul often moved on when persecution made his public ministry impossible (e.g. Acts 13:49–51), using circumstances as one aspect of his guidance.

However, we should not always be deterred by adverse circumstances, or overly swayed by comfortable ones. Circumstances must be taken seriously, but should not be seen as insurmountable or determining on their own; God can use or overrule them to achieve his purposes.

*Counsel and advice.* 'The way of a fool seems right to him, but a wise man listens to advice' (Proverbs 12:15). It is wise to seek the counsel and advice of others. Someone who knows us well can act as a sounding-board for our ideas and aspirations and offer a more objective view. Someone who knows about the job we are considering can tell us what it is like and help us to explore our fitness for it. A Christian friend can help us to review how our direction and aspirations align with God's purposes. But God requires *us* to decide and face the consequences of our actions, not our advisors.

*Direct guidance and 'signs'.* Gideon, unsure that he had been truly spoken to by God, laid a fleece on the ground, asking for it to be wet and the ground dry the following morning (Judges 6:36–37). Direct guidance (visions, God's voice) and signs are sometimes given by God, although they are the exception rather than the rule, and are usually given unexpectedly. They may confirm other guidance (as in the example above), or instruct us to do something that we would not have ordinarily done (as with Paul's vision of a man begging him to come to Macedonia; Acts 16:9–10). We are to test that they are from God by checking for their alignment with biblical principles and other aspects of our guidance.

Changing job and career, despite the reassuring comments I had received, was still like leaning backwards over a cliff edge on a rope to begin an abseil. I had been happy working as an oil explorer, but was keen to broaden my career and in particular to use some of the 'people skills' that others told me I possessed and that I enjoyed using. This was also in line with my desire to work in an area where I could use my skills to serve others more directly. So I started to signal my interest in personnel and community-affairs roles. Then circumstances prompted things to move more quickly; my personnel officer informed me he was moving and that his job was to be advertised, and that he saw me as a potential candidate. Following interviews, I mustered many reasons not to accept the job they offered me: 'It has all happened too quickly. I've only been in my present role eighteen months. I'll wait until the next opportunity arrives. I'm not sure whether this is the right role.' But friends I asked saw it as a good fit, and wasn't this just the type of role I had been looking for?

Some time before this all happened, someone had shared with me a 'picture' they had received in prayer. This showed that I would soon face a crossroads, but I was not to worry because I would know which way to go. Now it was happening and I was in a quandary! But when held together, the circumstances, my aspirations, the advice of people I trusted, my embryo skills and the opportunities the job offered left me with the underlying conviction that it was the right thing to do, despite my fears and excuses. After much heart-searching, I decided to step out in obedience to my understanding of God's guidance, and accept. My resolve was tested in the first few months of the new job, since it seemed to give me more hassle than satisfaction; but I could soon look back with confidence and say I had chosen the right job.

# Character to choose

## The mind of Christ

God's help in choosing, his guidance, is available to those who trust in him (Proverbs 3:5–6), who follow him (Psalm 23), and who are concerned with the things with which he is concerned (Isaiah 58:10–11). Aligning our lives with God in these ways means that we will increasingly be moving in the same direction as he is. Through seeking guidance in decision-making under the Spirit's tutelage, we build a godly character which helps us to make choices with the 'mind of Christ' (1 Corinthians 2:16).

Christian character enables us to use the tools described above with faith that God has work for us to do, with confident hope that we will find his will and fulfil the aspirations he has given us, and with patience and perseverance until we do.

## Humility, wisdom and discernment

To find the right job, we need humility: towards God, in recognizing that we do not have all the answers; and in relation to ourselves, so that we do not think more highly of ourselves than we ought (Romans 12:3). We need to be humble enough to seek and accept the advice of others, and careful not to advance ourselves at the expense of others, but rather to aim to serve them through our work.

Wisdom is a tool of guidance specifically promised to us (James 1:5). As Oliver Barclay states, 'the New Testament Christians expected to be guided by "wisdom", that is, by a sound judgment based on a truly Christian sense of values' (1978: 12). The wisdom referred to here is not 'earthly' wisdom, but wisdom 'from heaven' (James 3:15–17). 'It is the faculty that enables us to steer our way through life in a manner consistent with Christian character' (Barclay 1978: 16). How is such wisdom acquired? It is a gift of God (Proverbs 2:9–11) which is mediated through and taught by the Spirit (1 Corinthians 2:6–16). It grows in us through practice and through immersing ourselves in God's Word, so that the values by which we make judgments align with God's.

Discernment, closely related to wisdom, is the ability to distinguish finely between things, seeing them not only at face value but as God sees them. In 1 Corinthians 12:10 it is used in the context of distinguishing between spirits, when testing the authenticity of words and actions in relation to God's Spirit. In 1 John 4:1–6, discernment is referred to in the context of testing doctrinal authenticity. Applying discernment helps us to determine whether the work we are considering is of the Lord and the appropriate path for us at that time.

## Openness and obedience

Finding God's will presupposes an openness to God. Such openness helps us to comprehend the range of possibilities that may exist, and prepares us to be receptive to what God's path may be. It demonstrates our faith in God's ability to develop and use us, as well as to influence events so that our choosing is in line with his overall will. Being open gives us an enlarged rather than constrained view of the world, so that if a particular opportunity fails it is not the 'end of the world'. Openness to God enables us to cope with the fast-changing world of work. It enables us to respond to the call of God to serve him and others with the response, 'Here am I. Send me!' (Isaiah 6:8), thus preparing us for obedience to God's command. Coupled with obedience, it is characteristic of the spirit of servanthood epitomized by Jesus' words, 'yet not my will, but yours be done' (Luke 22:42).

When we have used various tools to find God's guidance, we come to the point of decision. We choose and follow through our choice in obedience to 'the command of God' (Barth 1961: 625). This command may have come in an indirect way (perhaps by applying wisdom to circumstances, or through the counsel of others), or more directly (through a sign from God, for instance, or by a strong inner witness). Either way, if it is God's command, it is the right step for us within his purposes, and the right choice to make.

## You chose your bed; now you have to lie on it

It doesn't end when you have made the decision and signed the contract. Even if the job was the one you wanted, you are likely to feel sad about leaving some things behind. Suddenly you see your old job in a different light, and mourn the loss of some of its familiar aspects – the people, your particular bit of workspace, tasks you were good at. (We thought about these aspects in chapter 6, on coping with change.) This is one emotional struggle to work through.

The second is when you begin the job and wonder what you have let yourself in for. After my first few days in a new job some years ago, I told Clare, 'I have made a terrible mistake. How could I have been so foolish? Why didn't I heed those doubts I had? I've really done it this time.'

But, with some support, I stuck at it and it became one of the most challenging and satisfying roles I have done. I believe it was very much part of God's purpose for me. When everything is strange and new, and you are vulnerable anyway because of the loss of a familiar routine, you forget the guidance you had and the positive features of the role. That is when your doubts loom large. I now brace myself for such feelings when I change role. I try to hang on to my conviction about the direction in which God is leading, and blinker out everything else until I have had time to settle and make a more considered evaluation.

But what if it really was a mistake? Well, it's not the end of the world. God has ways of helping us to get back on track. Again, it is wise not to react precipitately, otherwise you will get into a spiral of regretted decisions and become totally disorientated. Give yourself a little time for the emotions of change to settle. Talk it through with someone you trust, and seek God afresh. This may serve to confirm your original direction, in which case it becomes a question of seeing it through. It may result in looking again to find the right job for you at this time.

## The action column

1. Have you thought through how God wants to use the gifts he has given you? Do you have a vision for what you are aiming to achieve through your work? Dare to dream a little, and ask God to help you to identify some initial steps on the way to your goal.
2. Are you at a crossroads in your career? Are you looking for a new job? Test your options against the purposes of work we have looked at. Is it a good way to glorify God? To use your skills? To serve others? To support your dependants?
3. Use the tools God has provided to find his guidance: biblical principles, listening prayer, circumstances, counsel and advice, signs. Look to see how the results align with each other.
4. Ask God for wisdom and discernment as you decide. Be open to him, and, when you find God's will, follow it through in obedience as you make your choice.

# CHAPTER 9

# On the scrapheap?

*Responding to redundancy, unemployment and retirement*

## When work disappears

*Bad news*

'I read somewhere that in breaking bad news you need to get the key facts across in the first few minutes,' said Roy.

'Yes,' I agreed. 'That's what they will be listening for. I would do a quick introduction then get to the point.'

We had been frantically busy in meetings for two days. The time had come and we felt unprepared. But we had been thinking about it all day.

'Do you think I should go into the reasons?' Roy asked. We were a block away and the wind was cold.

'Not in detail. I would tell them the important stuff, then follow up with some background so they've time to think.' I was trying to anticipate their reactions, and to clear my mind so that I could help.

'How much do you think they know?' Roy wondered, struggling to hide his concern.

'I don't think it has leaked out, but they will have guessed from what has *not* been said.' I had picked up some of the gossip. They knew what was going on.

'They'll be aware that some of our people are looking at the plant in the US this week,' Roy commented. His voice was firmer, as if he was bracing himself for what lay ahead.

'They're not daft,' I said. We turned the corner and were outside the building which housed the plant.

'This is where the rubber hits the road,' said Roy, attempting a wry smile.

I nodded. 'Up to now it's been strategy and numbers and cost savings. Now it's people.' We were about to take away the livelihoods of thirty workers, and I felt sick. Companies merge, rationalize, downsize. People get hurt.

We entered the control room and it went quiet. There were some familiar faces but too many I didn't recognize, and I felt guilty. Nervous glances, a few smiles. We stood on our own at one end. They were in working clothes: boiler-suits, jeans, safety shoes. I was glad I had worn a jumper instead of suit and tie.

Roy started to speak, and they listened attentively. He spoke well and sincerely. Their expressions didn't change.

'... And so we have decided to close the plant.'

There, he had said it. Now it was out. Now they knew for sure. One swallowed, another shuffled. A youngster looked across to one of the older men, but he looked away.

I nodded supportively, played my part, and tried to show we had acted conscientiously. We were desperate not to be cast as the villains. Management had done its job, professional and to the point; compassionate but firm. Unwavering outside. Inside, crying.

'When will the plant be closed?' one of them asked.

Roy told them, making it clear it wouldn't end there and then; 'There will have to be a transition. We've got to complete work programmes and move equipment. It will probably take us through to the end of the third quarter.' Some faces brightened.

'What if I get a job? Could I go and still get the package?' asked a middle-aged man, the importance of the issue overcoming his reticence to speak. They were weighing up options, working out what it would mean for them. I would have done the same.

'Yes, we will be as flexible as we can.' Roy answered, glad that he could say something they wanted to hear.

'What about jobs elsewhere in the company?

'We will be networking all your names,' I said. 'Here, and at other sites. But as you know, there are reductions in most of the other areas too.'

I had given the appropriate answer and I could guess what they were thinking: 'It's all right for you, you smoothy.' I wanted to tell them I didn't have a job either.

'Why does our plant have to be the one that goes? We've heard they can't do all the things we can.' It was the team leader. Until now he had been silent, unobtrusive, watery-eyed, as he struggled with the brutal facts of industrial merger. Now, hardly moving, he dominated the room, his posture defiant.

'What were the criteria used to decide?' was his final question. Although softly delivered, it landed like a gauntlet thrown down.

Two others rallied to the cause, quoting technical details that only the engineers could have told them. It was as if they had started to believe they could change the decision and roll back the corporate forces which were pulling these two organizations together like giant magnets.

'We have a good two-shift system, and the team work well together. It seems wrong to close this site,' another spokesman went on.

Then the dream ended. A young fair-haired boy spoke up. 'What you're really saying is that we've all lost our jobs, ain't you?'

We winced as the ice-cold wind of reality cut through their denial and our polite euphemisms. 'Yes, I'm afraid that's the bad news.'

## Traumatic transitions

Being made redundant, undergoing a period of unemployment and retiring can be traumatic experiences. When the change is unwanted, it can often be accompanied by shock and loss of self-esteem, and can easily lead to depression and despair. They are among the most traumatic work transitions we can undergo.

At the beginning of this book, we saw that the Bible teaches that work is both good and necessary for our well-being. It can yield fulfilment and comradeship, provides for our material needs and enables us to serve others. People therefore have both an obligation and a right to work. According to David Brown, 'If the right to meaningful work is a fundamental right of man, then the right to work itself is an even more basic right' (1983: 63). If our primary work is taken away through redundancy, it can be seen as an attack on our very humanity. Donald Hay concludes that 'involuntary unemployment, however caused, is an evil' (1975: 15). Redundancy itself (the process of losing a job) is not necessarily an evil; where there are valid reasons and it is handled justly, it may be the right (sometimes the only possible) course of action. For some, redundancy may be a welcome opportunity for early retirement, retraining or a change of job. It is still a process of loss, however, and all the more distressing if it leads to unemployment.

Pope John Paul II states that unemployment, which he defines as the lack of work for those capable of it, 'in all cases is an evil ... which, when it reaches a certain level, can become a real social disaster' (1991:

para. 18). Where full employment is not possible, the state has a responsibility to provide assistance to fulfil an even more fundamental need: for subsistence. Such support is provided in many western countries, but it is a poor substitute for employment and usually makes only a small contribution to basic needs. Thus redundancy and unemployment affect not only the individual but also his or her spouse or partner, dependants, friends, community and society.

It is not surprising that redundancy, particularly if followed by a period of unemployment, causes us anguish and has potential for harm. John Stott states, 'It is a shocking experience to be declared "redundant", and still worse to have to think of oneself thus' (1999: 197). The experience is made worse by a society which idolizes paid employment for its own sake or as a means to wealth, status and power. Consequently, redundancy can be like entering a dark tunnel. Some are initially optimistic while they investigate new opportunities, but for many, if there is lengthy unemployment, the tunnel leads to depression and despair.

Retirement is similar to redundancy in that paid work activity ceases. However, retirement usually comes with some dignity towards the end of a person's working life, either at a set age or by choice. By contrast, redundancy can occur at any time and is often involuntary, and, like unemployment, tends to carry a negative social stigma. In times of recession these distinctions become blurred, as people are asked to take early retirement, voluntary redundancy, or some combination of both. People retiring with a pension and savings usually have the means to live without further paid employment, whereas those made redundant usually do not.

If work is 'purposeful activity' (as defined in chapter 2), retirement and redundancy can occur outside of the arena of paid employment. People retire from voluntary work or from church committees. They face 'redundancy' when their children start school, go away to university or leave home for good. In the sections below I concentrate on loss of paid work, since this most clearly focuses the issues; but they are also relevant to loss of unpaid work.

## Into the tunnel

The psychological effects of redundancy are well known. They follow a pattern which usually includes *shock*, followed by *optimism* (job-searching, a feeling of being between jobs), then *pessimism* (unsuccessful job-searching, seeing oneself as unemployed), and finally *fatalism* (hopelessness and apathy, giving up looking for a job) (Argyle 1989: 295). From a Christian viewpoint, John Stott speaks of shock, depression and pessimism, and fatalism (1999: 199), while Michael Moynagh has five 'steps into despair': shock, denial, search, despair and resignation (1985: 11–20).

### Shock

Whether anticipated or unexpected, losing your job is a shocking experience. It is usually hearing the bad news that signals a change for the worse. Clive had been told that his job was at risk, but like everyone else he hoped that when push came to shove, he would survive. He placed the opened letter on the table between us, and his face went blank as he attempted to come to terms with its message: 'We write to confirm with regret that your engagement with the Company will terminate by reason of redundancy on …'

'It's not real until you see it in black and white,' he said.

People attest to feeling numb, angry, or deeply distressed. Psychologists liken it to the loss of a close relative or friend. Self-esteem, status, income, security, purpose, routine, comradeship and career prospects can all be lost along with the job. This can be damaging and shocking.

My boss was phoning from the airport. My job was to go to someone else, based in America. He tried to reassure me, but I just felt numb. 'There will be another job,' he said. 'You won't fall out of this process. The plan is for you to transition your current role for six months.'

Six months! Handovers were usually less than six days, sometimes six hours. It meant there was nothing else available. For the rest of the day, I had a sinking feeling in my stomach, uncertain about the future and especially about how I would tell Clare when I got home.

'Darling, I no longer have a job. Dear, my job has been given to someone else. Clare, don't worry. I'm not redundant; I just don't have a job any more.'

As I drove home, I couldn't seem to find the right words. Worse, I felt embarrassed and belittled, as if I had failed.

### Denial or optimism

John, an experienced engineer, was shocked and surprised when he was informed that he did not have a job in the new organization, and that no suitable opportunity had materialized in another department. He struggled to comprehend how, given his record and service, the organization could do this to him. Even on his last day in the office, he continued to ask about the possibility of an alternative position. Such denial probably delayed by two or three months his adjustment to the loss, and his efforts to find another job.

Some people experience feelings of optimism as they think about new job opportunities, relieved that there is some certainty about their old job at last. But this can be short-lived as they come to see the reality of their predicament.

### Loss of self-esteem

The term 'redundant' means 'no longer needed or useful'. Your value to the organization has been questioned, which can make you feel worthless, even humiliated. A negative self-examination usually follows. Your self-esteem is lowered, and with it your confidence. 'If you are not earning, then you begin to feel less than a complete person. You begin to doubt yourself. You are not wanted, so you must be no good. It produces a loss of confidence and initiative' (Charley 1984: 10). You compare yourself with your peers who have kept their jobs. You feel guilty about no longer being able to support your family. You fear that your skills are outdated. You start to regret past career decisions. You feel embarrassed about the loss of your job status.

As I underwent the transition of my job to another person, I went from receiving up to a hundred e-mails a day to just a few. I understood the awful truth that no-one is indispensable. As my level of utility and influence decreased, so did my self-esteem. I had thought that the status of my job meant little to me, but when someone took it away, I felt demoted. When other responsibilities I had held were inadvertently given to someone else, I felt angry.

### Stress

Facing redundancy is stressful because of the uncertainty it prompts and the life-changes it causes. Uncertainty can begin long before you are made redundant, as jobs become threatened and rumours circulate. Some people feel a sense of relief when their fate is actually confirmed, though a new period of uncertainty begins as you search for a job. It is well documented that most stress is induced by major life-changes. Losing a job comes high up on Rahe's scale, used by psychologists to measure stress (Meadows 1988: 18), as do the associated effects such as a reduced financial position, starting a new job or moving to a new location.

### Depression

The effects of redundancy can lead to depression. You feel sad and pessimistic, and lose interest in life, particularly if there is little prospect of securing another job. The evidence suggests that depression deepens as the period of unemployment lengthens (Argyle 1989: 292). The inertia of depression makes it even harder to find another job. 'The unemployed become bored and apathetic, especially if they find they cannot organise their time, and just sit around doing nothing' (Argyle 1989: 291).

### Despair

Feelings of despair and hopelessness can be the eventual toll of redundancy, particularly if it results in long-term unemployment. If you are unable to get another job, it is easy to lose hope to the point of becoming completely demoralized. Research shows that people in such a state are more susceptible to a deterioration in health, heavy drinking and suicide (Argyle 1989: 293–295). This is the bottom of the change transition curve (described in chapter 6). Some people, even if they do not find another job, come to terms with the loss and resign themselves to being unemployed, and hence start to come off the bottom of the cycle, although they may continue to feel very negative about their predicament.

## Light at the beginning of the tunnel?

It is, however, possible to see light at the beginning of the tunnel. We need to make a Christian reassessment of some commonly held perceptions of self-esteem, the work ethic and security.

### Self-esteem

Our view of ourselves is often very closely related to the work we do. In fact, 'Self-esteem is so tied up with work that often a person made redundant will go on seeing himself in terms of his previous occupation' (Moynagh 1985: 90). Work contributes to our self-esteem, but should not be regarded as its basis. Rather, our self-esteem is based on the value invested in us by God, not for what we do or have achieved, but because of who we are – persons created in God's image and dearly loved by him. Self-esteem through Christ comes from equal sonship before God (Galatians 3:26), not from work status. Hence to Paul's statement, 'There is neither Jew nor Greek, slave nor free, male nor female …' (Galatians 3:28), one might add, 'employed nor unemployed'. Your work is what you *do*; while it contributes to your self-esteem and character, it does not define your worth. Even if it disappears, you are just as valuable to God.

## The work ethic

The 'Protestant work ethic' underlies many people's attitude to work, emphasizing a moral duty to work and a link between prosperity and God's blessing. Unemployed people can thus feel guilty and a failure. To make matters worse, 'Those who have been schooled in the values of the so-called "Protestant Work Ethic" (industry, honesty, resourcefulness, thrift, etc.) tend to despise those who are losers in the struggle to survive, as if it were their fault' (Stott 1999: 202). Research suggests that those whose view of work conforms to the Protestant work ethic 'believe in individual explanations for unemployment, suggesting that people are unemployed due to laziness, lack of effort, unwillingness to take on certain jobs, or move to places of work, etc.' They also tend to believe that 'social security (welfare) recipients who are unemployed should be working, as welfare encourages idleness' (Furnham 1990: 179).

Such a reaction is unfair, since many people are unemployed through no fault of their own and would work if they could. It is important to note that Paul's statement 'If a man will not work, he shall not eat' (2 Thessalonians 3:10) 'was addressed to voluntary not involuntary unemployment, to the lazy not the "redundant"' (Stott 1999: 202).

## Security

'If I lose my job, how will I pay the bills? My job is my security.' Paid employment is the usual means of obtaining life's necessities (near the base of Maslow's hierarchy of needs; see chapter 5), so a degree of security is vital. 'When such a fundamental aspect of well-being as security is neglected … serious dehumanisation sets in, especially when the load of that insecurity is not equally shared amongst all who are involved with the enterprise' (Dow 1979: 18). However, even when the *means* of security are removed, God remains as its *source*. He can provide security at the most fundamental level and, ultimately, for eternity. He is able to muster any means to care for his creatures, a truth articulated by the psalmists (e.g. Psalm 18:2), and reiterated by Jesus (Matthew 6:25, 32–33). The famous affirmation, 'The LORD is my shepherd, I shall not be in want' (Psalm 23:1), alludes to the experience of Israel in the desert for forty years where God provided for their needs. We too can have the same confidence in God as the caring shepherd.

## Finding a way through

The Bible makes it clear that as Christians we are not immune from suffering. It follows that we are not immune from the effects that redundancy can have upon us. However, we can be sure that God will help us through them. Although it may be difficult to see at the time, he can use them to good effect as, in a profound way, we share in the sufferings of Christ (1 Peter 4:12–13). Some of the ways of handling change which we looked at in chapter 6 are applicable to coping with redundancy. These are highlighted in the diagram, and I have described elsewhere a devotional approach to coping with redundancy (Curran 1995a).

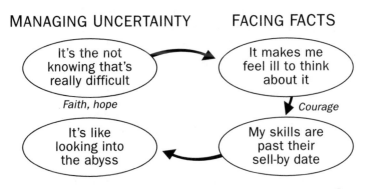

### Finding a way through redundancy

MANAGING UNCERTAINTY

It's the not knowing that's really difficult

*Faith, hope*

FACING FACTS

It makes me feel ill to think about it

*Courage*

It's like looking into the abyss

My skills are past their sell-by date

LOOKING INTO THE FUTURE
*Patience, perseverance*

TRANSFERRING SKILLS
*Openness, seeking*

## Managing uncertainty

'It's the "not knowing" that's really difficult,' a colleague said. She had been told that her job had disappeared, and was waiting for responses to a number of applications. When redundancy looms in a workplace, there is uncertainty about how many jobs will go and who will be affected. For those made redundant, there is uncertainty about what may lie ahead. For those remaining in the organization, the uncertainty is not over, since redundancies are nearly always accompanied by restructuring. Uncertainty disturbs us because it makes planning for the future difficult, and we put life on hold. We feel that we have lost control, and can fall prey to fear and stress. We cannot make all the uncertainty disappear, but we can identify some solid ground on which to build.

First, we still have a future, although it may be different from the one we expected. We are assured of this through *hope* – a confident trust and expectation concerning the future, based on God's character and promises. Under it, all life's other hopes can find their place and their meaning. Such hope is an anchor in times of trouble (Hebrews 6:19). Hope can strengthen us through uncertainty, and assist us in finding a way back from depression and despair, because it offers the promise and possibility of a future. In Psalm 42, the psalmist expresses how downcast he feels, and finds the answer: 'Put your hope in God' (verse 5). Jeremiah's letter to the Jewish exiles in Babylon seeks to reassure fearful people that despite their apparent helplessness and lack of a future, God has plans for them: '"For I know the plans I have for you," declares the LORD, "plans to prosper you and not to harm you, plans to give you hope and a future"' (Jeremiah 29:11).

Secondly, the way ahead is to grasp what certainties there are, to make reasonable assumptions and to be patient where uncertainty is too great to permit a decision. Starting to plan again, albeit in a tentative way, maybe looking only to the immediate future, can enable us to reassert some control on life. A good place to begin is with your campaign to find another job. We can do this because we have *faith* in God, who holds the master plan and whose promises are certain (Hebrews 11:1).

We can also take practical steps to deal with the stress which often accompanies uncertainty: talk it through, take regular exercise, eat a balanced diet, have sufficient sleep (see chapter 3).

## Facing facts

We had spent the day as a personnel team working out how we would implement a thousand redundancies. At the end we talked about the loss of many of our own jobs. 'It makes me feel ill to think about it,' one friend said. This is a common reaction of people facing redundancy. It may prompt 'loss-avoidance' behaviour: denial, a refusal to accept what is happening. We need to face the facts, however painful they are, so that as we express our loss, we come to terms with our situation and move beyond it.

## Grieving the loss

Following loss, we go through a time of grief and mourning before healing can start and we can face the world again.

King David grieved the loss of his friend Jonathan (2 Samuel 1:26). Many psalms express grief caused by difficulty, personal tragedy, persecution or defeat (e.g. Psalms 35; 38; 42). Jesus himself showed his grief at the loss of his friend Lazarus (John 11:33–36). To express our deep sadness for a loss is the appropriate and 'blessed' thing to do, for through it comes comfort (Matthew 5:4). God is the ultimate comforter who, through his Spirit, comes to 'bind up the broken-hearted' and 'comfort all those who mourn' (Isaiah 61:1–2).

Grief is not to be confused with an ongoing state of depression or despair. Grieving is the necessary human process that enables us to come to terms with loss and get the healing process under way. It should not become a way of life. It is a cup to be lifted, drunk, and then put down as we lay the loss to rest, so that we can then continue to live our lives again. We continue, changed but not defeated. Therefore we should not be surprised to feel sad because of our loss, or be afraid of expressing it. In fact, not to do so may indicate that we have not really begun to come to terms with it. But in our sadness we must remind ourselves that all is not lost, and that God keeps his arms around us at these times.

*Courage* is needed to survive the effects of redundancy and to face both the facts and the future. Courage is strengthened and fears are allayed by turning to God: 'Cast all your anxiety on him because he cares for you' (1 Peter 5:7).

## Transferring skills

John's role as training manager disappeared in a massive round of job cuts. Despite the organization's insistence that it was the job, not the person, that had to go, John's evaluation of himself was, 'My skills are past their sell-by date.' Skills and abilities can, however, be adapted and transferred, added to and used in other contexts. Many view redundancy as being thrown on the scrapheap. Maybe a *compost* heap is a more helpful picture; the skills we have can be transformed and put to good use again.

It is important then to identify your transferable skills: those generic skills that can be used in many roles – an ability with figures, or with your hands, an aptitude for working with others, organizational skills and so on. You have a unique combination of and competence in these, and even if your main professional or technical skill is no longer required, you will be able to take the underlying aptitude with you. Some of your skills may be in need of adaptation and new ways of application, as when a mechanic uses his knowledge of engines to teach motor mechanics. You may need to add some new skills; old dogs can learn new tricks!

The picture of the compost heap, of material being reclaimed, transformed and used again, reminds us of God's work. He redeems and transforms our lives. He offers us forgiveness and eternal life, making us more Christ-like as we follow him. God came as redeemer to the exiled Jews who were thrown on the scrapheap as a defeated people, having lost their land, livelihood and self-esteem. He promised to restore them to their land so that they would again give him glory (Isaiah 43:1–7). God acts as our redeemer too, guarding us through troubled times, and restoring us so that we can again use our skills to his glory.

We need to be looking actively for new opportunities as doors are closed on past ones. *Patience*, which we need during a period of unemployment, is not synonymous with inactivity. Rather, the waiting time is a time to push doors, re-evaluate skills and look for new ways to serve God. Chapter 8 outlined some ways of going about this.

### Looking to the future

Betty was distraught. As we stood by the coffee machine, she told me how her husband, who worked for another company, was also being made redundant. 'It's like looking into the abyss.'

The future can look completely empty as your job and all it means are swept away. However, there are new opportunities to be had, and for some people redundancy may be a blessing in disguise. I bumped into Betty a year or so later. She was back at the site, arranging flowers in the restaurant. She explained that with her redundancy money she had done what she had always wanted to do but had never before had the courage; she had started her own florist business and had won the contract to supply the site with fresh flowers.

We can look to the future because of the hope God has given us, and we can start to move towards it as we step out in *faith*. It is faith that enables us, as it enabled Abraham, to move from deliberation to action: 'By faith Abraham, when called to go to a place he would later receive as his inheritance, obeyed and went, even though he did not know where he was going' (Hebrews 11:8). But we also need *patience* and *perseverance*. With patience we can put aside the disappointments and find peace amid the turmoil, as the psalmist advised: 'Be still before the LORD and wait patiently for him' (Psalm 37:7). Patient trust in God yields some firm ground on which to stand (Psalm 40:1). With perseverance, we will see the situation through, despite difficulties, until the promise is realized. 'You need to persevere so that when you have done the will of God, you will receive what he has promised' (Hebrews 10:36).

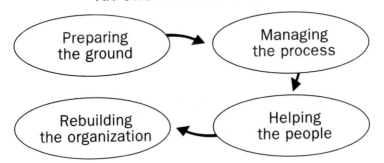

# Handling redundancy

## AN ORGANIZATION'S ROLE

Preparing the ground → Managing the process

Rebuilding the organization ← Helping the people

## The organization's role

### *Treating people with respect*

Organizations have a responsibility to treat people with respect as they leave employment with them. It is one of the ways the 'psychological contract' with employees can be honoured. It is also an important way of reassuring those who remain that the organization is still worth working for. I have written about this elsewhere (Curran 1995). Here I will simply highlight some of the key aspects of this role. It is all the more poignant if, as you make others redundant, you are facing job uncertainty yourself.

Making employees redundant is not like disposing of outdated equipment. It threatens their future career, livelihood and security. The incident described at the opening of this chapter illustrates some of the difficulties of representing the organization in handling the redundancy of others. As Christians, Roy and I knew that as we carried out company policy we were responsible to do all in our power to ensure a caring, compassionate and just approach. If you are called upon to manage or be involved in the redundancy of others, here are some practical ways of ensuring such an approach.

### Preparing the ground

Once the redundancies are announced, your aim is to reduce uncertainty for people, and to help the organization through an arduous period and back to business after it. So good preparation is needed: timescales, allocation of responsibilities, deciding where the cuts will fall, working out the numbers and skills affected, and forecasting likely future skills demands. Undertaking the job losses in one major reduction, although hard to achieve, is usually preferable to 'death by a thousand cuts' which prolongs uncertainty, generating discontent all around.

Involving people, including managers and staff who are leaving themselves, is a way of giving those affected some control over the way they and others are handled. It often prompts a positive response, rather than the resentment that comes when people feel that things are 'done to' them. When a research organization I worked with was dismantled and reorganized in the early 1990s, six of the seven most senior managers lost their jobs. Despite their own loss, when given the responsibility for seeing the process through, they worked harder than they ever had before in ensuring that the redundancy of others was well handled.

### Managing the process

Providing as much information as possible through early, frequent and honest communication helps people to manage the change and to plan and make decisions. While there may be sensitive pieces of information that cannot be released until the appropriate time, giving as much information as possible creates a clearer picture of the future and reduces speculation and fear.

There are alternatives to enforced redundancy, such as redeployment, 'natural wastage' (people who would have left anyway for various reasons), early retirement and voluntary redundancy, which can be advantageous to both individuals and the organization. A voluntary programme can contribute to achieving the necessary reductions, softening the blow of redundancy, and reducing or removing the need for an enforced programme. However, an organization will usually reserve the right to keep key skills.

To uphold fairness, the criteria used to select people for redundancy need to be clear, and applied evenly, with a process for appeal. This often involves ranking employees on the basis of skills, experience, performance, service, or some combination of these. This is one of the most difficult tasks, because so much depends on the judgments of supervisors or managers, ideally using objective criteria, but sometimes coming down to 'who knows who'. In takeovers or mergers, company politics or former affiliations can easily sway decisions.

As a human-resources manager during a merger, in selection sessions I found myself constantly reminding others (and myself) to consider *all* the candidates, to focus on who was best for the job, not which company they had come from, and to stick rigorously to the stated process. My colleague Daphne spent many hours working with managers in ranking and selection discussions, testing their decisions against our selection criteria. I can't say we got it right on all occasions, but I think the overall outcome was fairer because of our efforts. Getting other managers to 'peer review' decisions, and senior managers to overview the overall outcome, adds further safeguards.

### Helping the people

If the job of breaking bad news falls to you, you may feel responsible or guilty, or take people's angry or distressed reactions personally. The difficulty is all the more acute if you work in a small organization where you have had to make the strategic decisions and decide who will leave, *and* you have to deliver the message. Some practical tips:

- Make time to see people individually, being sensitive to the location and timing of the conversation.

- Be well prepared with information (severance terms, benefits, details of outplacement help).
- Listen. Be sensitive to people's reactions (shock, anger, distress). Be ready to provide appropriate support, or allow them to go home if necessary.
- Give a clear and honest statement of the facts: why the post is going, why the individual's skills are no longer required, how the decision was made, the overall numbers involved, timescales, and how redundancy payments have been calculated.
- Don't raise false hopes. Give a realistic picture of redeployment options.
- Don't make promises that cannot be kept or over which you have no control.

Some organizations have the resources to help people enter the job market – a daunting experience for those who have had a long career with a single employer. This can include professional counselling, and training in CV preparation and interview skills. Counselling can be an important way of helping people to express their loss, form their ideas about the future and rebuild their confidence. If your organization is not in a position to provide these, then try to direct people to sources of such help.

Being flexible about leaving dates is a way of showing sensitivity, since people vary in how they handle the actual leaving. Once he knew he did not have a job, Mark, an engineer, wanted to move on as quickly as possible. He soon found himself another job, and the best thing for him was to step into the future. Arrangements were made for him to complete or hand over outstanding work. Julia, a training professional, wanted time to adjust to leaving the company that had employed her for more than twenty-five years. She worked her notice period with colleagues in the familiarity of her work environment.

Of course, these factors need to be balanced with contractual notice periods, the needs of the organization, and the morale of remaining employees, so that a just and caring outcome is achieved. If a person is required to stay for an extended period, for example to complete a project, it is only fair to make some commitments about help into the job market at the end, perhaps a terminal bonus, or earlier release if he or she finds another job.

### Rebuilding the organization

Following redundancy in an organization, those who remain also need help, and the community of which they are a part needs rebuilding. As a leader or manager, you will need to rekindle trust and morale if the business and its employees are to be successful in the future. 'This company is not what it used to be,' I heard many employees say following the cuts of the early 1990s, and it was probably true. To perpetuate a myth that since the redundancies are over, all can resume as before, can be unhelpful, even dishonest. While many elements of an organization's ethos and culture may continue (such as the quality of its products, its style of doing business), the new realities must also be communicated so that a new 'psychological contract' is understood by all.

'Those who have gone are the lucky ones.' This can be the reaction of those remaining, particularly if they see former colleagues leaving with large redundancy packages and quickly securing other jobs, while they themselves remain in uncertainty with a greatly increased workload. Good leadership is required to motivate people towards new goals, and to protect employees from unreasonable pressure.

'Morale has never been as bad as this before.' This sums up the feelings of many, and reflects their mistrust, sense of loss, even guilt as they attempt to come to terms with what has happened. Like a period of mourning, this has to be worked through; but if it is prolonged it will affect individuals and their work. If you are in leadership, your role is to help people to refocus on their work as well as to take seriously their feelings and concerns. You need to encourage those with whom you work to begin to look to the future again and to play their part in rebuilding their work community.

## Retiring: end of work, or transition?

### When you retire ...

When you retire, life can be less stressful, with more time for family, relaxation, leisure and other activities. Psychologists, comparing the unemployed with the 'normally' retired, reveal dramatic differences between these two groups despite the similarities in their situations. Why? Probably because retirement is generally an accepted and honoured social status (a reward for a lifetime's hard work), whereas unemployment is regarded negatively (Argyle 1989: 305–306). Studies reveal that those with a purpose in life and strong interests are able to adjust to retirement and continue to find satisfaction.

However, if retirement is unwanted, for example due to ill health or as part of job cuts, it can result in effects similar to those of redundancy. These effects can be more acute, however, since age or physical impairment can make further employment, if desired, harder to find. Even those who welcome retirement have to make adjustments. They need to come to terms with the drop in income coupled with the end of their earning ability. They also face the challenges of structuring a day once filled by employment, coping with ageing or with failing health, and spending more time with the family or alone instead of with work colleagues. They may feel bored, lonely, useless or old. They may experience a loss of self-esteem: it can be a shock to move from being a chief executive or the family's principal breadwinner one day to chief washer-up the next.

### A change in purposeful activity

A Christian view of retirement takes the notion of reward for a life's hard work one step further, seeing it as an end to one type of work (employment) rather than an end to all work. The Bible upholds the principle that 'the worker deserves his wages' (Luke 10:7) and of reward for service rendered (Matthew 25:23). Receiving a pension as deferred wages and having more time for rest and other activities are consistent with these principles. While the balance may swing towards more leisure, work (purposeful activity) remains an important ingredient as we continue to seek ways to serve God and others, thus maintaining a balance of work and rest. As Keith Tondeur observes, 'The concept of "putting someone out to grass" is not biblical.' Although the nature of his or her work may change, 'a Christian never retires from active service' (1996: 136).

The characteristic attitudes of hope, seeking and openness can help in retirement. Hope reassures us that although our period of paid employment is over, we have an important and valuable future in God's eyes. A seeking and open attitude towards God's purposes and the future is vital since we may now have a greater opportunity to choose what we want to do with our time and energy than at any other time in our life.

A good place to start is with a self-appraisal of abilities and resources. Then comes the search for the way in which God wishes to use us in our retirement (the principles outlined in chapter 8 can help here). This may mean continuing along well-trodden paths, or it may mean utilizing skills in new and perhaps surprising ways. As with all purposeful activity, once the task is defined, our responsibility is to serve God faithfully in it (Colossians 3:23–24).

I asked Ivor, a friend and retired prison officer, what advice he would give to someone preparing for retirement. 'Try to find an interest in life,' he replied, 'and if it can supplement your pension, so much the better. Don't become a couch potato. Keep your mind and body active, and, as a Christian, keep your spiritual life active.'

He told me how, after he had ruled out various part-time options, his wife Caroline had suggested that he start his own gardening business, doing what he enjoyed most. I asked if he had put any plans in place before he retired. Ivor said he had finished his job with the prison service at 12 noon and by 2.30 on the same day he was working in someone's garden.

## The action column

1. Have you just been made redundant? Don't be surprised at the sense of shock and loss you feel – it's part of dealing with change. Find ways of expressing your sadness. Inject some certainty into your situation by planning a job campaign. Seek God's guidance. Remember, there is hope because God has plans and purposes for your life.
2. Are you unemployed? Are there ways of transferring your skills or learning new ones? Find support. Ask God to grant you faith and courage, patience and perseverance.
3. Are you about to retire? Start thinking *now* about how you will use your time. Ask for God's guidance as you consider what 'purposeful activity' you will embark on. Is there a way of phasing the transition?

# CHAPTER 10

# Leading the way

*Directing, inspiring, motivating, enabling,
caring ... serving*

## The leadership people deserve

'You are not giving the people in this organization the leadership they deserve,' my boss told the management team. His words struck our consciences because we knew he was right. Leadership properly interpreted is not a thing exercised for its own sake or for status, but rather an awesome responsibility and a privilege bestowed. Something is owed to the power bestowing it and to the people being led.

Where were we going wrong? For one thing, we dabbled in the detail, and thus did not give others the opportunity to grow. We failed to give them precise overall direction so that their activities could be well co-ordinated. We were not communicating regularly or clearly, or taking responsibility for problems or failures. We shied away from some of the tough decisions, and did not always abide by decisions we had made collectively. Management was not spoken of in glowing terms and was not always trusted, but we each convinced ourselves that it was the other managers on the team that were at fault, not us.

My colleagues were all experienced and respected individuals concerned to do a good job. But it did not make for good leadership. That the term 'manager' is, in some organizations, being replaced by 'leader' is perhaps part of the explanation. Leading is different from managing. Managing is a broad term; one can manage almost any resource including people and money. A manager's role can include being a figurehead, liaising, monitoring, disseminating information, being a spokesperson, being an entrepreneur, handling disturbances, allocating resources, negotiating *and* leading (Mintzberg, in Statt 1994:

336–337). But being a leader is primarily concerned with *direction* and *people*, and hence is focused on vision and inspiring others. One definition which captures both the 'task' and 'people' dimensions of leadership is 'exercising influence over other people in pursuing collective goals' (Statt 1994: 325). Work requires leadership to give it vision and direction, and to motivate and energize people to get things done.

## What makes a leader?

What makes for good leadership? Is it personality? Or is it style? What part does the context play? Should a leader focus on the task in hand or the people being led? Is the term 'leader' just a trendy word for manager?

### Personality and character

Throughout history leadership has been regarded by many as the crucial factor in promoting success in social enterprises. Just as the elders of Israel insisted to Samuel that they needed a king like other nations (1 Samuel 8:4–22), so through history people have assumed that success lies in great leaders – the so-called 'Great Man' theory. Emerging from a world of absolute monarchs, military models and autocratic landowners and industrialists, it is not surprising that great national leaders have been used as role models for leadership in modern work.

Do leaders, then, have distinctive personality traits? Research reveals that leaders *can* be more intelligent, energetic and flexible, and display greater alertness, originality, personal integrity and self-confidence than group members, and can possess a higher need for achievement, responsibility and task-orientation (Guest, in Warr 1987: 180). But the links between such traits and leadership behaviour or success are not so well established. Some people seem to be 'natural leaders' and end up leading in any situation in which they find themselves. This suggests that some essential qualities are needed for leadership. But this does not preclude others developing these qualities.

What are these essential qualities for leadership? Many organizations have attempted to define them. The lists vary, largely because of cultural factors and the context in which the leadership is exercised (e.g. industry, the military). John Adair, however, lists some generic or transferable leadership qualities (1997: 3):

- *Enthusiasm* is essential in motivating others towards a goal. Leaders can summon up the energy even when the situation is discouraging.
- *Integrity.* This speaks of wholeness, trustworthiness, values; it is what encourages others to trust a leader.
- *Toughness.* Good leaders are demanding, resilient, tenacious, able to set high standards and demanding goals.
- *Fairness.* They treat everyone justly and impartially, and have no favourites.
- *Humility.* They are not boastful or arrogant.
- *Confidence.* People look for confidence in a leader; it helps them to trust in his or her direction. But overconfidence can result in arrogance or foolishness.

These qualities are a mixture of personality traits (such as enthusiasm and confidence) and qualities of moral character (such as integrity and humility). They are largely consistent with the Christian view of leadership described later in this chapter, although the Bible puts particular emphasis on some characteristics, such as integrity, fairness (justice) and humility, and adds others, such as obedience, wisdom, trustworthiness and, importantly, love. The Bible's portrayal of toughness is a powerful combination of courage and compassion in relation to people, and faith, hope and perseverance in sticking to the task.

Personality and character are certainly part of the story in the making of good leaders. And the range of qualities needs to include moral character to be fully effective. Dictators are high on toughness, enthusiasm and confidence, but they alienate many whom they purport to 'lead' because people fear rather than trust them, so that their leadership is often reduced to coercion. But personality and character are not the whole story.

### Leadership style

Leadership is not only about who leaders *are*, but also about what they *do* and *how* they do it – their style. Some leaders simply announce their own decisions. Some ask for the opinions of those they are leading. Others share problems and accept a collective decision. Leadership covers a spectrum of styles, ranging from autocratic, through con-sultative, to democratic.

Some argue that a democratic style yields better results through producing employees who are more engaged, empowered and

## Leadership: a spectrum of styles

| Autocratic | Consultative | Democratic |
|---|---|---|

◄──────────────────────────────────────────►

| *The leader decides and tells the group* | *The leader shares problem then decides* | *The leader shares problem and accepts the group's decision* |
|---|---|---|

motivated. Others believe that the firm and clear decision-making of an autocratic style is more productive. Whatever the preferred style of a leader, the context is also important, as is the way the members of the team operate. I like to be involved in decisions that affect my job, but I would prefer to be led out of a burning building autocratically rather than by consultation! Sometimes, only the leader has the information or skill to decide. In other situations, urgency requires immediate and decisive action. More often than not, however, better decisions are made when the skills and input of others are taken into account.

Each of us will have an individual style as a leader, linked to our personalities, skills and what is important to us. However, effective leadership requires the ability to vary our style when the context requires it.

Leadership style also depends on the attitudes, skills, knowledge and experience of those being led. A team of highly experienced professionals will not usually take kindly to being told how to do their jobs, whereas a group of trainees will, initially at least, require a higher degree of directive leadership.

### Task-focused or people-focused?

A further aspect of leadership style is the balance between the need to accomplish the task and concern for the people being led. These were found to be dominant factors in descriptions of leadership behaviour (Halpin & Winer, in Statt 1994: 330). They raise a moral question about leadership: 'Is effective leadership that which gets the best results according to organizational criteria or that which gets the most positive response from subordinates?' (Guest, in Warr 1987: 179). A Christian response is that both functions are important, and need to be fulfilled with Christian principles in mind. Christian leadership is directed towards good goals and treats people well on the way to those goals.

### Leaders or managers?

Much has been written on the nature of management and on what makes a good manager. It is a function, or rather a collection of functions that an organization needs in order to operate effectively, but it is not synonymous with leadership. Management in the modern sense has its origins in nineteenth-century industrialization, which required the constituent tasks in a process to be separated out and allocated to a succession of workers. The manager supervised the process and ensured that each task was done. A manager is thus someone in whom the organization vests authority and accountability for supervising the work of others and for managing resources.

In what ways is leadership different? Richard Higginson describes a commonly held view of management as comprising '*planning, organizing, controlling* and *evaluating*', and contrasts this with leadership which 'is about setting a direction and motivating others to follow; it is about *aligning* and *inspiring*' (1996: 26).

The tasks of leadership and management represent a range of necessary functions. The way they are performed depends on how jobs are organized, and on the personalities and abilities of those in leadership and management roles. Many organizations assume that those in formal management roles will also be leaders, but leaders are not always good managers. I once worked for an inspirational leader, who spent his time and energy charting the direction of the business and motivating people with a deft touch. He was successful because he surrounded himself with capable people who could manage the finances, control expenditure, ensure that objectives were met, and so on. When his chief of staff moved on to another role, things didn't get done, and the leader quickly had to get someone else to perform those necessary management functions.

Most of us are probably good at some aspects of managing and at some aspects of leading. Roles often require a combination of both. I am concentrating on leadership rather than management in this chapter for a number of reasons. First, much of what is called 'managing' can be undertaken by workers empowered to plan and control more of their own work. This recognizes their creative talents, and allows them to own more of the whole task and thereby to be more satisfied in carrying it out. Empowerment is a key ingredient of leadership. Secondly, the leadership function is more fundamental than management, since it deals with the venture's overall direction, and includes motivating others towards its goals. The Bible depicts people fulfilling many functions as they work together towards particular goals, but it gives special attention to leadership. Thirdly, while an organization appoints formal management and leadership roles, leadership can be exercised from any point within the organization, and often is. Again, this aligns with the biblical view that it is a leader's *function*, not his or her position or status, that is important in achieving a task. As Christians, we will want to offer moral leadership through our work and example, whatever our position in the organization. Some of us are formally appointed leaders; others are regarded as 'born leaders' because of our personality and abilities, but we are all called to exercise leadership in some aspects of our work.

### What makes a poor leader?

Pinpointing what makes a good leader can be tricky, but most of us will have experienced poor leadership, or are aware of times when we ourselves have not given people the leadership they deserve. Some of the following leadership types may be familiar; they are all based on real people I have met, or characteristics I have at times found within myself:

- *The big ego:* for this leader, status, the trappings of power and the appearance of success are the key concerns. The team's direction and purpose are defined by what will further this boss's career.
- *The bungie boss:* this character is in and out of the role so fast that there is no time to form relationships, create direction, sustain change or live with the consequences of his or her decisions and actions. This ex-boss leaves a string of uncompleted objectives and a disorientated and destabilized team.
- *Genghis Khan:* this autocrat loves to tell people what to do, wants to make all the decisions and is always right. Such a boss squashes the views of everyone else, prevents good ideas from surfacing, and usually gets only compliance.
- *The control freak* is the leader who must be in control of everything and who gets cross if things are done without his or her knowledge

or say-so. People feel they are in a straitjacket; unable to manage their own work, they soon give up ownership of it.

- *The dabbler:* always meddling in the detail of his or her subordinates' jobs, this boss cannot leave them to get on with tasks delegated to them, and is unable to see the big picture. This character never has enough data to make decisions.

- *The decathlete:* the perfectionist who cannot delegate because no-one else can do things to quite the same standard in quite the right way. The result is that the skills and creativity of the team are stifled and the boss suffers burnout.

- *The upwardly focused:* always wanting to appear in a good light, this boss refers decisions upwards instead of taking responsibility and risks, and is more concerned with being a good subordinate than with being a good leader. Team members become cynical, and finds ways round the boss to the person who is really leading.

- *The appeaser:* fearful of offending people through challenge, conflict or confrontation, this boss avoids difficult situations and tough decisions at all costs. Poor performance goes unchecked, negative relationships are propagated, and people feel unfairly treated.

- *The very early-retired boss* does not want to lead anyone anywhere. The status quo rules. This boss, whose motto is 'Anything for a quiet life', just wants to see out his or her time (which could be the next twenty years) in peace. New ideas are unwelcome, progress is stunted and performance mediocre.

- *The bombshell boss* loves to drop startling news on the team to keep them awake. This boss uses information to show off his or her connections and importance, but gives direction in the form of 'received instructions' with little added. The team lurches from one crisis to the next, and loses confidence in the boss.

## Leadership in the Bible

What can we learn from the Bible about leadership structures and styles? How can we apply it to the world of work? There are many different examples of leadership in the Bible. They span a variety of cultural settings, represent different organizational structures, display a variety of leadership styles, and seem to utilize people of varying personality types. They often reflect the cultures of their day, although they also introduce some elements that challenge those cultures.

## In the Old Testament: 'after his own heart'

The world of the Old Testament and its institutions and settings was in many aspects unlike our own. Its patterns of leadership related to a sequence of contrasting situations: from the patriarchal leadership of nomadic tribes to that of a settled agricultural nation; from leadership by 'charismatic' judges to that of hereditary kings; from the spiritual leadership of the priesthood of an established temple religion to that of itinerant prophets. While a definitive pattern for leadership in our day may elude us, there are some important principles upon which the New Testament builds and from which we can learn.

- Leadership patterns are very varied, related to the culture of the time and relevant to the task in hand (for instance, the 'charismatic' leadership of Moses during the exodus gave way to the more settled leadership of judges, then kings, in the promised land).
- Once the nation was established, the principal leaders were kings, priests and prophets, although elders were present throughout (Numbers 11:16–17; 1 Samuel 8:4). Charismatic leadership existed alongside established hereditary leadership; God used both.
- While Israel's leadership patterns were similar to those of the nations around it, its leaders were subject to God, a fact brought to the attention of Israel's kings by successive prophets (for example, Nathan rebuked David, 2 Samuel 12; Elijah brought God's judgment on Ahab, 1 Kings 17:1).
- Leaders were often called and equipped by God for specific tasks (such as Abraham, Genesis 12:1; Moses, Exodus 3; Amos, Amos 7:15).
- Empowerment by the Spirit was crucial (as in the cases of Moses, Numbers 11:17; Gideon, Judges 6:34; and David, 1 Samuel 16:13).
- Delegation occurred (e.g. Numbers 11:14–17).

Leaders were implicitly called to render service to God. It was more explicit in the calling of some (such as people of lowly origin like David). As established forms of leadership became corrupt, the prophets looked forward to the coming of an ideal leader, the 'Messiah', who would fulfil the roles of prophet, priest and king (Jeremiah 23:1, 5–6, 11; Micah 5:2, 4; Zechariah 9:9–10). The Messiah's leadership would be through suffering and service, bringing justice and righteousness (Isaiah 42:1–4; 61:1–3), and would ultimately be glorious and powerful (Isaiah 52:13 – 53:12; Daniel 7:13–14).

The Old Testament reveals a variety of personalities as leaders: a cunning schemer like Jacob, a boaster and a dreamer like Joseph, the reluctant Moses, the youthful and brave David. They were all called to some form of leadership and shaped by God for the task. Good leadership is not the preserve of any one personality type. However, some characteristics appear to be common to good leaders and necessary for successful leadership. They were either inherent in the person or developed for the task with God's help. These include:

- faith (e.g. Abraham, Genesis 15:6; Hezekiah, 2 Kings 18:5–6);
- obedience (e.g. Abraham, Genesis 12:1–5);
- trustworthiness (e.g. Joseph, Genesis 39);
- courage (e.g. Joshua, Joshua 1:6–9; David, 1 Samuel 17:32–37);
- wisdom (e.g. Joshua, Deuteronomy 34:9; Solomon, 1 Kings 4:29–34); and
- justice (oppressive and unjust leaders are judged, e.g. Isaiah 3:12–15; Jeremiah 25:34–38).

These are only some of the characteristics that people who love God are to develop as they grow more like him (as we saw in chapter 4). Those listed here are the ones most appropriate for the functions of leadership. Taken together, they describe a person of integrity aligned to God's values and character. Samuel's words concerning the choosing of David are a fitting summary: 'The LORD has sought a man after his own heart and appointed him leader of his people' (1 Samuel 13:14).

### New Testament leadership: 'I have come as one who serves'

The New Testament offers us the examples of Jesus' leadership and of the early church leaders who followed in his steps. The theme that stands out is leadership through *service*. In contrast to secular models of leadership, where rulers lorded it over their subjects, Jesus taught: 'Not so with you. Instead, whoever wants to become great among you must be your servant, and whoever wants to be first must be slave of all' (Mark 10:43–44). He rejected the Jewish rabbinical schools' emphasis on status (Matthew 23:6–11), emphasizing a person's function rather than position. 'He saw ministry not in terms of status but in terms of function. The pattern he set was the pattern of service' (Green 1983: 18).

Much of Jesus' model of service was drawn from the Servant Songs found in Isaiah 40 – 55. His messiahship was that of a suffering servant rather than of a political liberator. The understanding of servanthood in these songs – obedience, fearless witness and innocent suffering – is all found in the ministry of Jesus. 'Jesus avoided all the usual titles that might describe the importance of his person. He understood his life as a way of obedience involving lowliness and suffering, in the light of the ways of all righteous men, of all God's servants who had already followed the way of obedience in Israel' (Schweizer 1961: 23). He clearly expected his disciples to follow this pattern of service in their ministry and leadership (Mark 10:43; John 13:14–15). Paul understood this and said as much: 'Your attitude should be the same as that of Christ Jesus ... taking the very nature of a servant' (Philippians 2:5, 7). Implicit are the qualities of humility and obedience, courage and compassion, and underlying them all, love.

Jesus lived out his leadership of service, leading his disciples and all those who followed through serving them with his time and energy. 'I am among you as one who serves' (Luke 22:27). He graphically displayed this principle in taking on the slave's job of washing their feet, thus turning on its head the established notion of greatness related to status (John 13:1–17). His service was motivated by love (verse 1) and undertaken through humility (verses 4–5).

At first glance, leadership exercised through service does not seem very inspirational or authoritative. Yet we see men and women of all types responding to Jesus' call to discipleship, ready to leave everything to follow him. And we see him teaching and dealing with his opponents with astounding authority (e.g. Mark 1:22; Matthew 23). His leadership did not lack decisiveness or power, as shown by his resolve to journey to Jerusalem despite the dangers (Matthew 16:21–23), and his eviction of the traders from the temple (Matthew 21:12–13). Clearly, leadership exercised through service to God and others can be distinctive and effective, resulting in a commitment that can far outweigh the compliance often resulting from more status-driven forms of leadership. Leadership should carry authority and power; Jesus acknowledged this, and granted authority to the disciples. However, the Christian contention is that 'Leaders have power, but power is safe only in the hands of those who humble themselves to serve' (Stott 1999: 431).

Jesus appointed a group of twelve disciples to share his ministry and leadership. The twelve functioned as a team, and local leadership in the early churches seems to have followed the pattern of a leadership team, sharing the various functions of leadership. Delegation and empowerment occurred, and although the twelve are depicted as a close-knit group, Jesus encouraged them to remain a fully open circle (Mark 9:38–40).

Following Jesus' death and resurrection, the church grew and spread, led by apostles, elder-bishops and deacons, with prophets, evangelists, teachers and others performing specific functions. As in the Old Testament, settled leadership (particularly elders, modelled on the elders of Jewish communities) existed alongside more charismatic or mobile roles. Paul did not seem disturbed by this, but was more concerned that each part of the church should fulfil its function (1 Corinthians 12 – 13).

1 Timothy 3 describes characteristics required of leaders in the church. Among other things they are to be 'temperate, self-controlled, respectable, hospitable, able to teach, not given to drunkenness, not violent but gentle, not quarrelsome, not a lover of money' (verses 2–3). The passage goes on to mention the ability to manage one's own family, and being of good reputation. In other words, leaders must be 'above reproach'. Although this passage is aimed at church leadership, its emphasis is not on spiritual abilities or theological knowledge, but on the integrity and wholeness of character required to draw out the respect and trust of others, and is thus applicable to leadership more generally.

While the comments in 1 Timothy 3:11 are normally regarded as referring to deacons' wives (as in the NIV), the Greek text says literally 'their women', which may refer to female deacons. Phoebe is referred to as a servant (deaconess) of the church in Cenchrea (Romans 16:1), and other women appear to have been prominent in churches that met in their homes (Romans 16:3–5; Acts 16:13–15, 40). This implies that despite the male-dominated leadership culture of the day, the Christian church had begun to challenge this assumption.

### Biblical principles of leadership at work

It is not possible to take the biblical material on leadership structures or styles and use it as an exact blueprint for either church leadership or leadership at work today. The world of the Bible represents many different cultures and, as in the world today, different styles of leadership may be appropriate in different settings. However, there are certain principles and qualities that stand out as characteristic of Christian leadership. What Philip King says of church leadership can be applied to Christians in wider leadership: 'Our task ... is to fashion forms of leadership that are consonant as far as possible with the culture of the day but are also consonant with those universal Christian principles by which culture is to be modified and purified' (1987: 48–49). Jesus did this by turning his back on the authoritarian and status-driven styles of leadership of his day and instead advocated a servant style. Such principles include the following:

- Leadership is to be characterized by serving.
- Leading is one function among others that have to be performed as a group attempts to achieve a particular goal. Its function is more important than the office, status or position often attached to it. Hence it can be performed from different points in an organization, not just the top.
- Leaders are to provide vision, direction, oversight and care.
- Leadership is to be shared.
- Leaders are to enable others to perform their functions, and where possible to delegate tasks that enable others to develop and grow.
- Leaders are to set an example by their own character and conduct.
- Leaders include both men and women.
- Leadership structures and styles can be varied and flexible, fit for the purpose, meeting the needs of the task appropriately within their own cultural setting.
- Leaders are accountable to those whom they serve, and ultimately to God.

## Leading through serving

Many of the aspects of leadership described at the beginning of this chapter can be illustrated by biblical examples, suggesting that they each highlight something of the enigma of leadership. In the Old Testament, charismatic leaders are shown as changing the course of Israel's history. It is difficult to pinpoint specific personality types as correlating with good leadership, but the most effective leaders appear to be those who are open to God and empowered by his Spirit. Being trustworthy, just, wise and courageous are some of the characteristics needed. In the New Testament, leadership is described as a gift, implying that it is a quality with which a person is endowed, or perhaps one that is granted for a particular task. In the former sense it can be a character trait that someone can develop; we call such people 'born leaders'. Those who have this gift are to 'govern diligently' (Romans 12:6–8).

A variety of leadership styles can be seen in the Bible, sometimes connected to personality traits (the enthusiasm of Peter's leadership, connected to his apparently impetuous personality), sometimes to the situation (compare Jesus' autocratic style in clearing the temple with his participative style in teaching the disciples, often by example).

Jesus was able to hold together the 'task versus people' dilemma of leadership. He had a definite mission and there were tasks within it from which he would not be deterred. Yet he always found time for people (those in his own team, and those to whom his ministry was directed) as he pursued his mission. How are these held together? By the concept of leadership through serving. In task-accomplishment, such leadership is serving God; in concern for people, it is serving those whom God has created and loves. Sometimes we hear people in high office speak of their leadership role as service to the organization, community or country. What they mean is 'serving through leading'; service in some form is an outcome of their leadership role (usually a role of high status and much vested power). The New Testament emphasis is on 'leading through serving', where serving is the means of leadership as well as its goal. Richard Foster expresses it like this: 'Our leadership flows out of servanthood; our first and primary drive is to serve, and our desire to serve motivates us to lead' (1985: 229).

Leaders inspire people towards a goal by exercising a range of functions relating to both the task and the people involved in it. Christians are to work out biblical servant-leadership in each of these functions, as shown in the diagram.

### Bringing direction and vision

To lead is to show the way, to give direction, to bring vision. It requires an understanding of what the end product is, or at least what it might be, and having a strategy to achieve it. John Stott describes it as 'a deep dissatisfaction with what *is*, and a clear grasp of what *could be*' (1999: 423). It means having an overview that looks beyond the day-to-day, and the ability to define clear objectives to move towards the goal. Objectives and strategy emphasize the 'task' side of leadership. No-one can be a leader unless others follow. To fulfil a corporate task efficiently and well requires everyone involved to catch the vision and become committed to it, and therefore motivated to achieve it. To bring this about, a leader needs to inspire people by communicating clearly and by winning their trust and respect. Leaders who stand out in this regard can paint a picture of their aim and, despite obstacles, lead others towards it. Martin Luther King's 'I have a dream' speech is a wonderful example of inspiring others through powerful communication linked to his individual stature.

# Functions of leadership

WHAT LEADERS *DO:*

Inspire people ...

... towards a goal

The Christian qualities of faith, hope and perseverance are pertinent to nurturing a vision: faith enough to take the first steps towards it, hope that enables us to hold on to the vision despite setbacks, and perseverance to keep at it despite opposition until it is realized. These are the Christian equivalents of the 'toughness' described by John Adair earlier in this chapter, enabling leaders to hold the vision in a firm but Christian way.

Many of the leaders in the Bible had a clear vision of their task (for instance Moses, Exodus 3; Isaiah, Isaiah 6) with which they inspired others, bringing direction and purpose. Jesus had a clear view of his mission (Luke 4:18–21), and a certain knowledge of where it must take him (Luke 9:18–22; 18:31–34). While the disciples did not then understand the full extent of his mission, his strong sense of purpose and the way he communicated it to them inspired them to follow him. He obviously believed passionately in the vision and pursued it with enthusiasm and commitment. The belief that what one is doing is worthwhile becomes contagious.

Bringing direction and vision as a servant means building and shaping a vision through dialogue, enabling others to follow through listening to them and allowing the vision to become *their* vision. Jesus communicated his vision, listening and responding to the concerns of his listeners, often using parables which left the listeners to draw their own conclusions. In work, direction and vision can originate from corporate strategy, or be generated by the leader, or come from within a team, or spring from a mixture of these. The more people are involved in the shaping of a vision, the more committed to it they will be. For Christians, it is important to test any vision that we propagate or follow for consistency with Christian principles.

In whichever way the vision originates, it is vital that the leader and the team own it as theirs. This is why communication and dialogue are such important elements of leadership. We don't have to be a Martin Luther King; there are many ways to communicate, and even Moses needed help in communicating his vision (Exodus 4:10–17). Communication does not stop with the vision, but needs to characterize its implementation and the culture of the team; it is a key way of showing respect for people, of involving them, and of getting them to contribute and share their feelings and views. Keeping the messages simple and memorable helps. Vision needs to be translated into challenging, achievable and measurable goals. It is essential to align everyone's individual goals with the overall vision, so that everyone's contribution is consistent with and complementary to it – so that everyone is rowing in the same direction.

Visionary leadership entails demonstrating by example as well as telling in words. A servant leader 'must be a playing captain and not just a coach who shouts from the touchline' (King 1987: 130). Jesus often led the disciples by example (e.g. in serving, John 13:15; in sacrificial love, 15:12–13; in suffering, Luke 9:23; in ministry, John 14:12). Paul saw that the example he set was an important part of his leadership (Acts 20:33–35), and he exhorted others to lead by example (1 Timothy 3:1–7; 4:12). Primarily, leaders should exemplify integrity of life; the Bible stresses trustworthiness, honesty and dependability above particular skills. Characteristics such as self-discipline and commitment are also important. The way we go about our work and the commitment we show towards it will set the tone for the work of others.

### Enabling others

Leadership exercised through serving will enable others to use and develop their gifts in the achievement of work goals. The biblical model of the human body as a picture of the church powerfully illustrates that the gifts and abilities of each are needed if the whole is to function effectively (1 Corinthians 12:12–26). An organization works best when the potential of its people is released, a fact emphasized in many of the 'cultural change' programmes under way in many companies. The biblical model lists leadership as one function among others (Romans 12:4–8); it stands not necessarily above, but alongside, assisting other functions to play their part. Just as Jesus identified himself with his disciples (in fact, with the whole of humanity), putting aside the status and privilege of a leadership position, servant-leaders are to identify themselves with those whom they lead. Industrial structures may place people in hierarchies related to levels of responsibility (though delayering in many organizations is beginning to change this), and place much weight on senior management positions. But this does not preclude identifying with those led and thereby serving them. Many enlightened managers have rediscovered this truth through approaches such as 'managing by walkabout', or by simply rolling up their sleeves and getting involved in the day-to-day work when required.

Delegation (asking others to do a task on your behalf) and empowerment (handing over a task so that it becomes theirs) are other ways of enabling others (see chapter 3). Both need care. People need to be challenged, but should not be given too difficult a task, or have unwanted tasks pushed on them. The task needs to be clearly explained, responsibilities and accountabilities clarified, training and support provided, and some reviews of progress built in. The leader can confidently delegate and empower if he or she knows that people understand the vision and know the boundaries within which they can operate. My boss Robin said to me a number of times, 'It's my job to create the *space* in which you can do what you are good at.' He gave the overall direction and set the boundaries, but within them he gave me freedom and his delegated authority to be creative. He used his influence to protect the space within which I worked.

Delegating to and empowering others often involves leaders in a teaching or coaching role. 'Coaching' is the fashionable term, suggesting a friend alongside rather than a guru above. What is important is the imparting of knowledge and experience when the person is receptive to them, usually when he or she is close to the task and its problems. When Jesus demonstrated his servanthood to his disciples by washing their feet, he also described himself as their 'Teacher' (John 13:14–15). Like a coach alongside, he was unselfish in passing on to them his knowledge, to the extent that he could say: 'I no longer call you servants, because a servant does not know his master's business. Instead, I have called you friends, for everything that I learned from my Father I have made known to you' (John 15:15).

## Caring for people

I first came across Chris when he was chief geologist. I remembered him because he took an interest in me and what I was working on, and called me by my Christian name. Years later, when I came to work in an organization in which he was chief executive, his first words to me were, 'Hello, Peter.' He was responsible for an organization of several hundred operating in many countries, but he had remembered my name. In fact, as I soon found out, he made time for people, held regular communication meetings which were recorded so that those working elsewhere could be kept informed, always ensured that his staff were treated fairly, and insisted that his management team put development of their people high on the agenda. A colleague said of him, 'He is the sort of leader people will walk through fire for.' And we did.

To be a leader of others also means carrying responsibility for them. This is often formalized in management roles through reporting relationships, but it is implicit in any leadership role. If people follow you, you have some responsibility for where and how you lead them. The Bible illustrates this side of leadership using the picture of the *shepherd*. In the Old Testament, God is described as a shepherd (Ezekiel 34; Psalm 23), and Jesus took on a similar mantle, describing himself as the 'good shepherd' (John 10:1–18). Jesus commissioned Peter to lead the embryonic church with the words, 'Take care of my sheep' (John 21:16). Elsewhere in the New Testament, church leaders are exhorted to be shepherds (e.g. 1 Peter 5:1–4), and Paul was no exception. Despite his missionary task and its challenges, his pastoral concern weighed heavily on him: 'Besides everything else, I face daily the pressure of my concern for all the churches' (2 Corinthians 11:28). 'The ministry of seeking, healing and watching over others is the essence of servant leadership' (King 1987: 129).

Shepherding can be seen as an antiquated, agricultural picture of leadership; the dictatorial leadership of weak and foolish sheep. But the metaphor is focused not so much on the character of the sheep as on the shepherd, who has to fulfil a demanding and hazardous role. As well as providing direction, he has to go in search of those who are lost or in danger. It requires courage to protect those being led, and compassion to care for their needs. This is the 'people' side of leadership *par excellence.* Courage in leadership at work is shown in willingness to tackle difficult situations such as disciplining poor work, or handling redundancies, and in standing up for your team against injustice or to champion their view. It can also take courage to admit you are wrong. Compassion is shown in concern for the well-being of others: getting to know and appreciate them as individuals, being aware of their concerns, and treating them with love, fairness and respect. 'In everything, do to others what you would have them do to you' (Matthew 7:12).

The Old Testament underlines the responsibility of those in positions of authority and power to protect the vulnerable; in fact, their performance will be measured by how well they do this (Proverbs 31:8–9; Zechariah 7:9–14; Psalm 72:1–4). My boss Lyn stood up for me when something I had done had angered a senior manager. She not only argued my case; she took the invective that had been directed at me, despite the risk to her own reputation and standing. Jesus spoke of the self-sacrificial role of a leader: the good shepherd is willing to lay down his life for the sheep (John 10:11). Paul spoke of being 'poured out like a drink offering' through his service to the church (Philippians 2:17).

Leaders have a duty to protect people by being champions of good working conditions, fair pay and appropriate training, and by creating an environment in which people do not overwork. Whether or not these produce more highly motivated employees and a more impressive bottom line, they constitute the right way to treat the people whom God has given into our care in the work setting.

Some argue that work organizations are not set up to provide pastoral care. In fact, many companies bring in external counsellors to help staff with personal problems, or to face major change such as redundancy. They can be appropriate when independent and professional help are needed. However, there exists the danger that many leaders abdicate their 'shepherd' role and neglect to treat people as whole beings, seeing them simply as resources from which work is to be extracted. A platoon leader in the forces has a mission to accomplish, but he knows that it is to the peril of all if he neglects the care and morale of his soldiers.

### Making decisions and being accountable

Good leaders involve their team in decision-making, delegating to or empowering others when there is the opportunity to do so. However, leaders also need to be able to make decisions when required, and to be accountable for them. A leader who puts off making decisions, or refuses to decide because there is not enough information (there is never a full data set!), letting events take control by default, does not inspire confidence. Sometimes the decisions to be made are very demanding: making people redundant, resolving conflict, or confronting injustice. In these cases they are often the rightful responsibility of those in leadership, and should not be shirked.

Leaders are accountable for their decisions in their sphere of activity. In industry it may be argued that accountability is too narrowly focused on a few leaders. A chief executive may get all the blame when a company performs poorly, and huge rewards when it does well. Actually the responsibility is far more widely spread, and so should be the accountability. However, at whatever level, there has to be someone with whom the 'buck stops'. As Christians in leadership, we should not try to pass the buck if the accountability is ours. In fact, we are called to go further: to act in a self-sacrificial way by drawing accountability towards ourselves if it means protecting others from unjust treatment. Like Jesus, we can entrust ourselves to God, 'who judges justly' (1 Peter 2:23).

## Stewarding resources

Many leaders in industry would see the managing of resources (money, material and people) as their key role. A Christian view takes this further. Since God is the ultimate source of all the earth's resources, and because he has delegated responsibility to us to subdue the earth and take care of it, stewarding resources is a serious matter. A number of Jesus' parables illuminate what it means to be a good steward (e.g. the talents, Matthew 25:14–30; the shrewd manager, Luke 16:1–12). It entails being faithful and loyal to those in authority (ultimately God), treating those under one's authority well, and using resources prudently to create value.

Leaders in the work setting are responsible both to those who work for them, and to those for whom they work in the stewardship of resources. Finding the balance can be tricky; money spent on training or pay rises for employees has to be balanced with the leader's responsibility to the organization and its shareholders to manage costs and produce a return on investment.

Leading involves bringing vision and direction, motivating, enabling and caring for others, stewarding resources and making decisions. To do this in a Christian way, through serving, means leading by example, valuing the opinions of others, being willing to sacrifice one's own desires for the benefit of others, not being obsessed with one's own status or position, wanting others to grow and flourish, and protecting them from harm, through self-sacrifice if necessary. It requires characteristics such as trustworthiness, fairness, humility, faith, obedience, wisdom, self-discipline, perseverance and openness to God.

## The action column

1.  Think of a good leader you have worked for. What was it about this person's style and character that made you want to work for him or her and that inspired you to do the best you possibly could?
2.  How does your own leadership match up to biblical principles?
3.  As a leader, what functions do you perform best? Think how you could improve in your weaker areas, perhaps through getting some coaching, watching someone else, undergoing leadership training, or gaining specific experience.

# CHAPTER 11

# Reaching for the skies?

*Handling ambition and wealth, status and power*

## Ambition – snake or ladder?

*The desire to achieve*

'Ambitious, resourceful, determined and with the drive and ability to progress to a more senior level' read a job advertisement for a sales and marketing director (*The Daily Telegraph*, 22 April 1999). Organizations are on the look-out for so-called 'ambitious' people because they deem them to be driven to achieve goals and bring the organization success. Ambitious people are viewed in different ways. Many admire them because they appear hard-working and thrusting, they gobble up challenges, and often seem to get what they want. Others view them as self-seeking, even ruthless, to be regarded with suspicion or as a threat.

'You're not ambitious enough,' someone said to me. 'Don't you want the top job?'

I avoided answering the question, not sure if I wanted the top job or not, and hoping to appear modest.

'You're the ambitious sort. What is it you're aiming at?' someone else asked. Obviously, I wasn't modest enough!

What is the Christian view on being ambitious? As Christians, we can struggle with the tension between wanting to do our jobs well and achieve things (which are worthy aims) and wishing to remain modest and unselfish in our attitudes to success and career progression. Is ambition a ladder that helps to fulfil work's purposes for us and achieve our potential, or a snake that appeals to our vain and selfish human nature with the lure of status, power and riches?

This chapter examines what it means to be ambitious, its relation to Christian character, and how to handle position, wealth and power, often viewed as the outward signs of achieving in work.

## Ambition and honour

An 'ardent desire for distinction' is how the *Concise Oxford Dictionary* defines ambition. Being ambitious in work usually means having a strong desire to achieve or succeed, often driven by a future goal. It can be in competition with others, and its success is often measured by an 'onwards and upwards' trajectory, accompanied by the rewards of wealth, status and power. Some Christian traditions view ambition as self-centred and materialistic, whereas others consider prosperity and success as signs of God's approval.

St Thomas Aquinas saw ambition in the context of a desire for honour or recognition, and listed three ways in which such a desire could be excessive: 'one can seek it without deserving it, or without acknowledging God's part in it, or without using it for the good of others. Ambition covers all these types of excessive enterprise, and is clearly sinful' (1991: 424). Instead, he extolled *enterprise* ('thinking big'), a subsidiary virtue of courage, which is also concerned with recognition, but 'not so much with recognition itself as seeking to do things worthy of recognition' (1991: 424). However, if being ambitious is defined broadly as the desire to achieve goals, and involves doing things well to achieve those goals, then it deserves our attention. Granted, if the goals are purely one's own recognition and position, then Aquinas' criticisms need to be heeded. But if the goals are worthy, and if we pursue them with integrity, then being ambitious in this sense is legitimate.

Ambition is often related to achieving distinction or honour. To honour is to appreciate worth or to express esteem for a person or office-holder. Aquinas described honour as 'a certain gracefulness and beauty of spirit' (1991: 428) which 'is owed to people of excellence', especially God, 'whose excellence is unparalleled' (1991: 400). What does the Bible say about honour? The fifth commandment instructs people to honour their parents (Exodus 20:12). This concept is further extended in that honour is to be given to those to whom honour is due (Romans 13:6–7), since all authority ultimately comes from God. Being made in God's image means that all people are worthy of honour in its broadest sense (1 Peter 2:17; Genesis 1:26–27). God desires honour for his people (Deuteronomy 26:19), and, as Barth says, he bestows 'unsurpassable honour' on man by calling him to himself (1961: 648). When someone bestows honour on us, it is a strong motivation to act honourably. Honour in hierarchical societies and institutions (such as the military) has been closely associated with status and position. However, as the Bible passages quoted above show, it is not restricted to this context. In fact, those who expect honour because of their position, but behave dishonourably, are condemned by Jesus as hypocrites (Matthew 23).

If there is a case for honouring people – giving due recognition – what of Aquinas' charge that ambition is sinful because it is the desire for such honour? Ambition falls into error when it leads people to concentrate on themselves to the exclusion or detriment of others. When the statement 'He's very ambitious' is made in a derogatory way, it often describes a person who will stop at nothing to get to the top, even if it means treading on others. This is the 'selfish ambition' Paul instructs us to avoid (Philippians 2:3). For ambition to be righteous, its goals need to be good and aligned with a Christian's overall purpose, and these goals need to be pursued in just and honest ways which show respect for others. To have the ambition to excel at work or to reach a position of influence can have a positive effect on someone's work, providing challenge and purpose. As long as we remain clear about our goals (to work for God's glory, not our own), and go about achieving those goals in a Christian way, ambition can stir us to serve better.

I have a Christian friend who, having worked for thirty years in the same industry, reached a senior position. He was greatly respected by all who worked with him. When I asked him about his career and whether he felt he had achieved what he had set out to achieve, he said he had always worked hard because he saw that as his duty. He didn't mind that he hadn't had the top job, but would have accepted it had it come along. His 'ambition' was always to do his best, rather than to seek honour or position. But both had come his way and he had handled them well.

Receiving due recognition is good when it is not the goal itself but an outcome of pursuing some worthy goal. Many 'great' people view honour in this light. They pursue worthy goals ambitiously, and when they are recognized by others for attaining them, they are often surprised, since they were not seeking such recognition. Honour in this positive sense is good for us as recipients because it affirms us in the work we are doing, raises our self-esteem, and makes us aware that both we and our hard work are appreciated. It is also good for us to bestow honour. Through being generous in praise, appreciating and recognizing the efforts and achievements of others, we reinforce the importance of exemplary acts that teach us how to live godlier lives, as well as encouraging skills development and good performance. This is the essence of constructive feedback, so important for both coaching and motivating.

At the end of the school concert, Mrs Bridge, the head teacher, said: 'What a marvellous performance! Every one of you has played an important role in this. You should be very proud of yourselves. You are all very special.'

The hall erupted in applause. The children beamed and their emotional tanks were fully topped up. To be recognized is powerful medicine.

### The attitude of Christ

Gordon MacDonald draws a distinction, based on Jesus' choosing of his disciples, between those who are *driven* and those who are *called*. (1985: 38–53). He lists the characteristics of driven people, who are gratified by accomplishment, preoccupied with power and status, caught in the pursuit of expansion, highly competitive and abnormally busy. He cites King Saul in the latter years of his career as an example of a driven person who directed all his energies into holding on to his throne. Jesus seems to have avoided those who were driven because they were full of their own plans and objectives, and who used others to achieve them – this is ambition in its vain and selfish sense. Rather, Jesus called those who were drawn to him and, as the martyred theologian Dietrich Bonhoeffer stated; 'When Christ calls a man, he bids him come and die' (1959: 79). This is the calling to humility.

The competencies that organizations desire of their workforce often include being ambitious and having the will to succeed. They tend to look for the type of ambition that focuses on personal success, on the presumption that those driven by the desire for personal success will also meet the organization's objectives. They do not usually look for the quality of *humility*. Yet this is one of the hallmarks of Christian character, in keeping with the fact that service is at the heart of the way Christians are to live and work. It is humility that prevents the legitimate ambition to achieve godly goals from turning into vain ambition.

'Do nothing out of selfish ambition or vain conceit, but in humility consider others better than yourselves,' wrote Paul (Philippians 2:3). He went on to describe the example of Jesus and exhorted the Philippians to have the same attitude as Christ (2:5–11). Jesus took the form of a servant and made a particular point of serving others (e.g. John 13). Humility does not preclude being recognized or ambitious, but it is the opposite of seeking honour for one's own sake, or of pursuing work goals selfishly.

'Blessed are the meek, for they will inherit the earth,' Jesus said (Matthew 5:5). Is humility then a means to an end that is far from humble? Not necessarily, since it is possible and appropriate to be humble even when exalted and honoured. However, we run the risk of taking pride in our humility; it then becomes something else. Elsewhere in the New Testament, humility is praised as a truly Christian quality. Jesus described himself as 'gentle and humble in heart' (Matthew 11:29), and Paul urged the Ephesians to act likewise (Ephesians 4:2). Humility is listed as one of the qualities with which Christians are to clothe themselves (Colossians 3:12), and is conspicuous by its absence from any of the contemporary Greek lists of virtues. Here is a truly distinctive Christian quality.

Not all Christians are of lowly position in earthly terms, but all are called to humble themselves before God, and to follow the example of Christ in practising humility. In work, whatever our position or achievements, we are to reject vain boasting and self-centred pride, remembering that the true source of our abilities and success is God. James links humility to acting wisely, but distinguishes between heavenly and earthly wisdom. Humility comes from heavenly wisdom, whereas 'bitter envy and selfish ambition' are linked to earthly wisdom (James 3:13–16). The contrast is stark; the way of the world which envies the achievements of others and pursues personal success by any means versus the way of Christ, which is 'first of all pure, then peace-loving, considerate, submissive, full of mercy and good fruit, impartial and sincere' (James 3:17).

Sometimes humility gets confused with low self-esteem. But it is not about putting ourselves down, or a false modesty designed to impress others. Rather, it involves raising our evaluation of others (Romans 12:10). True self-esteem comes from the value and worth invested in us by God, not from what we do or have achieved. Paul stated that Christians are to think of themselves (in the sense of their abilities) no more highly than they ought, but with 'sober judgment', openly and honestly (Romans 12:3). We should be realistic and confident about our abilities and achievements, and honest about our shortcomings. Humility does not preclude you displaying confidence in what you can do, or describing your skills and abilities to others. Jesus was not afraid to speak the truth about himself (e.g. John 8:12), or to declare what he could do for people (e.g. Luke 4:18–21; Matthew 11:28-30). Yet despite his divine position and remarkable deeds, he set the example of serving others with humility.

When seeking work, or advertising goods or services, we need to articulate what we have to offer and present ourselves confidently and clearly. There are accepted formats for advertising and for professionally presenting a CV that highlight strengths to best effect; the 'rules of the game' are understood by customers, applicants and employers alike. While it is valid to use these, Christians should do so honestly with no intention to mislead.

Ambition, when directed at worthy goals and pursued with integrity and humility, can help us to serve God better and achieve his purposes in our lives.

## Wealth: treasure-hunting or fair reward?

### *Creating wealth*

Michael Douglas played Gordon Gekko in the 1980s film *Wall Street.* In a powerfully delivered monologue, Gekko espouses the creed that 'Greed is good' since, he reasons, it drives people to achieve. As the morality tale unfolds, his young protégé, played by Charlie Sheen, begins to experience the destructive side of the quest for riches, and expresses his doubts. In a heated discussion he asks Gekko, 'How many yachts can you water-ski behind? How much is enough?' We are left questioning, 'What is it all for?' From parading itself as the elixir of life, wealth is shown to be a hollow thing when it becomes a person's *raison d'être.* Yet in order to live in the world and enjoy its blessings, we need to create and handle wealth.

God has put humankind in a responsible position over the world, requiring us to utilize its resources in good and beneficial ways. One of the outcomes is that through our work we create wealth, although only God truly creates. 'It is true that in a strict sense, talk of *creating* wealth is misleading: God creates the resources, and everything human beings do with them is secondary – what we do is to increase or multiply the wealth' (Higginson 1992: 17). We utilize what God has created by extracting and processing resources and by developing and producing goods and services, and in these senses we 'create' wealth. Not all wealth creation is good, since some products are harmful to people and the environment, and others involve harmful processes or dubious motives.

The wealth that is created through work can be used in opposing ways: it can encourage greed and be distributed in ways which increase division and injustice, or it can be distributed fairly and used to enrich life.

It remains part of our responsibility through work to create wealth. This is how life's necessities are supplied. Kenneth Adams comments on wealth creation: 'Its purpose is nothing less than the good and noble task of eliminating material poverty everywhere' (1991: 5). Work provides for material needs, but also a little more; the wealth it generates gives the opportunity to improve human life, ideally enriching it and making it more satisfying for everyone. The Bible warns of the dangers of wealth, but upholds God's wonderful provision of the world for us to enjoy, celebrate and delight in, since 'The earth is the LORD's, and everything in it' (Psalm 24:1).

## Loads of money versus treasure in heaven

Wealth offers trappings which can ensnare. Some organizations use large salaries and perks to recruit people, financial incentives such as big bonuses to motivate them, and 'golden handcuffs' of various types – stock options, pension schemes, the promise of large severance packages – to retain them. Such an approach can encourage the belief that money and material benefits create happiness. People want not the promise of treasure in heaven, but treasure now, in exchange for selling their soul to the organization. The monetary and material rewards of work can become today's equivalents of the golden idols of the Old Testament, and they are worshipped with no less devotion. To God, their worship is just as idolatrous.

The Bible has a lot to say about wealth, because the way we handle it has an impact on our relationship with God. Wealth is not to become our master, since we 'cannot serve both God and Money' (Matthew 6:24). The 'love of money' is described as 'a root of all kinds of evil' as it lays us open to temptations and harmful desires, and it has the potential to corrupt and ruin us (1 Timothy 6:6–10). The Old Testament prophets attack the rich who oppress the poor (Amos 2:6–7; 4:1–3), and this theme is taken up by New Testament writers (James 5:1–6; 1 Timothy 6:3–10, 17–19). To chase after riches, to put one's trust in wealth or to neglect the needy will bring disaster and condemnation (Proverbs 11:28; 28:20; Luke 12:16–21; 16:19–31). Jesus said it was difficult for the rich to enter God's kingdom (Matthew 19:23–26) because material wealth easily usurps the place of God in our lives. Who hasn't thought, 'I wonder what it would be like to win the lottery?' Of course, we reason, 'I would give it all away ... well, most of it.' A Christian's heart is to be set on God and eternal things, free from the love of money (Matthew 6:19–21; Hebrews 13:5).

However, 'It is not possessing riches that God condemns but clinging to them, coveting them and centring our lives around them' (Tondeur 1996: 15). Without conceding to those who subscribe to a 'prosperity theology' (that there is a direct correlation between a life pleasing to God and the accumulation of wealth), it is important not to decry productive work that results in wealth. The Bible describes the relation of honest and hard work to provision, even abundance (e.g. Proverbs 12:11; 14:23). At the same time the Bible denounces idleness (Proverbs 18:9; 19:15; 2 Thessalonians 3:6–13), and the squandering of the abilities and gifts God has given us (Matthew 25:14–30) as practices that can bring self-inflicted poverty. In some passages, there is an implied or explicit link between righteousness and blessing (Proverbs 21:21; 22:4), even material wealth.

God does bless some in this way, but, as Christians, we are not guaranteed a prosperous life, and prosperity is not necessarily a sign of God's approval. Neither have the poor necessarily displeased God. Blessing may come in material forms. If it does, we are to be grateful, just and generous, and to realize that we will be held accountable for what we have been given. We may find ourselves undergoing suffering or persecution, in which case we are assured of God's concern; where there is disadvantage, poverty, injustice or oppression there is a 'divine bias to the poor' (Sheppard 1983: 10). As Sir Fred Catherwood states, 'Some Christians will be rich for a few years here and some will be poor, some will be honoured in society and others will be killed' (1987: 140). Whatever happens, we are to find contentment, knowing that we can cope with, and live morally and justly in, all circumstances, because God is our strength. 'I have learned the secret of being content in any and every situation, whether well fed or hungry, whether living in plenty or in want. I can do everything through him who gives me strength' (Philippians 4:12–13).

Work *is* a source of wealth, but if we are to avoid the love of money, work is not to be viewed as merely a tool to create more and more wealth. To meet our material needs and a little more is certainly a purpose of work, but is not its *only* goal. Because work can yield virtually unlimited wealth in a capitalist system, wealth can easily become our master, thus influencing our choice of job (the one with the highest salary), the decisions we make in work (to increase profits and decrease costs, whatever the effects on people, in order to benefit our own personal wealth), the way we treat others (as means to generate profit); and, ultimately, our character (we become greedy, selfish and acquisitive). How are we to avoid entrapment in the Aladdin's cave of personal gain? The biblical approach is to handle wealth *justly*, *generously* and *gratefully*, and thereby to recognize that wealth is a gift of God's creation, to be earned fairly and used responsibly, as well as appreciated and enjoyed.

Fundamental to handling wealth in a distinctively Christian way – and it will be distinctive in a world bent on materialism – is to acknowledge that it all belongs to God: 'Recognizing God's ownership of everything is a key element in allowing Jesus to become the Lord of our money and possessions' (Tondeur 1996: 6–7). This means *all* of our wealth, not only the part we label 'giving'. Such an attitude enables us to hold our wealth lightly and to fulfil our role as stewards of what God has given. We are stewards of the world and its resources, of the time and talents given to us, and of the wealth that God allows us to control.

## Handling wealth justly

How should the wealth created through work be handled? The capitalist system is viewed by many as the most efficient in encouraging wealth creation, yet it tends to distribute wealth unevenly. Shareholders and directors often benefit in a disproportionately high way and, as Richard Higginson points out, 'personal affluence is the inevitable side-product of utilizing certain sorts of talent in a capitalist system concerned with the creation of wealth' (1992: 17). Socialist (and communist) alternatives which have attempted to enforce a more even distribution have largely failed, amid charges of stifling initiative and squandering resources. In a market economy, wage levels are mainly determined by scarcity, and the sky has become the limit for some senior executives who, like film stars and professional footballers, are able to earn vast sums. The reward given to people in the caring professions, where making a profit is not the purpose of the enterprise, also needs consideration. And what of work of a voluntary nature: caring for an elderly relative, or raising children?

The Christian principle of *justice* is important in the distribution of wealth. Justice makes us question what it is that we reward. Is the reward itself fair? Are people able to share in the outcomes of the enterprise? How are differences in pay justified?

# Handling wealth justly, generously, gratefully

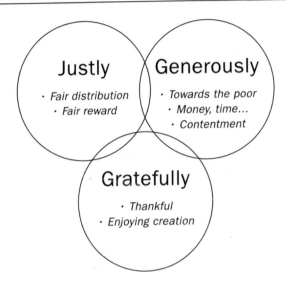

First, *what is rewarded?* Fair reward for work needs to reflect both the *inputs* that a person brings to the job (time and skills) and the *outputs* of the job (quality and achievements). The balance between these elements depends on the job. For a doctor, extensive training, specialist knowledge and expert skills will be major factors. For a factory worker, the important things are skills, time worked and productivity. The main factors to consider are as follows:

- *Time:* hours worked need to be compensated for, but hours expended do not necessarily mean that a person has worked efficiently or well.
- *Training and expertise:* the education, skills and abilities a person brings to the job.
- *Individual contribution and effort:* the energy and commitment brought to the job, and how contribution relates to ability.
- *Quality of work:* the standard of the product or service and of its production or delivery.
- *Objectives met:* how well the employee achieves what is required through meeting targets, timelines, budgets and so on.

Secondly, *is the reward for the work done fair?* A 'fair day's work for a fair day's pay' is in line with the biblical principle that a 'worker deserves his wages' (Luke 10:7). If justice is to be served, work done should be rewarded. Defining what is fair, in a world where a day's pay in the developed world can equate to a month's back-breaking labour in the developing world, is perplexing. For better or worse, the capitalist system results in a market for a particular job or skill: the amount society is willing to pay. One way of defining a fair day's pay is therefore to compare it with the going rate for others doing the same or similar work. This can help, but the results need to be treated with caution, as markets are influenced by many factors, and many jobs are in sectors where the 'market' is determined by government policy (e.g. health workers), which are subject to public-sector wage restraints.

The market approach cannot therefore be left alone to decide what is just. As Charles Handy comments, 'The market is a mechanism for sorting the efficient from the inefficient, it is not a substitute for responsibility' (1994: 15). Other questions to be considered are:

- Does the reward earned enable a person to make a reasonable living?
- Does it reflect the training, skills and experience brought to bear?
- Is it commensurate with the effort employed and the hours worked?
- Is it fair when compared to others doing similar work?
- Would I do this work for the reward it yields?

Thirdly, *is there opportunity to share in the success of the enterprise?* 'Do not muzzle the ox while it is treading out the grain', Paul exhorted Timothy with reference to the treatment of elders in the church (1 Timothy 5:18, quoting Deuteronomy 25:4). This principle establishes that those engaged in work should be allowed to share in the results of their labour. 'The hardworking farmer should be the first to receive a share of the crops' (2 Timothy 2:6) conveys a similar principle.

In agrarian societies, the link between work and material reward is direct. Crops provide food, or income when sold. In industrial societies, where people sell their labour, this link is often lost. The reward comes through remuneration rather than from sharing the products, and most of the wealth generated goes to the organization and its shareholders. Nevertheless, the principle of allowing those who partake in the enterprise to share in its success can still be upheld. Schemes that encourage employee share ownership, or that pay bonuses when the company performs well, can be appropriate ways of doing this. They can also have a positive effect on the enterprise: employees feel more closely aligned with its goals. If these schemes are to be truly just, however, there must be a real sharing of the success, not just a token gesture while the real profits go to senior executives and large shareholders. And, as in any financial matters, there is the danger that such schemes will slip from 'just reward' to an appeal to greed (as discussed in chapter 5).

Many organizations are making a higher proportion of pay 'variable' and dependent on the success or otherwise of the business. This carries the danger of eroding basic wages so that employees have less that they can count on as regular income. While it is fair that the outcomes of an enterprise (good and bad) should be reflected in the rewards given to those engaged in it, this must be balanced with the principle that 'the worker deserves his wages'.

Finally, *what are the criteria for justifying differences in pay?* There are good and just reasons for pay differentials between individuals and groups. However, there comes a point on the scale of differentiation when the argument of justice begins to cut the other way. For the managing director to earn ten times more than the shop-floor worker may be justifiable, given the differences in the roles, but to earn several hundred times more is open to question, and needs to be judged against such criteria as

- job responsibility and size, and accountability;
- knowledge, experience, skills and ability brought to the job;
- hours worked and effort expended;
- performance in the job and results achieved; and
- hardship of working conditions or danger.

Differences in pay between those with the same skills but working in different sectors are more difficult to justify. Why should accountants working in the building industry be paid far less than their counterparts in the City? There may be various reasons, such as profitability, an organization's ability to pay, or higher risk. But the root of such differentiation lies in the capitalist market system, which prices jobs primarily on scarcity or financial value. In such a system, this cross-sector differentiation will persist, although it often needs challenging, particularly in support of workers in sectors who have little control over their pay (for instance, in the public and voluntary sectors).

The 'market' is also used to justify the increasingly high salaries which companies claim they have to pay their senior executives to get the right people into these top jobs. Principles of justice need to be applied at both ends of the pay market, so that the low-paid are not exploited, and so that the highly paid cannot be accused of being 'fat cats', warranting a rebuke like that delivered to the 'cows of Bashan' (Amos 4:1).

## Handling wealth generously

The Old Testament commands *generosity* towards the poor (Deuteronomy 15:1–11) and this is emphasized in many aspects of the Mosaic law, including the giving of tithes, interest-free loans to the needy, not reaping the fields to the very edges, and not gathering the gleanings after harvesting. The wisdom literature holds up such generosity as a characteristic of a righteous person (Proverbs 14:21; 21:13; 22:9). Paul said about the rich: 'Command them to do good, to be rich in good deeds, and to be generous and willing to share' (1 Timothy 6:18). To those whose special ministry is contributing to the needs of others, Paul said they should give generously (Romans 12:8). Such generosity was demonstrated within and between the New Testament churches (Acts 2:44–45; 2 Corinthians 8:2). Generously sharing wealth will inevitably result in a limiting, even lowering, of our own standards of living so that the poverty of others can be alleviated. This generosity finds its basis in a generous God (Romans 8:32) and has love as its motivation (1 John 3:17–18). It is to be undertaken voluntarily (2 Corinthians 8:12; 9:7) and sacrificially (2 Corinthians 8:2–3; Mark 12:41–44). And there is a wonderful principle built into the Bible's approach to generosity: those who give will not go without. 'He who gives to the poor will lack nothing' (Proverbs 28:27).

Generous giving is not a duty of the rich alone, but is expected of all Christians as they are able. One way of resisting secular patterns of acquisition is to give proportionally more as income rises, which takes one beyond a legalistic interpretation of the Old Testament concept of tithing. This is to live with 'enough' rather than 'excess'. In giving, 'We are trustees of our income and capital for Christ and when we look at it to see what is due each year, we should look with the careful eyes of trustees, making absolutely sure that we are caring for the true interests of the real owner, who has given us his trust' (Catherwood 1987: 153–154). While we are not to give because it brings reward, blessing in one form or another (not necessarily material) is nevertheless an outcome of generous giving (Proverbs 22:9; Luke 6:38; Malachi 3:10).

You may say, 'But I don't earn a fortune. I can barely make ends meet as it is.' There are opportunities to be generous other than financially. Some good friends of ours express their generosity through wonderful hospitality for which they are renowned; examples of this are found in the New Testament (e.g. Lydia, Acts 16:13–15; Priscilla and Aquilla, Acts 18:1–3, 26). Possessions can be shared so that a wide circle of people can benefit. The giving of time, energy and expertise is often viewed as secondary to financial giving, yet it can be more effective and more demanding.

Organizations too are called to be generous, not only to enhance their reputation but because they have a moral responsibility towards the people they employ, the communities in which they operate, their shareholders and other stakeholders. They can express generosity through granting opportunities for training and jobs, paying fair wages, sharing in the success of the enterprise, providing adequate redundancy pay and retraining opportunities if work disappears, investing in the community, giving to charities and so on.

For those who strive after wealth, contentment is elusive. Yet those whose lives are focused on God, who are generous and willing to share, find contentment because they 'take hold of the life that is truly life' (1 Timothy 6:19). Contentment comes through trusting in God's love and provision (Hebrews 13:5–6), so that we can hold material things lightly and learn to be content whether in plenty or in need (Philippians 4:11–13). John V. Taylor uses the word 'simplicity' to describe the kind of life characterized by generosity and contentment. 'Our enemy is not possessions but excess. Our battle-cry is not "Nothing!" but "Enough!"' (1975: 82). Paul says that 'godliness with contentment is great gain. For we brought nothing into the world, and we can take nothing out of it. But if we have food and clothing, we will be content with that' (1 Timothy 6:6–8).

### Being grateful

Peter showed us the absurdity of the way we talk about things we have spent money on and enjoyed. 'When someone asks us about our holiday in Florida,' he said, 'we say how great it was, then quickly add how cheaply we got the flights, or what a good package deal it was, and how next year we will self-cater.'

There is a lot of guilt among Christians concerning the possession and use of wealth. This is not surprising, given the inequalities and need we see around us: the person we pass in the High Street, who is sleeping rough; the family next door who lose their home because of redundancy; the grinding poverty of people in lands struck by conflict,

206 *All the hours God sends?*

famine or disaster. These needs are real enough, and the Lord requires us to handle wealth justly and generously with regard to them. But to leave it there misses out an essential element of biblical teaching. We are also to recognize that the treasures of the world come from God; as the hymn goes, 'All good gifts around us are sent from heaven above.' So we are to be grateful for them, to celebrate them and to enjoy them. 'He is not ordering us to live a life of poverty, He is challenging us to live a life of obedience and gratitude' (Tondeur 1996: 11).

The Old Testament speaks of a fellowship offering of thanksgiving (Leviticus 7:11–13), and the Psalms encourage us to 'give thanks to the LORD', a theme picked up by the New Testament, which instructs us to be thankful and to pray with thanksgiving (Colossians 3:15; Philippians 4:6). How would you feel if every time you gave your children Christmas presents, they spent the rest of the year feeling guilty? Thankfulness, not guilt, is the appropriate response to good gifts.

In chapter 2, I emphasized the importance of rest and showed how biblical rest includes celebration. The Bible particularly stresses the importance of celebration and festivity as ways of commemorating God's deeds and goodness. And as Jesus showed in his reaction to Mary's gift of expensive perfume, it is sometimes appropriate to mark significant occasions without regard for the cost. 'It was intended that she should save this perfume for the day of my burial. You will always have the poor among you, but you will not always have me' (John 12:7–8). We are to celebrate good things; the fruit of our labours is worth celebrating.

While self-sacrifice and service characterize the Christian life, the Bible portrays the beauty and abundance of creation as something for us to enjoy (e.g. Genesis 2:9, Psalm 104). Jesus endorsed this principle through his desire that people should live life to the full (John 10:10), by the way he shared his own joy (Luke 10:21; John 15:11), and by the way he enjoyed wining and dining in the company of others (Luke 7:33–34). When Jesus turned water into wine at Cana, no doubt it sent a spiritual message to his disciples about his identity, but it also enabled the guests to continue enjoying the wedding party (John 2:1–11). 'At the heart of God's creation is something extravagant and gratuitous, going beyond what is strictly needed for survival' (Ryken 1989: 188). Creation has the potential to yield more than is required for our basic needs, and when this happens we should not feel guilty, but enjoy it.

In his letter to Timothy, Paul captures the balance we need to apply. Rather than putting their hope in wealth, the rich are 'to put their hope in God, who richly provides us with everything for our enjoyment', and 'to do good, to be rich in good deeds, and to be generous and willing to share' (1 Timothy 6:17–18). Justice, generosity and enjoyment are woven together when it comes to handling wealth.

## Position: secular status or God-given authority?

### The thickness of the carpet

A senior manager joined the team. 'Where's my office?' he asked.

His colleague, also a senior executive, pointed to a desk in the corner of the open-plan area.

'I'm not sitting there,' the manager protested. 'I should have an office.'

'Well,' his colleague responded, 'if you want to discuss it with the boss, he sits on the end over there.' The boss was a company director and shared the open-plan space.

There was a time when status at work was indicated by visible signs such as one's own office, having tea brought on a tray and the thickness of the carpet. Everyone deferred to the boss, and did what he (there were few women in such positions then) said. Times are changing, but status and its symbols still tug at us, and we feel cheated if they are taken away.

The disciples argued about who among them would be the greatest. Position, and the status and respect it would bring, were important to them. Jesus brought a child before them to illustrate that greatness comes through humble service, not through position (Luke 9:46–48). He did not deny the need for some people to be in positions of authority over others. Speaking of his own position, he said: 'You call me "Teacher" and "Lord", and rightly so, for that is what I am' (John 13:13). But, for Jesus, the emphasis was on the function rather than the position, and this is shown by his desire to serve. This is the pattern for Christian roles in the church, including leadership; the function, not the status, is emphasized (see chapter 10).

The Bible recognizes that if people are to live together in society, it is necessary that some should be in positions of authority. The way authority is established and upheld varies greatly across time and place; leaders can be warrior kings, hereditary monarchs, emperors, dictators or democratically elected politicians. In work organizations, positions of authority range from supervisors and team leaders to managers and executives, with chief executives, directors and chairpersons in the upper echelons. With position comes power (the topic of the next section). But position itself deserves some attention. I said earlier that the Bible upholds the principle of honouring the good and those who earn our respect. But what of those who are placed in authority over us in work? What if, instead of rising to their position by merit, they have been elevated for some other reason (being godson of the chief executive, or skilled at 'looking good' in front of the boss)? What if they are less able than we, or make decisions with which we disagree? How are Christians to treat those in authority over them?

The Bible teaches that we are to submit to those in authority over us for one very good reason: because God has established such authority. 'Everyone must submit himself to the governing authorities, for there is no authority except that which God has established. The authorities that exist have been established by God. Consequently, he who rebels against the authority is rebelling against what God has instituted, and those who do so will bring judgment on themselves' (Romans 13:1–2). Paul goes on to say that this is why we pay taxes (an echo of Jesus' comment to 'Give to Caesar what is Caesar's and to God what is God's'; Mark 12:17); the authorities are God's servants. What if they do wrong? Well, they are accountable to God, and just as God has established them and gives them their authority, he can take it away. As Isaiah reminded the Jewish exiles, 'He brings princes to naught and reduces the rulers of this world to nothing'; to him, 'the nations are like a drop in a bucket' (Isaiah 40:23, 15). Whether the authority is vested in kings reigning in God's name, like the Old Testament kings, or in rulers of godless nations, such as Cyrus (Isaiah 45:1), God can use them for his purposes.

The Bible makes it clear that such submission is applicable to work as well as government. 'Slaves, obey your earthly masters in everything; and do it, not only when their eye is on you and to win their favour, but with sincerity of heart and reverence for the Lord' (Colossians 3:22). Just as work is to be done well because it is service to God, masters (bosses) are to be obeyed because in submitting to them, we are submitting to the Lord. We are to do this not just to look good when the boss is around, but loyally and sincerely because we are really serving Christ himself (verse 24). This requires obedience – not a popular concept in the empowered workplace of today, or in a society where few people hold to absolutes and where values are relativized.

But what about when the boss gets it wrong? Or if we are asked to do something we think is unwise, or downright unethical? Paul tells

Titus to 'Remind the people to be subject to rulers and authorities, to be obedient, to be ready to do whatever is good' (Titus 3:1). The call to obedience is qualified by the phrase 'to do whatever is good'. When we are asked to do something which is clearly wrong, we should refuse or suggest an alternative approach. If it is something unwise, we are right to question or, when appropriate, challenge. But as Mark Greene points out, 'unless some more important principle is being flouted, we are to obey our boss' (1997: 115–116).

Part of the challenge for Christians who reach influential positions is managing the status that comes along with it. It so easily panders to our pride and vanity. 'Look at how important I am now.' *Not* being promoted can also cause us problems. On two occasions I have been denied promotion at the time *I* thought it was due. Whether the denial was justified or not, I quickly found myself concocting articulate arguments to the effect that I had been poorly treated, and getting belligerent about taking my case higher. What lay behind my reaction? Some injustice, possibly, but it was more about my hurt pride and comparison of myself with (envy of?) others.

The other great challenge of position is handling power.

## Power: road to corruption or force for good?

### *The means to make things happen*

Work gives people power – power to create and change things, power to transfer vast amounts of money at the press of a computer key, power to influence markets and materials, power over products and people. Organizations concentrate this power as a lens focuses the light of the sun, so that it can be used to embark on enterprises of mind-blowing size and complexity, to change the consumer habits of millions of people, and to create hundreds of jobs or discard them just as quickly. Some organizations are more powerful than sovereign states in the resources they can bring to bear, the projects they can undertake and the lives they can affect. The market capitalization of Microsoft is $476 billion; it dominates the software used in computers the world over, and has an effect on nearly every business and home that has a computer. It must be scary to head such a vast organization. The few times in my working life I have had direct power over people or funds, I have felt its pull. It inflates you and beguiles you into thinking it is something to do with your own identity and ability – as if somehow *you* have generated it. If you cannot persuade people by sound argument or good influence, power tempts you to take the easy way; you just order them to do what you want. But it also enables you to change things. Is power, then, the road to corruption or a force for good?

Power is the capacity to effect intended results, the means to make things happen. God is himself all-powerful (Matthew 26:64), and he shares some of his power with us to fulfil the task of subduing the earth. It can be used responsibly in the service of God and others, and in the care of the world, or for selfish, evil ends. Power can corrupt, but refusing to use power can have negative effects too, since 'By using power humans order their common life, specify the goals of society and distribute its goods. Not to share in power means not to share in the life of the community' (Cox, in Macquarrie and Childress 1986: 490).

The New Testament invites Christians to be filled with God's power by the Holy Spirit (Romans 15:13; Ephesians 3:16–19). Such power not only fosters appreciation of God and his love, but also helps us to live for him in the world and stand against evil powers (Ephesians 6:10–13), which can be embedded in the social structures of human life including work organizations (Dow 1979: 20–24).

## Types of power

Five types of power have been identified in the work setting (French & Raven, in Statt 1994: 33).

- *Legitimate power* derives from a person's role; it is the authority to sign cheques, allocate resources, make decisions, or say, 'Do this because I'm the boss.'
- *Reward power* is the ability to give people a pay rise or recognize their efforts in some way, to give them a promotion or put in a good word that will help their progression.
- *Coercive power*, the twin of reward power, is the power to drop people off the project, dock their pay, halt their career, or fire them.
- *Expert power* is based on the possession of knowledge or skills highly valued by others. 'I know most about this, so you had better heed what I say.'
- *Referent power* derives from an individual's personality, integrity or charisma, which inspires affection and loyalty and thus enables him or her to exercise an influence over others.

In the working world, power is often associated with position – *legitimate power*. It may be the power of a worker over his or her tasks for the day, or the power wielded by a chief executive who controls people, money and resources. The legitimate power of leadership and management roles usually also includes the power to *reward* or *punish*. A manager who was about to retire said he had got stuck because the director had had something against him. 'I don't know what I'd done, but he never forgot it and I got sidelined.' But reward and punishment power exist outside legitimate power. Every time we praise a colleague's performance, we enhance the reputation of that person, and influence others to see him or her in that light. Of course, every time we malign someone we do the opposite.

With the increasing importance of technology, some regard technologists and scientists, who exercise *expert power*, as the potential power-brokers of the future, comparing their role to that of the rise of capitalists at the end of the age of feudalism. This may become the case, although currently direct power in work is most usually invested in management roles. The idea of restricting knowledge to experts is counter-cultural in many organizations today, when it is realized that the rapid sharing of knowledge is crucial to success. But it remains true that expert knowledge brings power. Some are reluctant to share their expertise because they want to retain their power, or to realize the market value of their knowledge. Being labelled a 'scarce resource' gives people power. The demand for IT specialists was so great in the late 1980s that some of those we interviewed would attempt to dictate their own terms.

We may not have the power of position or expertise, but we all exert some power through the relationships we have, the respect in which we are held and the example we set. This is *referent power*. This enables us to influence the way others behave and to sway the decisions they make.

We all wield power. How are we to handle it so that we are not corrupted by it and so that we use it for good?

### Handling power

God uses his power in wholesome ways through, for example, creating (Genesis 1 – 2; Psalm 104), empowering others (e.g. Isaiah 40:29–31), and opposing oppression and injustice (e.g. Amos 2:6–16). Similarly, we can use our power to good effect, particularly in our work, to carry out our responsibilities and thereby to serve God and others. For example, Joseph used the power of his position to prepare the nation for famine; Moses used the power given to him to combat the injustice of Pharaoh, and Jesus' followers utilized power in healing and restoring people and in building the church.

If power is to be used well in work, it must be directed towards good ends, motivated by service and implemented with justice. Sometimes it needs to be used authoritatively to accomplish an essential task or promote just treatment (think of Jesus cleansing the temple; John 2:13–17). The irresponsible use of power through coercion or manipulation can deny others their dignity, preventing them from acting responsibly themselves.

Power can be intoxicating and can make us proud and arrogant. To realize that a single instruction can buy or sell an enterprise, move large amounts of money across the world, or create or destroy the jobs of whole communities can instil a feeling of self importance, even omnipotence. As Richard Foster comments, 'Pride makes us think we are right, and power gives us the ability to cram our vision of rightness down everyone else's throat' (1985: 180). Even limited power over a single work project or a small team needs to be exercised with care and humility. This is because when we are entrusted with greater resources than our own, we have the potential significantly to affect events outside our own immediate sphere, and can be easily tempted to use power for our own ends. When we have little accountability to others, we are particularly susceptible to the corrupting influence of power. We need to follow Jesus' example in resisting the use of power for selfish ends (Matthew 4:1–11), and to realize that in all the power we wield, we are ultimately accountable to God.

The sin described in the Garden of Eden typifies the desire for power. Despite being given everything necessary for a good life, Adam and Eve wanted to be like gods themselves. 'For us, it is never enough to enjoy good work. No, we must obtain supremacy; we must possess; we must hoard; we must conquer' (Foster 1985: 175). Rather, we are to follow God's example in using power to empower others. John Goldingay says: 'Power is a little like wealth. You do not have to feel guilty about finding yourself in possession of it, as long as you use it to give it away, use it for other people's benefit' (Goldingay & Innes 1994: 8).

The story of the apostles Peter and John healing the crippled man outside the temple gate is an example of the good use of power. In response to the man's request for money, Peter said, 'Silver or gold I do not have, but what I have I give you. In the name of Jesus Christ of Nazareth, walk' (Acts 3:6). In explaining the healing to the crowd, he continued: 'Why do you stare at us as if by our own power or godliness we had made this man walk?' (Acts 3:12), and he went on to speak of God's power which had glorified Jesus. We may draw some principles from this:

- Power is *bestowed*. It is when we start to think of power as emanating from ourselves that the rot sets in. We need continually to acknowledge the source of the power we handle.
- We are *accountable* for the way we use the power given us – to our boss and organization, and ultimately to God.
- Power is to be used *responsibly* and for good ends, to serve others and ultimately God. It should be motivated by love, not advancement of self, and mediated by humility. 'Humility is power under control' (Foster 1985: 202).
- We should see ourselves not as possessors of power but as *channels* through which it flows and can be directed (and when appropriate, limited).

You may not feel very powerful in the role you perform at work; you may not manage thousands of staff or control large sums of money. However, you channel power in a number of ways: through the example of your work and character, through wielding influence during times of change and through leading projects and people. And in all of this, as a Christian you are a channel of the most dynamic power there is: the Holy Spirit. Paul's prayer for the Ephesians was 'that out of his glorious riches he may strengthen you with power through his Spirit in your inner being' (Ephesians 3:16); we too should recognize and appropriate the power 'that is at work within us' (verse 20). The prayer at the end of the Church of England's communion service acknowledges our need for God's power in our work:

> Send us out
> in the power of your Spirit,
> to live and work
> to your praise and glory. Amen.

## The action column

1. Are you ambitious? If so, examine your goals and the way you go about achieving them. If not, why not? Ask God to fire your ambition to serve him.
2. Think about the wealth you create through work. Challenge

yourself to handle it justly, generously and gratefully.

3. Are you more concerned with the status and respect your position brings than with the good you can do from that position?

4. Think about the power you wield, directly or indirectly, in work. How can you use it as a force for good?

## CONCLUSION

# A Christian path through the world of work

### It is the Lord Christ you are serving

It is possible in a single day to encounter many aspects of the journey we have undertaken at work: pressure, the struggle to balance work and family, working with people we may not choose as colleagues, coping with mind-boggling change, or leading others. Some may be isolated events such as choosing our next job, or being made redundant; others may be ongoing, such as handling power and influence, or being a witness through our words and actions.

Some of these experiences are difficult, even traumatic, while others are among the most invigorating challenges we will encounter. The good news is that there is a Christian path through the world of work.

In all facets of work, our chief aim is to *serve God*. We thereby glorify him and play our part in fulfilling his purposes for the world. By bringing his love and principles into the working world through the quality of our work, our character and our witness, we are his ambassadors in the most accessible mission field there is.

As we serve God in work, we also align our path with God's so that his purposes for us are fulfilled, and we find sustenance and satisfaction in our work. By using our skills in work we develop them and achieve the things God has for us to do. By facing the daily demands, awesome challenges and never-ending problems of work, we develop our character and keep our hopes intact, 'because we know that suffering produces perseverance; perseverance, character; and character, hope' (Romans 5:3–4).

To work is to serve God, whether we have a hugely responsible job

215

216 *All the hours God sends?*

or a humble one, and whether or not it brings great rewards on earth.

> Whatever you do, work at it with all your heart, as working for
> the Lord, not for men, since you know that you will receive an
> inheritance from the Lord as a reward. It is the Lord Christ you
> are serving (Colossians 3:23–24).

# Bibliography

John Adair (1997). *Leadership Skills*. London: Institute of Personnel and Development.

Peter Adam (1988). *Guidance*. Grove Spirituality Series 27. Nottingham: Grove Books.

Kenneth Adams (1991). *Christianity and Wealth Creation*. Amersham: Comino Foundation.

Michael Argyle (1989). *The Social Psychology of Work*. 2nd edn. Harmondsworth: Penguin.

Aristotle (1976). *The Ethics of Aristotle: The Nicomachean Ethics*. Eng. trans. Harmondsworth: Penguin.

Oliver R. Barclay (1978). *Guidance: Some Biblical Principles*. 5th edn. Leicester: IVP.

Karl Barth (1961). *Church Dogmatics* III: *The Doctrine of Creation*, Part 4. Edited by G. W. Bromiley and T. F. Torrance. Eng. trans. Edinburgh: T. and T. Clark.

Dietrich Bonhoeffer (1959). *The Cost of Discipleship*. Eng. trans. London: SCM.

William Bridges (1991). *Managing Transitions: Making the Most of Change*. Reading, MA: Addison-Wesley.

Isobel Briggs Myers (1980). *Gifts Differing*. Palo Alto, CA: Consulting Psychologists Press.

David Brown (1983). *Choices: Ethics and the Christian*. Oxford: Blackwell.

John O. Burdett (1991). 'What is empowerment anyway?' *Journal of European Industrial Training* 15.6: 23–30. MCB University Press.

Sir Frederick Catherwood (1987). *God's Time, God's Money*. London: Hodder and Stoughton.

Steve Chalke with Penny Relph (1998). *Managing Your Time*. Eastbourne: Kingsway.

Julian Charley (1984). *Pastoral Support for the Unemployed*. Grove Pastoral Series 19. Nottingham: Grove Books.

Curran, Peter (1995a). *Coping with Redundancy*. Farnham: CWR.

————(1995b). *Handling Redundancy*. Grove Ethical Studies 99. Cambridge: Grove Books.

217

Graham Dow (1979). *Dark Satanic Mills?* Nottingham: Shaftesbury Project Publications.

————(1994). *A Christian Understanding of Daily Work.* Grove Pastoral Series 57. Nottingham: Grove Books.

Richard J. Foster (1985). *Money, Sex and Power: The Challenge of the Disciplined Life.* London: Hodder and Stoughton.

Adrian Furnham (1990). *The Protestant Work Ethic: The Psychology of Work-Related Beliefs and Behaviours.* London: Routledge.

Sumantra Ghoshal & Christopher A. Bartlett (1996). Rebuilding behavioural context: a blueprint for corporate renewal. *Sloan Management Review*, Winter.

Terry Gillen (1997). *Assertiveness.* London: Institute of Personnel and Development.

John Goldingay & Robert Innes (1994), *God at Work.* Grove Ethical Sudies 94. Nottingham: Grove Books.

Michael Green (1983). *Freed to Serve.* London: Hodder and Stoughton.

Mark Greene (1997). *Thank God it's Monday: Ministry in the Workplace.* 2nd edn. Bletchley: Scripture Union.

David Guest, Neil Conway, Rob Briner & Michael Dickman (1996). *The State of the Psychological Contract in Employment.* Issues in People Management 16. London: Institute of Personnel and Development.

Stanley Hauerwas (1984). *The Peaceable Kingdom: A Primer in Christian Ethics.* London: SCM.

Charles Handy (1994). *The Empty Raincoat: Making Sense of the Future.* London: Hutchinson.

————(1996). *Beyond Certainty: The Changing Worlds of Organizations.* London: Arrow.

Alison Hardingham (1992). *Making Change Work for You.* London: Sheldon.

Donald A. Hay (1975). *A Christian Critique of Capitalism.* Grove Booklets on Ethics 5a. Nottingham: Grove Books.

Marion E. Haynes (1996). *Make Every Minute Count: How to Manage your Time More Effectively.* London: Kogan Page.

Robert Heller (1998). *Motivating People.* London: Dorling Kindersley.

Peter Herriot, Wendy Hirsh & Peter Reilly (1998). *Trust and Transition: Managing Today's Employment Relationship.* Chichester: ©John Wiley.

Frederick Herzberg (1968). *Work and the Nature of Man.* London: Crosby Lockwood Staples.

Richard Higginson (1986). *Key Themes in Roman Catholic Ethics: Nature, Character and Rules.* Grove Booklets on Ethics 60.

Nottingham: Grove Books.

————(1993). *Called to Account*. Guildford: Eagle.

————(1988). *Dilemmas: A Christian Approach to Christian Decision Making*. London: Hodder and Stoughton.

————(1992). *Living with Affluence: Prosperity, Prayer and the Christian Business Person*. Grove Spirituality Series 40. Nottingham: Grove Books.

————(1996). *Transforming Leadership: A Christian Approach to Management*. London: SPCK.

Tim Hindle (1998). *Manage your Time*. London: Dorling Kindersley.

Arthur F. Holmes (1979). *All Truth is God's Truth*. Leicester: IVP.

————(1991). *Shaping Character: Moral Education in the Christian College*. Grand Rapids: Eerdmans.

Barrie Hopson, Mike Scally and K. Stafford (1992). *Transitions: The Challenge of Change*. Stroud: Management Books 2000.

James Houston (1979). *I Believe in the Creator*. London: Hodder and Stoughton.

Pope John Paul II (1991). *Laborem Exercens*. In *Proclaiming Justice and Peace*, edited by B. Davies and M. Walsh. London: HarperCollins.

Susan Jones (1995). *Coping with Change at Work*. London: Thorsons.

Ian Kessler & Roger Undy (1996). *The New Employment Relationship: Examining the Psychological Contract*. Issues in People Management 12. London: Institute of Personnel and Development.

Philip King (1987). *Leadership Explosion*. London: Hodder and Stoughton.

C. S. Lewis (1963) *The Four Loves*. Glasgow: Collins Fount.

Gordon MacDonald (1985). *Ordering your Private World*. Godalming: Highland Books.

John Macquarrie & James Childress (eds.) (1986). *A New Dictionary of Christian Ethics*. London: SCM.

Iain Maitland (1995). *Motivating People*. London: Institute of Personnel and Development.

Abraham H. Maslow (1954). *Motivation and Personality*. New York: Harper & Row.

Peter Mayhew (1985). *Unemployment Under the Judgement of God*. Worthing: Churchman Publishing.

Peter Meadows (1988). *Pressure Points: How to Survive with the World and the Church on your Back*. Eastbourne: Kingsway.

Michael Moynagh (1985). *Making Unemployment Work*. Tring: Lion.

Stephen Neill (1984). *Crises of Belief: The Christian Dialogue with Faith and No Faith*. London: Hodder and Stoughton.

Organization for Economic Co-operation and Development (1994). *The OECD Jobs Study: Evidence and Explanations*. Part I: Labour market trends and underlying forces of change. Paris: OECD.

Hugh Ormiston & Donald M. Ross (eds.) (1990). *New Patterns of Work*. Edinburgh: Saint Andrew Press.

Thomas J. Peters & Robert H. Waterman Jr (1982). *In Search of Excellence: Lessons from America's Best-Run Companies*. New York: HarperCollins.

Plato (1974). *The Republic*. Translated by D. Lee. 2nd edn. Harmondsworth: Penguin.

Michel Quoist (1963). *Prayers of Life*. Dublin: Gill and Macmillan.

Alan Richardson (1963). *The Biblical Doctrine of Work*. 2nd edn. London: SCM.

Alistair Ross (1993). *Understanding Friends: Getting the Best Out of Friendship*. London: Triangle.

Leland Ryken (1989). *Work and Leisure in Christian Perspective*. Leicester: IVP.

Michael Schluter & David Lee (1993). *The R Factor*. Sevenoaks: Hodder and Stoughton.

E. F. Schumacher (1974). *Small is Beautiful*. London: Vintage.

————(1979). *Good Work*. London: Jonathan Cape.

Eduard Schweizer (1961). *Church Order in the New Testament*. London: SCM.

Cynthia D. Scott and Dennis T. Jaffe (1992). *Empowerment: Building a Committed Workforce*. London: Kogan Page.

David Sheppard (1983). *Bias to the Poor*. London: Hodder and Stoughton.

Jane Smith (1996). *Empowering People: How to Bring Out the Best in your Workforce*. London: Kogan Page.

David A. Statt (1994). *Psychology and the World of Work*. Basingstoke: Macmillan.

John Stott (1999). *New Issues Facing Christians Today*. London: Marshall Pickering.

Derek Tasker (1960). *Vocation and Work*. London: Mowbray.

John V. Taylor (1972). *The Go-Between God: The Holy Spirit and the Christian Mission*. London: SCM.

————(1975). *Enough is Enough*. London: SCM.

Thomas Aquinas (1991). *Summa Theologiae: A Concise Translation*. Edited by T. McDermott. London: Methuen.

Keith Tondeur (1996). *Your Money and Your Life: Learning How to Handle Money God's Way.* London: Triangle.

Miroslav Volf (1991). *Work in the Spirit: Toward a Theology of Work.* New York: Oxford University Press.

Paul J. Wadell (1992). *The Primacy of Love: An Introduction to the Ethics of Thomas Aquinas.* New York: Paulist.

Steve Walton (1994). *A Call to Live: Vocation for Everyone.* London: Triangle.

Peter B. Warr (ed.) (1987). *Psychology at Work.* 3rd edn. Harmondsworth: Penguin.

David Westcott (1996). *Work Well: Live Well: Rediscovering a Biblical View of Work.* London: Marshall Pickering.